MORE

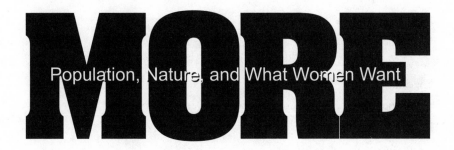

MORE

Population, Nature, and What Women Want

By Robert Engelman

ISLANDPRESS

Washington • Covelo • London

ISLAND PRESS is a trademark of the Center for Resource
Economics.

Engelman, Robert.
  More: population, nature, and what women want / by Robert
Engelman.
       p. cm.
  Includes bibliographical references and index.
  ISBN-13: 978-1-59726-019-0 (cloth : alk. paper)
  ISBN-10: 1-59726-019-3 (cloth : alk. paper)
  1. Fertility, Human. 2. Population. 3. Women—Attitudes.
  4. Nature—Effect of human beings on. I. Title.
  HB901.E64 2008
  304.6'2—dc22   2007040649

Printed on recycled, acid-free paper ✪

Manufactured in the United States of America
10 9 8 7 6 5 4 3 2 1

Keywords: demography, environment, evolution, reproduction,
women's health, contraception, midwife, cultural development,
social history, gender relations

To Colleen and Lucy, and in memory of Jinny

Contents

Preface

C hance remarks from two very different women inspired my years working on population and on this book. I don't know how I arrived at the presumption I could or should write about any aspect of the intentions of women, but the journey began with meeting these particular individuals.

For a time during the 1980s, I worked in Washington, D.C., as a newspaper reporter covering science, health and the environment. A U.S. population activist named Sharon Camp happened to suggest that if all the world's women could determine for themselves when and when not to have children, population problems would resolve themselves with no need for governmental "control." As a journalist I was skeptical, but it struck me as a rare statement of plausible hope amid gathering environmental risk. Within a few years of that conversation I left reporting to initiate a program on population and the environment at Sharon's organization, then called the Population Crisis Committee and later Population Action International (PAI).

Not long after I took that job, I met Wanga Grace Mumba, head of the Environment and Population Centre in Lusaka, Zambia. "The environment," I once heard Wanga say, "begins in the womb of a woman and ripples out all over the world." That image became a central one for my work over the next fifteen years.

When it comes to human numbers, one day is pretty much like the next. Another added increment of 215,000 people (births minus deaths) living, breathing, eating, working, and doing the rest of their business on the planet, just like yesterday.[1] As a newspaper reporter, I had been intrigued by the obvious gap between the importance of demographic trends and their marginalization in journalism and public discourse. How is it, I wondered, that some people can effortlessly recall sports statistics or argue over the appropriate number of guests to invite to a party, but when asked how many people are on the planet miss the figure by two or three zeros? Why is it that the news media track the growth of economies almost daily, but the growth of populations once or twice a year? Why do most historians and environmentalists ignore demography? And why, when a few brave pundits do take on population, is their message most likely that the real "population crisis" is not growth but decline?

Once I moved into the field of population and reproductive health, I gained some insights into the questions that brought me there. These observations inform the pages that follow, but the book is far more a first word than a last one on the intriguing connection between population growth, environmental change, and the lives of women. In part a journey into the literature of demography, anthropology, archaeology, and history, it is in equal measure a creative exploration of possibilities about the future of humanity and nature.

For help in the several scientific disciplines that I trespass into, I particularly thank Barbara J. King, Anne Pusey, Anthony Davis, Joyce Powzyk, Susan C. Antón, Leslie Aiello, Joyce Marcus, Daniel Sarewitz, Louise Barrett, Cara Wall-Scheffler, Michael Smith, Christine Mauck, and Dean Falk. All patiently answered questions and clarified key points. Peter Engelman, associate editor with the Margaret Sanger Papers Project at New York University, and Sherrill Redmon, director of the Sophia Smith Collection at Smith College, advised me on my research on Margaret Sanger. David Coleman, Martha Campbell, Robert Wyman, Elizabeth Leahy, J. Joseph Speidel, Barbara J. King, Malcolm Potts, Colleen Cordes, Joyce Marcus and Sandra Yin read the manuscript in part or in its entirety and made many helpful suggestions.

This book would not exist had not Todd Baldwin, editor in chief and associate publisher of Island Press, approached me with the idea of a book for general readers on population. Todd supported me through the long process of conceptualizing the book, and early in the writing process brought in editor Emily Davis to help. I'm tempted to apply the metaphor of the midwife, a figure who shows up from time to time in the pages to come, but I'll resist and simply say that Todd's and Emily's careful and sensitive handling of the ideas, the prose, and the author were essential to the book's completion. My appreciation also goes to Julie Van Pelt and to Katherine Macdonald for careful copy and production editing.

Special thanks are due to a range of dedicated people in the population and reproductive health field beyond those already mentioned and to my richly rewarding employment at PAI. Amy Coen, president and chief executive officer of that organization, generously allowed me to spend working time on this book, and PAI supported expenses for travel and research assistance. My colleagues trusted me to write something of value that would aid the organization's ambitious mission, which is to make family planning and broader sexual and reproductive health and rights available to all people everywhere. I especially thank PAI's librarian, Mary Panke, and Zachary Miller and Dan Mesnik, then on her staff, for their swift, untiring responses to my many requests for help. Former PAI staff researcher Jennifer Dusenberry devoted several months to locating and helping me digest a vast amount of information, and her own analysis of the factual material often steered me away from misinterpretations I might otherwise have made.

Elizabeth Leahy of PAI took up the same task with care and skill in later months. Among the many who have worked at PAI at some point in their careers, I particularly thank Joe Speidel and Sharon Camp for bringing me to the organization, which they headed in the early 1990s, as well as Richard Cincotta, Sally Ethelston, Wendy Turnbull, Vicki Sant, Susan Rich, Craig Lasher, Shanti Conly, Catherine Cameron, Tod Preston, Nada Chaya, Terri Bartlett, Susan Howells, Sarah Haddock, and Carol Wall. Former board chair Robin Duke welcomed me to the field with characteristically open arms. I owe thanks as well to Christopher Flavin, president of the Worldwatch Institute, and my colleagues there for supporting my continued work on this book after I moved to the institute in 2007. Appreciation goes to the Jake Family Fund for supporting outreach on this book.

Through my friend Betsy Taylor, then president of the Center for a New American Dream, I learned about the Mesa Refuge writers' program at Point Reyes, California, a philanthropic venture of Peter Barnes. I'm grateful to him, Pam Carr, and the Common Counsel Foundation for the luxury of their hospitality when I especially needed two weeks of rich and well-fed solitude for thinking and writing.

As a man writing about women, I owe special debts to more of the latter than I can possibly mention here. I doubt I would have stayed in this field so long had I not been inspired early on by reproductive-health specialist Jennifer Mukolwe of Kenya. Both Jennifer and Wanga Mumba died tragically in the late 1990s while active in their work on women's sexual and reproductive health and rights. The late Gordie Wallace, who effortlessly saw connections between demographic change and the practice of female genital cutting (which she may have been first to bring to the attention of the rest of the world), was a particular inspiration. The late Perdita Huston brought the lives of women in developing countries powerfully to light in her books. Guadalupe de Vega and Julia Henderson were role models for what passion and decades of work can accomplish in the field of population and family planning. Karen Rindge, then with the National Wildlife Federation (NWF), had the courage as a North American woman to speak up on the importance of family planning despite a tent full of opposition at the UN Conference on Environment and Development in Rio de Janeiro in 1992. NWF's Sidonie Chiapetta, whose work ranged from educating Americans about population to helping Mexicans understand the value of composting toilets, lost her life while traveling to make a presentation on population and the environment at a midwestern community gathering. The late Peggy Curlin, president of the Centre for Development and Population Activities (CEDPA), fought tirelessly for better access to reproductive health care. Among countless others who have taught me, I particularly thank Fatoumata Batta, Denise Caudill, Nancy Wallace, Catherina Hinz (who generously assisted me with literature in German), Petronella van den Oever, Wren Wirth, Cynthia Green, Erika Vohman, Edith Eddy, Lesley Riddoch, Susan F. Martin, Wendy Thomas, Frances Kissling, Cat McKaig, Joan Dunlop, Susan Gibbs, Judith Bruce, Teresa de Vargas, and Sharon Pickett. Joanne Omang suggested that I title this book *What Women Want*, which inspired part of the subtitle. The names of other women to whom I owe gratitude emerge from the pages ahead.

Many men, of course, helped shape my ongoing education in this field as well. Among them were George Benneh, Norman Myers, Steven W. Sinding, Jagdish Ghimire, Nicholas Danforth, Stephen Viederman, John Bongaarts, Anrudh Jain, Stan Becker, Benjamin Gyepi-Garbrah, John Bermingham, Partha Dasgupta, Carl Haub, Emmanuel Mtiti, Ed Ruddell, Robert Wyman, Ekisa Anyara, Jethro Pettit, Fabian Drixler, George Zeidenstein, Peter Donaldson, Fred Sai, Michael Teitelbaum, Peter Gubbels, Joseph C. Wheeler, Frederick A. B. Meyerson, Godfrey Mbaruku, and the late Jack Parsons, Edwin Martin, Robert Fearey and Marshall Green. Lester Brown and James Hansen were early inspirations for my interest in population and climate change. Peter Gleick joined me in an early exploration of population and water resources that shaped much of the population-environment research that followed. My brother John Engelman provided key insights that influenced my questions and my thinking. Our late father, Gerald Engelman, taught me throughout my childhood never to take easy answers at face value. And I thank Tom Outlaw, Jim Nations, Jim Baird, and the larger-than-life Mechai Viravaidya, who regularly imbue this serious work with gags and laughter and remind me that sometimes planet savers, like the girls Cyndi Lauper sang about, just want to have fun.

Finally, of course, there are the women who accompany and endlessly teach me in life. My education about girls and women—and especially about their rights, power and capabilities—began at birth as the son of Annabel "Jinny" Johnson Engelman and the younger brother of Janet Engelman, and later as the older brother of Elizabeth Engelman. Having thanked my PAI colleagues, I must add that this book was written mostly at home. For the gift of their patience and unconditional love, not to mention encouragement and advice that informs every page of this book, I give the most heartfelt thanks of all to my best friend and wife, Colleen Cordes, and to my daughter Lucy Cordes Engelman. Both are quick to catch me in false assumptions or hypocritical behavior in regard to women, gender relations, and fathering. To them and in memory of my mother—who skillfully nurtured me, her third child, into my own adulthood—I lovingly dedicate this book.

Introduction: Uncrowding Eden

Let's face up to the fact that our population growth is putting our city on a collision course with the environment, which itself is growing more unstable and uncertain.
    —*Michael Bloomberg, mayor of New York City*

My strongest hope resides in the speed of transformation. For instance, the demographic projections based on the high birth rates of 20–30 years ago have not been confirmed, allowing us a more encouraging view on the growth of cities for the next years and decades.
    —*Jaime Lerner, former mayor of Curitiba, Brazil*

Some travelers call the southwestern corner of Uganda the Switzerland of Africa, but the quaint tourist name belies the rugged landscape's hazards. Just outside the thickly forested Bwindi Impenetrable Forest National Park, where half the world's last few hundred mountain gorillas cling to survival, farmers work their crops so far up the steep hillsides that sometimes, I learned when I visited some years ago, they hurt themselves falling off their fields.

Farmers in the world's poorer countries don't cultivate hazardous hillsides and farm at an angle because they can, but because they have to. They need every inch of arable land to support themselves. And their children often face equally dismal prospects in finding housing in the crowded cities where half of humanity now lives. These farmers and their families are suffering the consequences of, for lack of a better word, *overpopulation*. It's not a term used much these days and I don't especially care for it myself, with its implication that some of us already here should not be. But the reality remains that what most people call overpopulation is more evident, in more places, than ever.

Mayor Michael Bloomberg recently urged his fellow New Yorkers to "face up to the fact" that overcrowding undermines environmental stability. Members of Rwanda's nearly half-female parliament considered a national drive to achieve three-child families in the land-short African country, in the hopes that slower growth might prevent a repeat of its genocidal 1994 civil war. China, its 1.3 billion people clambering up the lower rungs of the consumption ladder, reached to Brazil for livestock feed, to the west coast of Africa for fish, and to Ethiopia for oil, where nine Chinese oil workers were killed by Somali insurgents. And as for the gorillas of Bwindi, they are far from the only apes that may miss the train to the twenty-second century. The 373,000 human babies born on the day you read these words will outnumber all the world's existing gorillas, chimpanzees, bonobos, and orangutans, our closest animal relatives.[1]

The most-covered story in the "population news" category, however, is one in which population received few mentions: final public acceptance that by using the atmosphere as a dump for waste gases, human beings are heating up the planet. Even as we have awakened to the scientific reality that human-induced climate change is real and happening now, we still pull up the covers and roll over in bed at the thought that this has any important connection to how many of us there are. In April 2007, *Time* magazine offered "51 things we can do to save the environment"; not one had anything to do with population. A report from the environmental group U.S. PIRG (Public Interest Research Group) called *The Carbon Boom* detailed state by state the rising emissions of heat-trapping carbon dioxide from 1990 to 2004 in the

United States. The word *population* did not appear in the report, even though the country's carbon dioxide emissions grew a hair *less* than did its population over the period, 18 versus 18.1 percent. As I neared completion of this book, serious talk began about the need to slash global and U.S. emissions of carbon dioxide by up to 80 percent within decades—with no discussions of how different population scenarios will affect our chances for achieving such a staggeringly challenging objective.[2]

Why so much silence on something so firmly entrenched in the foundations of the environmental, economic, and social challenges the world faces? Some resistance stems from the "impersonal reduction of humans to quantity," in the words of English historical demographer Peter Biller.[3] Who wants to be reduced to a number, or go out for a beer with one? Partly, population is just a sensitive topic. Any discussion of population growth quickly taps into an edgy confusion of feelings most of us harbor about contraception and abortion, about childbearing and family size, gender relations, immigration, race and ethnicity, and—not least—the intense longing, the pleasure, and the risks we can't avoid as sexual beings. Sexual taboos are getting harder to confront as a wave of religious fundamentalism grows in apparent response to the same chaotic global complexity to which population growth itself contributes.

Many doubt that we need to worry about population growth at all. Humanity has been growing steadily for centuries. For most people life gets longer and better, with tastier and more nutritious food, improved health, more affluence, and lots of cool gadgets and amusements. If population growth is a bomb, some have suggested, it seems to be a dud. Indeed, so dramatic have been the changes in childbearing in recent years, with the spread of effective modern contraception—supplemented in many countries by safe and legal abortion services—that the worry has shifted to countries like Japan and many in Europe where population has begun to ebb, or to nations that will need to draw many more immigrants to avoid imminent demographic decline.

It's almost amusing to see this new phase of "population crisis" based not on growth but on decline. The likelihood of future decreases in population drives far more writing, broadcasting, and blogging than does population growth, despite the fact that growth remains the overwhelming global dynamic and probably will for decades to come. On any given day, after all, more than twice as many people worldwide begin their lives (373,000, as noted above) as reach life's end (159,000). That's cold comfort all the same in countries from Belarus to South Korea, where women are having little more than one child on average. Politicians and demographers worry about the future of such countries' retirement programs, the vibrancy of their economies, and their capacity to project military power or defend their territories.

Fear of losing not just population, but "our" population, also underpins the angst many people express over the high levels of immigration that have changed the complexion of industrialized countries in recent decades. One of the cures offered for population aging or decline is simply to invite in more people from other countries. Already, foreign-born Americans are more numerous than the native-born in Miami-Dade County and in several cities in Florida and California. The U.S. Census Bureau projects that by 2070 there will be no majority race in the country.[4] Serious authors like Phillip Longman and Ben Wattenberg, and fearmongers like Patrick Buchanan, have called openly for a return to large families—implicitly or explicitly by native-born Americans—to stave off population aging, stagnation or an immigrant-driven continuation of growth.

Longman has called for lower Social Security taxes and higher benefits for parents, scaled to the number of their offspring, with the financial gap to be closed by the childless. He finds a dense and growing population optimal for combating global warming, apparently believing that per capita greenhouse gas emissions would fall in such societies as the urgency of the problem called forth innovative solutions from the greater number of smart people around. (One wonders where the smart people are among the 6.7 billion of us alive today.) And he argues that patriarchal families, being larger on average, will inherit the earth—as though we weren't all descendents of patriarchs, no matter our family's size.[5]

Not long after I began work on this book, I joined Ben Wattenberg on a radio talk show that focused on his just-published one, *Fewer*.[6] I think I was courteous in suggesting it might more accurately have been titled *More*, as this is the current and projected future reality of U.S. and human population trends. Wattenberg offered no prescriptions to reverse the demographic decline he foresees for most societies rooted in Western culture. He was just drawing attention, he said, to the sad fact that modern women find the attractions of contemporary employment and culture so enticing that they delay or forego altogether the joys of motherhood. The world, he argued, is poorer for their selfish choices.

Wattenberg is right that, when given the choice, women typically decide to have fewer kids. In every country in which a variety of contraception options is readily accessible, backed up by safe abortion for the inevitable cases of contraceptive failure, women average roughly two children or less— barely replacing themselves and their partners, and signaling a future of gradual population decline if there is no net immigration.

But he is shortsighted when he implies that more people equal greater prosperity. Why do housing and land get more expensive over time, while so many jobs find workers who will work for less money than the jobs paid two or three years ago? Could it have something to do with the fact that land doesn't expand, but the base of workers can, and does? What happens in societies in which people younger than thirty vastly outnumber those older, and the number of workers always outpaces the numbers of jobs? Why do we face an explosion of dangerous infectious diseases that no one had heard of thirty years ago? Why are there no real solutions to traffic congestion, the loss of open space, the endlessly rising din of urban life, the replacement of the soulful education of children with the soulless training of test takers, the dehumanizing indignity of talking to mechanical voices on the telephone and scrolling helplessly and with rising fury through "frequently asked questions" on the computer screen?

Our numbers take on special urgency as we face the reality that through human-induced climate change we are turning our long-hospitable home into a harsh and alien place, a "different planet," in the words of leading climatologist James Hansen of NASA.[7] It is the global transformation our descendents are least likely to forgive, whatever rates of economic growth they may manage to record in the insubstantial calculus of monetary currency. And of all the threats the world faces, other than nuclear war, climate change poses the greatest risks to humanity, perhaps even posing the danger that some future generation will fail to renew our species through parenthood.

Human annihilation probably isn't at the forefront of the minds of most women contemplating whether or not to have a child. But their own prospects, and those of their hypothetical children, factor heavily in the decision. Those opportunities and risks are clearly tied to the condition of the world in which they live and the number of other people trying to navigate it.

The three-way connection between individual women's lives, world population, and the health of the planet came into stark relief in my own travels, to Uganda and elsewhere in the developing world, during the fifteen years I worked for a policy research and advocacy nonprofit in Washington, D.C., called Population Action International. In Kenya in the fall of 2006, my PAI research colleague Wendy Turnbull and I spent unproductive hours trapped in traffic in Nairobi, often next to one of the dangerously crowded *matatu* buses that provide most of the city's public transportation. On one or two car trips we moved more slowly than the streams of purposeful pedestrians, heading to work along an uncompleted stretch of highway from their tin-roofed homes in a slum named Kibera. Featured in the 2005 film *The Constant Gardener*, Kibera has hundreds of thousands of people and sanitation so scarce that defecation is often accomplished in plastic bags that are then hurled away, an innovation the locals call "flying toilets." Dominating the Nairobi headlines were stories of nomadic squatters occupying ranchland in the northeast; civil conflict in neighboring Somalia; and the trial in Nairobi of a white landowner, charged with ordering the murder of a black worker discovered in the act of butchering a poached impala.

Shortly after our visit, writer Richard Conniff in large part attributed the poverty and tension that contributed to the crime to the environmental impacts—from lost forests and plunging lake levels to the decimation of Kenya's trophy wildlife—of a population explosion that had been building in Kenya for decades.[8] My Kenyan research colleague, a doctoral student in demography at Southampton University in England named Ekisa Anyara, lent that thesis some support based on his own tribal experience in western Kenya.

"I believe there is an intertwined synergy between population and environment to the degree that is little known to existing populations," Ekisa wrote me in an e-mail after I returned to the States. "My people have cleared the hills and rivers bare. We no longer have rain where it used to start. The bare soils constantly exposed to the heat and chemicals have continued to deteriorate and become unsupportive to varied vegetations including domestic crops. Certainly, knowledge of why there are no longer sufficient harvests despite expenditure of massive energies in preparing and tilling the land is peripheral in my and other districts."[9]

On our way to the country's northeastern coast, Wendy and I flew past Mount Kilimanjaro, where a thin strip of snow adhered diagonally to the summit like a sorry Band-Aid on a melting planet. We were traveling to this remote area of Kenya to study an innovation that may offer a ray of hope for people and nature. A project sponsored mainly by the environmental group World Wildlife Fund (WWF) in the Kiunga Marine National Reserve was bringing health and family planning services to communities that also were learning to conserve their dwindling populations of fish and turtles. Fishing is the main source of local livelihoods. Sustaining it in and around the reserve will determine whether these men and their families, like so many in rural areas of Africa, eventually abandon their birthplace for big cities and industrialized countries.

Visiting the villages of Mkokoni and Kiunga the next day, we learned that roughly half the women in this isolated area had embraced modern contraception. Some worried that this violated Islamic law, yet family sizes of three or even two children were nonetheless now common. Adopting more sustainable fishing practices while slowing the growth of the number of fishers offered a double prospect for a decent future along the wild green Kenyan coast. "A mother's priority is sustenance," one village woman told us, noting the economic benefits of smaller families and the greater chances of surviving and thriving when women pause for a few years between births. "Nothing is going to stop us from using family planning now."

If any message arises from the research that went into this book, it is this: Women aren't seeking more children, but more *for* their children, and we can be thankful for that. Avoiding unintended pregnancy and childbearing is an essential strategy for achieving the dreams that women hold for their children. Women's intention to bear wanted children and nurture them to adulthood, with the best possible future in mind, is a central theme of this book.

The pages ahead comb evidence, logic, and history to venture answers to two questions: What effects do more people have on the world? And what effect does more reproductive autonomy for women have on the number of children they have?

These questions are as old as humanity, and to fully address them we need to start at the very beginning. How can we begin to guess how population will affect our future without grappling with how it shaped our past? Delving into the darkest reaches of hominid prehistory and then traveling forward in time, this book will explore key moments in our long and tangled history of growth. Along the way we'll consider how the invention of the plow may have altered gender relations and women's standing, why men's control over women's childbearing appears to have shifted into a much higher gear around 500 BC, how women may have timed childbirths (or at least tried to) in the distant past, and what the witchcraft hysteria of fifteenth- through early eighteenth-century Europe may have had to do with contraception and abortion. We'll look briefly at two influential lives in population and birth control: England's Thomas Robert Malthus and the United States's Margaret Sanger.

We'll also ask, How strong is the link between women's control over their reproduction and low fertility? What connection might women's standing in society have to the development of culture and civilization in the past? And how might better access to contraception and greater equality between women and men influence the future of population?

Exploring the dynamic triangle of women's lives, human numbers, and nature may shed light on the history and likely future of women's opportunities, rights, and status. Just as importantly, it could help answer increasingly urgent questions about humanity's place in our fast-changing home. For even if there has been no single, global demographic detonation, that's no inoculation against the risks associated with a large and still-growing global population. After his premature obituary was published, Mark Twain noted that "rumors of my death have been greatly exaggerated." Yet Twain was mortal, and eventually his obituaries were accurate.

We don't know what the future will bring, but as I chat with experts about the melting ice fields, the hunting of gorillas for meat, and the emergence of strange new infectious diseases, I doubt that the biggest worry facing us is that our retirement checks would have been bigger if we had had more children. If it happens for the right reasons, a little uncrowding of the world—not too much, and not for too long—will be just what the doctor ordered.

During much of the time I was writing it, this book bore the working title *Uncrowding Eden*. I happened to share that with a colleague who was about to travel to Ghana, where the book's first chapter opens. "Of course," this practical and direct woman said gently after considering the title for a moment, "Eden was never crowded." Eventually I learned that it might well have been, a story told in chapter 4. But at the time I conveyed to her my own conviction that the Bible is mistaken in key details of the creation. The planet on which humans emerged, evolved, and expanded remains in its essence a paradise for humanity, despite the degradation we have caused. This is Eden. We live here. Like the people of Kenya's Kiunga reserve, who struggle to sustain their fisheries and to bear the next child at the right time, we can choose to stay.

ONE

Henrietta's Ideal

Demography is ultimately about sex, but never so much fun in its details.
  —Renee Pennington, American anthropologist,
    "Hunter-gatherer demography"

The street kids called her Condom Sister, but her real name was Henrietta. She seemed a confident seventeen-year-old when I met her a few years ago in Accra, the capital of Ghana in West Africa. During the day she played indoor games with friends and learned about AIDS prevention at a youth center for recent arrivals in the capital, those who had left or lost their families. In the evenings, she worked as a "peer educator," earning about $7.50 a month. That meant trolling the city's streets for young people to talk to, with her anti-AIDS T-shirt, her slogan "if it's not on, it's not in," and her talking points on the virtues of safe sex. Sometimes she carried a few Champions—a brand of condoms manufactured in Dothan, Alabama—to dispense to those who asked.

Despite her street moniker, which I thought might draw some unwanted attention or worse, Henrietta went about her work unmolested. The boys all knew, she told me, "that I control myself sexually." She was abstinent.

Henrietta had a dream for herself and planned to stick to it in a choreo-
graphed sequence of accomplishments: a job as a hairdresser, marriage, and
children one, two, and three—all arriving after she reached age twenty-four.
The half dozen other teenage girls I met along with Henrietta at the youth
center all expressed the same family-size ideal for themselves. I heard the
number three often in Ghana when I asked, as I do on such trips, how many
children women wanted to have before their childbearing days were over. In
Accra, on that visit at least, the goal was nearly unanimous among young
women: three children.

Good, someone who frets about world population growth might think.
Three children, after all, is less than the four the typical Ghanaian woman has
today and much less than the nearly seven that women there averaged from
1950 to 1975, when the country's population was growing by about 3 percent each year. And if all women waited until age twenty-four to have their
first child, that would slow the stream of new arrivals simply by stretching
the world's generation gaps. Henrietta and her friends' childbearing ideal was
a textbook illustration of a revolution in reproductive behavior that has been
occurring in Africa over the last two decades and in the rest of the world for
longer than that.

Here's how today's childbearing differs from the past: For most of the last
several centuries—and possibly for most of the last 200,000 years—women
have had an average of five or more live births each. Today the average is 2.6.
It is among the most remarkable behavioral shifts in history.

A common view in the world's wealthier countries is that women in
developing countries *want* to be pregnant much of the time and to mother
the ample broods that frequent pregnancy produces. There's no particular evidence that this has ever been the dominant sentiment among
women, however, and it's far from the reality today. Fifty years ago, fewer
than 30 percent of sexually active women of childbearing age worldwide
used contraception or had a partner who was doing so, and women had
an average of five children. Today, the comparable figure is above 60 per-

cent, and the average woman gives birth to just two or three children.[1] If contraception were a soft drink, some multinational corporation would be paying its CEO obscenely, but instead it's more a behavior and an attitude than a product, and it has spread all over the world.

But have birthrates fallen far enough? Many people worried about population growth would answer no, Henrietta's ideal family is still too big. For when two parents contribute three children to a population, and those three children grow up to have three of their own, each generation is 50 percent larger than the one that came before. To keep the population steady by only replacing themselves and their partners, women need to have about 2.1 children on average in wealthy countries and somewhat more than that in most poor ones.

Two parents have two children, replacing themselves in a population just fine. Why add the odd fraction of a birth to make "replacement fertility?" First off, demographers tend to calculate replacement fertility based on the childbearer: the woman. So birthrates are discussed in terms of children born per woman, not per couple. (The monogamous mother, the faithful father till-death-do-them-part, and their two-plus kids form just one among a diversity of family structures. Men can father all the children they please, and demographers, like a lot of other people, generally don't pay much attention.)

Then there's birth itself. For reasons guessed at but not well understood, under natural conditions about 105 boys are born for every 100 girls. The ratio tends to be even higher in first births and with young parents. So, one hundred women need to give birth to about 205 children to ensure that the next generation has the same number of potential childbearers. Already, we have a "twentieth of a child" in the replacement equation.

Then, in any large population, some children die before they grow old enough to have children of their own. You need a few "extra" births per hundred—a little bit in the bank or, as a colleague of mine calls his third child, a "spare"—to hedge against tragedy. If you figure that 1 out of 22 or 23 daughters will not live to see age thirty (roughly the midpoint of reproductive age), replacement fertility settles around 2.1 children per woman. Note, however, that this is the average number of children for *all* women, not the average for all women actually *giving birth*. In the United States, 18 percent of women complete their reproductive years without having kids.[2]

If we consider all the women in a population, mothers and nonmothers alike, it's easy to see that replacement fertility is rarely if ever a steady, stately 2.1 children per woman. Given differences in sex ratios at birth (influenced in some Asian countries by sex-selective abortion) and child survival rates, different populations require different numbers of children per woman to replace the parents' generation. In western Europe and Japan, where deaths of young people are quite rare, the replacement fertility rate may be as low as 2.06 children per woman. In the United States, the rate is a small fraction higher, 2.08, because young people in the States are a bit more likely to die before parenting than in most wealthy industrialized countries. But this variation from the lowest rate is minor compared to the 2.9 replacement fertility rate of Africa or the 2.7 rate of the world's least developed countries.[3] Obscure as the statistics are, replacement fertility rates quantify the failure to survive among the youngest and most vulnerable among us. We ought to be tracking how the rates change, but no one does.

Watching Children Die

Through much of human history, replacement fertility may have been as high as five, six, or even more, a grisly guess based on the fact that modern married women tend to have about this number of children when they aren't using contraception. (Some have many more. A small religious group known as the Hutterites was renowned for having a documented fertility from 1880 to 1950 of roughly ten children per woman.[4] But that's unusually high fertility, well above that of any country in known history.)

During much of the two thousand centuries since *Homo sapiens* became a separate species, population growth rates remained low.[5] As we'll see, our numbers jumped dramatically at key moments, but there were also periods of abrupt decline, and yet others of relative stasis. Some women in the deep past may have had some success in managing their own fertility, but it was likely high mortality, not low birthrates, that was the greatest check on growth. Throughout prehistory, women may well have watched half of their children die, needing to give birth six or more times just to keep the population from fading away.

Even today, having at least some three-child families is essential to survival of the species. The two-child ideal—once marketed by the population-movement slogan "Stop at two"—would condemn us to extinction if it really did become universal for long. Why? Suppose only a few young people die in your population, and the sex ratio at birth holds at the normal 105 boys for every 100 girls. Even under these ideal conditions, replacement fertility will always be just slightly above two children per woman. (Any 100 women will need to have from 205 to 210 babies to be confident they'll have 100 daughters who grow up to have children themselves.) Babies arrive, however, only in whole numbers. So if all women had precisely two children each, they wouldn't quite be replacing themselves and their partners. Then, add in the many women who have just one child or none at all. Such women make demographic room for others who have three, four, or a dozen children in populations that are nonetheless, *on average*, at or below replacement fertility. Without occasional above-replacement fertility, populations begin a long, dangerous slide. If you're the parent of three children and worry about population growth, you can take comfort in the fact that *someone* has to have three. It may as well be you.

There's an obvious corollary, however, to this celebration of the third child: if average fertility rates remain *well above* two live births per woman, death rates will eventually rise to levels any sane person would call catastrophic. Exponential growth cannot continue indefinitely on the finite surface of a planet. Not long ago, UN demographers calculated the population density of the world under the seemingly modest scenario that the average number of births per woman would remain at the current 2.6. In less than three centuries, this "constant-fertility" scenario would produce 134 *trillion* people on earth, pushing them onto every patch of terra firma from deserts to mountaintops at a density 143 times that of Hong Kong today.[6]

People who think about population often dream up these sorts of thought experiments to make tangible such intangibles, whether they're trying to prove human numbers are a problem or a nonissue. A favorite factoid for the nonissue side is that all of today's world population could fit into the state of Texas, with room for a house and a modest eighth-of-an-acre yard for households of five people each. They're right, though no one seems to have asked Texans how they feel about this idea.[7] The more important point is that once settled in the Lone Star state, the world's billions would quickly die of thirst unless they could somehow move the mouth of the Amazon River to Galveston. Eating red meat or even an un-Texan vegan diet would be out of the question.

Like all things in the physical universe, natural resources like water and soil can only go so far. The same is true even of the inventions and other innovations—more efficient engines, more productive varieties of food crops—that make resources useful to people. No one really knows any more than you do what the "limits to growth" might be for human numbers. You're free to pick 10 billion, a trillion, or some other "illion" that no one can relate to. But once humanity reaches that limiting range, whatever it may be, average fertility had better be low enough to stop or reverse growth. Otherwise, rising death rates will do the job without mercy.

"Limits to growth" hasn't been a very popular idea since a book with that title brought the scorn of economists and cornucopian thinkers in the 1970s.[8] But the idea that such constraints are out there is coming back.

There's not enough water for those alive today in the Horn of Africa, not enough atmosphere for those alive on earth to use fossil fuels the way we do in the United States. In Afghanistan and more than a dozen countries in sub-Saharan Africa, ill health, hunger, and violence make youth as risky a phase of life today as it was in Charles Dickens's London. Parents need to have more than three children per woman to replace themselves in such populations, since infants have only a two-thirds probability of making it to age thirty.

While it's too simplistic to blame rapid population growth for the high death rates in these countries, overcrowding is likely one of several interacting factors. Parents in Rwanda and Malawi, for example, divide their subsistence farms between so many sons that each tiny plot can barely support a family. Many in the younger generations look for alternative livelihoods, but these aren't easy to find in either country. Malawi suffers from recurrent famine, and more than one in three newborns fails to make it to mid-reproductive age. And some see the 1994 genocidal war of Rwanda as an example of what can happen when population densities reach intolerable levels in countries that lack decent government and decent economic options for their citizens.[9]

Even when birthrates hit the critical replacement value, whatever it is in a specific population, it takes time for human numbers to stabilize. Population change has its own momentum, like that of a speeding truck that skids along the pavement after the driver slams on the brakes. If most parents are members of a "youth bulge" in the population—maybe they're baby boomers—then even if they average 2.1 children per couple the sum of all people will keep growing. Only a small group of older people is leaving the population—not to put too fine a point on it, they're *dying* to leave it—while a big, bawling, baby-boom "echo" is being born, comparable in number to their parents. Until deaths equal births, with the generations of reproducers about equal in size to those dying, the beat of growth goes on.

Population momentum can also work in reverse, to keep shrinking populations from stabilizing even when couples are replacing themselves precisely. In a population weighted toward old people, the two children of a small generation of young parents may not be able to compensate for the large number of elderly dying. Demographers didn't pay much attention to this until they realized that some European populations could begin having more than two children per woman tomorrow—Germany, Italy, and Spain, for example—and still their populations would keep declining for decades to come because of this negative momentum.

Some writers fear that *below-replacement fertility*—any level too low to replace parents in a population—amounts to a sentence of demographic self-extinction, as in "Will the last Italian please turn out the lights?" Actually, below-replacement fertility has been nearly as common in human experience as above-replacement fertility. For our species, obviously, family sizes too small to keep population from shrinking have never been fatal and, except for some small groups, it rarely has lasted long enough to threaten survival. (European invasion and disease overwhelmed the Caribs in the Caribbean Sea and the aboriginal Tasmanians south of Australia. Such disappearances of small subpopulations were no doubt common in prehistory and early historic times.) Most countries today with fertility rates below replacement are still growing demographically, generally due to still-young populations or net immigration or both; although, among the dozen countries with the smallest families, population stability or decline is indeed the rule. Moreover, it's inaccurate to say that birthrates in low-fertility countries are in any kind of free fall. Most countries that have reached 1.1 births per woman have experienced leveling and even slight rises in fertility, suggesting that 1.1 births may be something of a fertility floor.

To be sustainable, then, a population will need some, but not too many three-child families. Human numbers are staggeringly sensitive to small differences in fertility. Two or three thousand years with 1.8 children per woman, and vines start to snake up vacant skyscrapers and break the windows. The same few millennia with 2.4 children per woman, and people are stacked up on each other's heads. Such sensitivity to small differences in fertility is one reason demographic trends and data merit attention. However you feel about population as an issue, whether the earth holds 5 billion or 15 billion people in 2100 will have an awful lot do with the how rapidly and dangerously the global climate warms, the survival of anything we can call wild, and much more besides.

Ephemeral Numbers

Right now *this* many people live in a place called Planet Earth: 6,633,975,438. Oops. It went up.[10] But seriously, you really don't want to consult this book, or any other, if you want to know the latest figures about national or world population. Demographers, someone once said, are accountants, but without the charisma. Demography itself, however, is endlessly dynamic. So a new book on population shares this with a new baby: it's only new until the next one arrives. In 1993 George Will, a columnist meticulous about numbers related to politics or baseball, wrote this sentence: "There are about 4 billion people alive now, and all will die more or less on a known schedule."[11] World population at the time was just shy of 5.6 billion. We can reliably guess that the demographic reference Will pulled from his shelf was copyrighted around 1974.

Population is an odd, amorphous thing. It's people, but it's anything but people-friendly. The 78 million people added to the world's population each year, for example, are not the sum total of babies born, they're only *some* of the sum, and it's impossible to say which particular babies they are. The "added population" is simply a mathematical construct derived from subtracting those who died in a given year, around 59 million people in recent years, from those born, around 137 million. Seventy-eight million is just a number, abstract but real nonetheless.

We're free to imagine this large number as creatively as we like. It's just over one-quarter of all the people who live in the United States, and also the number of those populating California, Texas, and New York combined. If all the additional people lived in cities—and cities are where most of this growth is gravitating—the world would need eight new ones every year, each almost the size of New York City.

As a musician, I wonder what population growth might *sound* like. I imagine this moment-by-moment addition to the world's sum of people as a kind of percussion or, in some hypothetical future world of accelerating hypergrowth, even a low-pitched but rising tone. Today the sound of population growth is a fast ticktock. If it were audible, the 2008 pace of individual additions to the human family would have the tempo of a swiftly played Irish slip jig, at 149 beats per minute. The sound, at least, would appeal to me.

But population needs a sound for loss as well. During most of prehistory, growth would have produced occasional ticks, balanced more often than not by some other sound—perhaps a bell's chime, like the sound of an angel getting his wings in the film *It's a Wonderful Life*—to indicate a decline in human numbers. On rare days, even in modern times, world population can shrink. One such day arrived without warning on December 26, 2004, when the deadliest tsunami in history took the lives of as many as a quarter million people in coastal Asia. Another 159,000 or so died for reasons having nothing to do with the giant wave, and the day's 373,000 births couldn't compensate for the departed. The next day's births, however, could and did. A much longer-term setback to population growth occurred in 1918, when that year's influenza pandemic wiped out as many as 40 million people. World population probably didn't regain its prepandemic levels until the early 1920s.

Demographers suggest that "almost all" world population growth is occurring in developing countries, a statement that leaves one with a picture of unchanging populations in wealthy industrialized countries while developing countries grow more crowded every day. But demographers can only say this because significant population growth in the United States, Canada, Australia, and the United Kingdom is almost perfectly balanced by population decline in Japan and parts of continental Europe.

The United States alone adds about 2 million people to the world's population each year through births that exceed deaths, and it takes in roughly another 1 million people born in other countries through immigration that exceeds emigration. You could say that the U.S. population-growth increment of 3 million more people each year amounts to about 4 percent of the world's population growth, but few demographers look at it that way. They prefer instead to wash out the *natural increase* (the term refers to deaths minus births within a country or area, ignoring any effect of international migration) of the United States, along with most other industrialized countries, by balancing it against comparable declines in Europe. But this is a demographic shell game, one that lulls many Americans into thinking that population growth is overblown, overhyped and "over there." The reality is that the United States is growing demographically only a bit more slowly than the world as a whole. No one has a clue when this U.S. growth might stop or how many Americans there will be when it does.

Most aggregation is by its nature subjective and distorting. Divide the world into urban and rural halves, for example, and effectively "all" future population growth will take place in the urban half. This makes it seem as if the women of the world's villages are all having 2.1 kids and population stability reigns. Actually, family size in most rural areas is significantly larger than in cities, so much so in parts of Africa, for example, that many inherited farm plots are now too small to feed a typical family.[12] The streams of rural migrants relocating in the swelling cities of the developing world contribute to an illusion that the world's population growth is now mostly taking place there, but the countryside still provides much of the fuel for that growth, and it will for decades to come. The point to recall is that each *place*—whether village or state or country—experiences population change specific to that place. And through migration, the demographics of any one place can influence those of any other.

Wild Cards

Migration itself is one of three demographic forces that are neither well understood nor well integrated into demographers' analyses and their projections of future population. An intellectual chasm separates scholars of historic human migration, most of whom see the process as linked to variations in local and regional population growth, and those who study contemporary international and *internal* (domestic) migration. Today, some experts in international migration argue that population growth or high density don't play a significant role in spurring people to move from one place to another. Migration is, in this view, chiefly a function of globalization, ease of travel, and the uneven pace of development. People, like capital, flow from areas of low to high opportunity regardless of what's happening to population.[13]

No one doubts, however, that migrants contribute to the population growth of the countries to which they move, and they often help fill gaps in the receiving countries' age structures as well. Japan and the European nations that face the prospect of declining ratios of workers to retirees could at least slow this decline by accepting many more immigrants than they do today. But these countries' governments must wrestle with widespread concerns among their electorates about the ethnic shifts such high levels of migration would produce. Mostly ignored in the debates on this topic is that maintaining current worker-to-retiree ratios through immigration would boost population densities in these countries to levels that before long would become intolerable. The reason: There are so many new retirees, due to longer life expectancies and the aging of baby booms, that if each retiree requires four or five workers for a decent pension, the number of workers countries must bring in becomes unimaginable. And workers tend to have children, perpetuating the population increase. The only force that could prevent further crowding would be precipitous declines in life expectancy, a case of the cure being worse than the disease.

In an increasingly interconnected world, with older and wealthier populations close to younger and poorer ones, large numbers of people will likely be on the move for years to come. Eventually, however, fading job prospects or problems related to ever denser populations—rising costs of housing and transportation, for example—could dampen immigration into some countries. So, of course, could improving job prospects in the countries from which large streams of people emigrate. Few people migrate to satisfy a lifelong aspiration or a yen for travel. What woman, giving birth, hopes her child will grow up and move to another country? Yet humans have always migrated, and no doubt always will. Best would be a world where development levels are roughly equal, few people are desperate to leave their countries of birth, and where migration to most countries is safe, legal, and in rough equilibrium with emigration out of them. That world is possible, but not yet in sight.

The second demographic wild card is the global HIV/AIDS pandemic, the future of which depends on how billions of people have sex over the next several decades and on whether governments get serious about preventing transmission. Already AIDS deaths exceed those of the Black Death of fourteenth-century Europe (when world population was a fraction of today's size). In southern Africa, Swaziland and Lesotho may now be losing population, no doubt the first countries on the continent to do so other than through war. Even more dramatic than population decline is an unprecedented hollowing out of age structure projected for the next few decades in these and other countries devastated by HIV. The ranks of the middle-aged appear likely to be thinned out, as though by a dark intelligence aiming at the most productive members of society. In most of the continent the sheer power of high birthrates is greater than that of deaths from AIDS, but other countries may join Swaziland and Lesotho in time.

Sometimes when I speak publicly on population, someone in the audience will ask, "Won't AIDS take care of the population problem?" I pause for breath before I respond. Which part of this rhetorical rattlesnake do I grab hold of first? *Take care of.* While lower birthrates have benefits well beyond the demographic ones, AIDS deaths disrupt entire societies, cultures, and nations and draw them toward chaos and state failure. Eventually I state the obvious: no threat attributable to population growth could or would justify the "solution" of increased death. Population activists strive to assure that falling birthrates, outcomes of intentional reproduction rather than inability to bear wanted children, are the overwhelming factor in slowing or reversing population growth. Population decline stemming mostly from premature death or involuntary infertility would be no sane person's triumph.

Reproductive health is a concept that elegantly brings all this together: intentional pregnancy, health care for mother and child, and prevention of the sexually transmitted infections that can contribute to AIDS deaths or infertility. Perhaps understandably, governments and international agencies spend almost all new funding for reproductive health on HIV/AIDS prevention and treatment. Few doubt that HIV/AIDS deserves more money and attention than it receives even now. But a comparable attention to broader reproductive health would combat HIV/AIDS as well as other sexually transmitted infections. It would also improve access to family planning services, which are not only needed for HIV prevention but also lead to positive demographic change.

Finally, a third wild card: the future of support from the world's governments for funding family planning. Demographers assume that birthrates will keep drifting downward, as they've been trending for decades, but there are no guarantees. In some countries in Africa there's scarcely a flicker of the fertility revolution sweeping the rest of the world. Women in Niger, for example, have 7.6 children on average, down from 8 in the 1970s, but actually fewer than the 8.2 children women reported as ideal in a 1998 survey. Their male partners dreamt at that time of having 10.8 children each, and those with more than one wife considered 15.3 children ideal.[14]

These are extremes in the fertility spectrum, with family-size ideals trending downward in most of the world's remaining high-fertility countries. There's good reason to believe that many women in high-fertility countries would welcome smaller families but don't have ready access to birth control or health services. For many developing countries, especially those in sub-Saharan Africa with large rural populations and financially strapped governments, it's no easy matter to build clinics and dispensaries, keep them consistently stocked with a full a range of contraceptives, and staff them all with capable health care providers. The world population projections produced by the United Nations and relied upon by journalists and analysts are based on the assumption that governments are making the right investments and will assure that the needed health care personnel and contraceptives are available. That's rosy and wrong: the gaps remain huge and hard to bridge, especially in rural areas, where 57 percent of the population of the developing world still lives.

Demographic possibilities for the next few centuries range from human extinction (global nuclear war, collision with a comet, a species-wide pandemic, name your catastrophe) to the theoretical "constant-fertility" population of trillions if average family size stays where it is today. But the standard UN projections, capably produced by expert demographers, are useful for thinking about the future in a world without major surprises: somewhere around 9 billion people by midcentury, and another billion less or more by 2100. You'd be a fool, however, to bet on any specific number.

Dodging the Stork

We do know with reasonable clarity what the human population is today and how it is changing. Today, the third child still prevails, and survives to parenthood, in most populations, and he or she will spur those populations to grow for decades to come. The prevalence of the third child does not occur because most women agree with Henrietta and want more than two children. Sex is a powerful drive and sexual intercourse takes place—anywhere from 100 million to 215 million times a day, but who's counting?[15]—mostly for reasons unrelated to any desire to launch new human life. Anywhere from a quarter to a half of all pregnancies worldwide are not welcomed at the time they occur by the women who conceived them.

Mistakes will be made. Birth control can fail, even when partners disrobe with the best of intentions to avoid pregnancy, and even with the best of contraceptives. Nor are couples who use no contraception always happy when the natural consequence of unprotected sex actually occurs. Many treat the resulting pregnancies as irreversible twists of fate, and lots of love results from these unplanned pregnancies, along with occasional child abandonment. But the magnitude of unwelcome pregnancy is well indicated by the roughly 46 million abortions that occur each year, roughly 1 for every 3 births. More than 40 percent of these abortions are illegal and most of these are performed in unsafe circumstances. More than 1 in 270 of the illegal ones end in a woman's death—not the sort of odds anyone would take lightly if she could avoid it—and many of the rest render women disabled or infertile or both for the rest of their lives.[16]

In a study of 144 women undergoing illegal abortions in Nigeria, half of them teenagers, only 25 percent of the women emerged from the procedures unscathed. The rest suffered one or more complications typical of ending a pregnancy in the shadows: anemia, sepsis, cervical tear, pelvic abscess, uterine perforation with peritonitis, injury to the gut, chemical vaginitis, laceration of the vaginal wall, vesicovaginal fistula—and, in 9 percent of the cases, death.[17] Botched abortions are among the reasons half a million women die from pregnancy-related causes each year. "To become pregnant is to approach the door of death," a woman told a colleague of mine in Bolivia, where women face nearly a 1-in-50 lifetime chance of dying in pregnancy or childbirth. In Afghanistan, the risk is 1 in 6.[18] Not many wars force combatants to face such dismal odds.

However you feel about abortion, the politics of which thoroughly dominate population policy today, you can't seriously claim that erecting barriers to contraception will make abortions less common. Quite the reverse: as access to safe and effective contraceptive methods improves, rates of abortion go down.[19] From a demographic perspective, it's worth adding that no country has ever reached sustained replacement fertility without the availability of safe and affordable abortion—even if only in an adjacent country, as is the case in Ireland and Poland.[20] Better access to effective contraception could undermine that correlation, but it's also possible that access to safe abortion is essential to ending population growth through lower birthrates. That's not an argument you can imagine helping the cause of abortion rights. But, then again, not many other arguments seem to be changing hearts and minds on the subject. Abortion will always be controversial, and it will always be with us. A sensible strategy—if sense were a part of the discussion—would be to make it safe, accessible, and likely to occur as early as possible in a pregnancy, while improving the effectiveness and reach of contraception. And, of course, support abstinence as an option, especially for the young. But to criminalize abortion is to ask for dead and maimed women and to bring on infanticide.

Some economists write about childbearing as though couples sat at the dining room table and worked out their mutual interest in having babies the way they might plan their investments or select a new refrigerator.[21] Baby making is nothing like buying a refrigerator, however; it's more like the appliance retailer bringing you a new refrigerator every year or two unless you've taken effective and consistent steps on a nearly daily basis to make sure none is delivered. Sexual intercourse is an act of intimate shared pleasure that occurs "many hundreds or even thousands of times more frequently than is needed to achieve the desired number of pregnancies," as University of California population and health specialist Martha Campbell and colleagues have written.[22] Rather than akin to ordering a refrigerator, more often the act includes steps—if nothing more than a prayer—to keep the delivery truck away from the door.

Despite the problem of unbidden pregnancy, a conservative estimate of 125 million women around the world—a population the size of Japan or Nigeria—are sexually active, do not want to become pregnant, and yet are not using any contraception. Why aren't they using it? Economists would say the absence of supply indicates an absence of demand. But contraception is not a soft drink. It's a money loser for many companies without some kind of partnership with governmental or intergovernmental agencies. Demand is hard to project. Product liability suits are a constant threat, distribution a headache, and quality control a never-ending challenge. For the consumer, especially the urban poor and most people in rural areas, there may be no convenient drug store, no affordable doctor, no nearby clinic or other source of contraceptives.

Sometimes, of course, there are clinics and pharmacies nearby, and sexually active people who don't want a new child still don't visit them. The reasons that unintentional pregnancy persists side by side with available birth control are complex. In many cases the failure to use birth control may stem from legitimate concerns about side effects or principled opposition to the idea of contraception. But too often, women forgo birth control because of senseless barriers: misinformation about side effects, low self-esteem, inability to oppose men's sexual demands, the lack of affordable contraceptive services within a reasonable distance, and the requirement of unnecessary tests or a physician's prescription to purchase contraceptives.[23] These are barriers that we could begin to break down if societies would commit to doing so.

Losing Control

"Population control" at times has meant what it says: governments or medical personnel trying to control women's reproduction for whatever reasons. Where this kind of control survives today, it does so despite opposition from the vast majority of reproductive health advocates, public health professionals, and demographers around the world. China, where coercion to enforce a one-child-per-couple policy has been documented, is an authoritarian outlier. Recent evidence offers hope that Chinese officials are backing away from coercive methods—even though the policy seems fairly well accepted by most of those affected.[24] In China and elsewhere, the glare of media coverage may have made more difficult the abuses found in some governmental efforts to reduce fertility.

It is not population *control*, a term I will not use in any positive sense in this book, that depresses demographic growth over the long term. Nor is it, in all likelihood, simple economic development and growth, as many economists assume. Instead, the main factor in regulating population is women's ability to manage their own fertility, ideally in agreement with their sexual partners. Those who hear this concept as a prescription for runaway population growth simply haven't followed the research on humanity's incredible shrinking family size. Those who see it a license for sex without commitment or responsibility are a more challenging source of opposition. I invite them to visit a well-staffed and well-stocked health clinic somewhere in Africa, Asia, or Latin America and see what reproductive health care really is.

For a population peak to occur through birthrate declines by the middle of the twenty-first century, families in which women bear three or more children will have to be in rough balance with families that have just one child or none at all. Few governments are moving with real urgency to enable more women and couples to put small-family intentions into effect. Until governments offer such support, no assumption that replacement fertility will arrive any time soon is a safe one—unless replacement fertility itself floats upward on a rising tide of death. For these reasons and more, few threats related to population are as worrisome as the prospect of setbacks for women's status and persistent barriers to their access to health services.

As the story of "Condom Sister" Henrietta suggests, women's childbearing patterns ripple out into the world through population and its influences. They also powerfully shape women's own destinies. It's astounding how many words have flowed in the population debate without much consideration of the lives of those who bear and raise children. The relative silence feeds a long-standing tension between advocates for women's health and rights and advocates for policies aimed at slowing population growth. Some women may worry that efforts to "control" population could turn them into instruments of government policies that have nothing to do with their own interests or, worse, into targets of outright coercion. This fear has roots deep in history—although, as we'll see, most reproductive coercion has aimed at getting women to have more children, not fewer. The tension between governmental and social interests in population and the individual interests of women and their partners' could dissolve with a better understanding of how those interests intersect. It's not population control, but a letting go of control over women's lives that could lead us safely between the Scylla and Charybdis of stressful growth and a fading decline. To begin to understand how this could work, we'll need to look into the past, as far back as the darkness of prehistory allows.

TWO

The Population Growers

Be fruitful, and multiply; fill the earth and subdue it; have dominion over the
fish of the sea; over the birds of the air, and over every living thing that moves
on the earth.
    —Genesis 1:28

Throughout most of humanity's past, the challenge was species survival.
How could the half-pint bipeds who appeared on the scene in Africa a
few million years ago secure themselves an ecological niche—as every successful species must—and hold on to it? They had no fangs, no claws, and
modest muscles at best. The earliest hominids to move on two feet may well
have been lumbering runners, unable to outsprint either prey or predators.
Such vulnerabilities may have caused more hominid species than paleon-
tologists have even found or named to blink out after relatively short tenures
on the planet. A few, however, survived and thrived long enough to leave
Africa and to master much different ecosystems in distant Asia and Europe.
One species—*Homo sapiens*, us—took over the world.

We can speculate about what led the more successful species—*Homo erectus*, *Homo neandertalensis* (the Neanderthals), and modern humans—to disperse around the planet. Learning to wield fire must have been important.

So was the development of tools, though some apes use and even craft tools, and none proliferated across varied ecosystems as humans have. For *Homo sapiens*, at least, the invention of language and art may have provided the sparks that ignited humanity's takeover. We may never know the combination of factors that brought us to where we are now: 6.7 billion strong and securely occupying all the world's continents.

We can be confident of one reason, however, though it rarely receives the credit it deserves. Women succeeded at safely giving birth and then nurturing helpless infants (on average, more than two) to their own early adulthood. Early population growth, which eventually enabled people to encircle the globe, is a direct outcome of those efforts. The fact that child care and feeding are almost universally women's work is a pretty obvious point, but its implications for population growth didn't come into view until the 1970s, when a number of women scholars began questioning the conventional wisdom about human evolution.

In the traditional view, human domination of the planet got its start because Man the Toolmaker—Benjamin Franklin coined this phrase[1]—kept honing his weapons and cooperative strategies for bringing down big animals. But this theory is looking more and more old-fashioned, especially as researchers observe contemporary primate behavior and unearth artifacts from ground where early hominids once lived and died. Current research suggests a more nuanced picture of cultural evolution—one that includes contributions from both sexes.

There's no particular reason to assign men the credit, we know now, for making the first human tools or even the first weapons. Among chimpanzees, females are the more likely sex to make tools. Researchers working in savannas in southeastern Senegal recently observed female chimps crafting simple spears from branches and using them to jab into tree hollows in search of tasty nocturnal primates called bushbabies.[2] Something similar may have been true of hominids and early humans.

Even after males assumed mastery of weapons and other tools, planetary domination would have eluded them without help. All the meat in the world won't keep children alive if they aren't born safely and nurtured with care and vigilance for fifteen years or more. That suggests some vital roles for women. We can get a sense of the technologies and cooperative strategies women devised, although we must rely on a certain amount of conjecture.

The vast literature on human origins grows out of archaeological and genetic evidence, contemporary behavior observed in great apes and humans, and simple logic.[3] Speculation on the origins of human attributes, from fur-free bodies to assisted birth, mostly falls into the realm of what the late biologist and writer Stephen Jay Gould called "just-so stories," after the explanatory tales made famous by Rudyard Kipling.[4] These stories are not facts, but if well reasoned they may stimulate interest, lead to testable hypotheses, and perhaps prompt thinking about choices open to us today.

Homo sapiens populations did, of course, "fill the earth," growing and spilling out across the landscape in ways no other large animal's populations ever had, until in a blink of an evolutionary eye we occupied every habitable nook and cranny on six of the world's seven continents. Our species wouldn't have survived without women's efforts—in fact, not without adaptations and innovations that almost surely belonged to women alone. The argument that women played an equal or even primary role in early population growth rests on the simple fact that in every known premodern society they performed the crucial task of assuring that babies and children stayed alive. This is not to say that any particular woman is obligated to perform this task, or that any man cannot do so. Each of us is, or should be, free to choose. It is to say that everywhere, at every time in the past, directly assuring a child's survival to adulthood has been a triumph for which women far more than men can claim credit.

Why Grow?

Demographers and paleoanthropologists tend to focus on the flip side of the question I'm developing here. Rather than asking why population growth began, they wonder why our numbers grew so slowly for so long after our species emerged. We can be certain of the low densities and glacial growth not just because bones and artifacts are so scarce, but because of the math.

From the emergence of *Homo sapiens* around 200,000 years ago to the height of the Roman Empire, population grew to about 300 million human beings, which suggests extremely low average rates of growth during that time. Suppose that 70,000 years ago our prehistoric ancestors numbered about 20,000, a reasonable guess (some estimates are even lower) based on genetic analysis.[5] This group—similar in size to the populations of some gorilla subspecies today—would have on average gained just 1 person per 7,000 every year to arrive at the estimated population of the world 2,000 years ago.[6]

That's not to say populations never grew rapidly in the past. As human beings spread around the world, many populations may well have gone through periods of explosive growth followed by catastrophic decline. Averaged out over time this looks like relative stability, but not for the people who lived through such boom-bust cycles.

Suppose our early population had grown consistently at about 2 percent per year, the growth rate around 1970. Within just 6,000 years a spherical mass of humanity would have been ballooning out from our solar system at the speed of light.[7] That's just one illustration of the power of exponential growth, and although the global growth rate has fallen to around 1.2 percent per year, we can be confident that even this lower rate won't last. Any growth rate significantly above zero, if sustained, eventually would make the earth so crowded that death rates would rise, and this would happen long before humanity began exploding toward the outer solar system. Behaviors that aren't sustainable—including having third surviving children—eventually stop.

But why grow at all? Why didn't human beings and their hominid predecessors become just another genus of apes—albeit apes that walked on two legs rather than four—that stuck to one kind of habitat in one region of

Africa or Asia? Why didn't we max out at 5 or 10 million individuals, as each of the ape (and, indeed, most large mammal) species most likely did? Why and how did we conquer every type of ice-free landform from tropical rain forests to deserts and balloon our numbers to hundreds of times that of other species similar to our own? The answers, or a start anyway, may lie in bipedal-ism itself, which emerged at least 4 million and perhaps as many as 6 million years ago. The unusual animal behavior of standing vertically and walking on two feet (only penguins share the stance) began among primates around the time that a particular line of apes split into subpopulations. One of these gave rise to today's chimpanzees and bonobos (sometimes called pygmy chim-panzees). The other led to a dozen or more species of hominids and humans, eventually including us.

The Oldest Profession?

Curiously, it may have been the business of standing on two feet itself that helped launch the demographic success of hominids and, eventually, mod-ern humans. The genetic and fossil evidence hints that hominids and chimps interbred for a million years or so, producing hybrid offspring whose fossils may confuse paleoanthropologists about human origins for years to come.[8] New candidates for the first bipedal primate nonetheless keep emerging from the sediment. One such candidate could even predate the time when primates divided into subpopulations, suggesting that some ancestors of chimpanzees briefly tried a humanlike erect posture and then returned to all fours.[9]

We know next to nothing about the social behavior of the earliest hominids, but we can make some suppositions. Fossil evidence and near-universal behavior among modern humans both support the hypothesis that a key aspect of human birth helped make us what we are today. The earliest cooperative relationship unrelated to food procurement or fighting may well have been that between a woman delivering a baby and a person assisting her. In all probability, the first career specialist was the midwife.

"For millions of years, primates have secluded themselves in treetops or bushes to give birth," note anthropologists Karen Rosenberg and Wenda Trevathan. "Human beings are the only primate species that regularly seeks assistance during labor and delivery."[10]

Why? The most compelling explanation for the near-uniformity of birth assistance—there are cultural and individual exceptions, but not many—is that giving birth alone would have led bipedal hominids to an evolutionary dead end. Giving birth in seclusion was and is more dangerous for us than for quadrupedal monkeys and apes because of our anatomy. Any mother who has anticipated or experienced a vaginal delivery knows that the large size of a human baby's head makes it challenging to push the baby safely through the birth canal. But the need for birth assistance may go back much further, back to the days when hominid heads were no larger than those of chimpanzees today. The origins of birth assistance may lie not so much in our social nature—indeed, birth assistance may have helped shape that nature—but in the anatomy of the human pelvis and birth canal.

As our ancestors began standing and moving routinely on two feet, their pelvic bones shifted significantly to support the full weight of a vertically carried upper body. Archaeologists can often tell even from partial remains of a fossilized pelvis whether a primate walked on two feet or four. It would be surprising if the new arrangement of bones, occurring in the part of the body where birth takes place, did not complicate the birthing process.

In supporting an erect posture, the new pelvic structure narrowed the gap between the tailbone and pubic bones. In a normal human birth, the infant's head must twist 90 degrees after entering the birth canal sideways and then pass through this narrow gap facing the mother's rear (usually with a slight tilt toward one side or the other). The back of the baby's head presses against the mother's pubic bones. If you've witnessed a conventional vaginal delivery, you may recall that the baby's head emerges facing the bed on which the mother lies, not the ceiling. Any other position makes the birth process risky for mother and child.

The "twisted" and rear-facing birth of humans contrasts with the quite literally straightforward birth of quadrupedal primates. These infants typically emerge with their faces in the same direction as their mothers'. The primate mother can look down at the little face as it comes into the light, reach easily to clear the mouth and nose of mucus, untangle the umbilical cord, and gently tug the new arrival up the front of her body to her breast. Bipedal mothers, by contrast, faced a new danger in doing what had once come naturally. They couldn't clear mouths and noses of mucus without twisting the infants' fragile necks. And guiding their babies easily to the breast proved just as risky.

"If she tries tries to accelerate the delivery by grabbing the baby and guiding it from the birth canal," Rosenberg and Trevathan write of the laboring human mother, "she risks bending its back awkwardly against the natural curve of its spine. Pulling on a newborn at this angle risks injury to its spinal cord, nerves and muscles."[11]

Even worse is the breech birth, in which the infant enters the birth canal feet or hips first. Such births occur in about 3 percent of human births, and more frequently when babies are born prematurely. Unassisted breech births would be 100 percent fatal, Trevathan suggests, and any genetic tendency toward such births would long ago have been selected against and eliminated, unless something—or someone—intervened.[12]

What to do? Historians of childbirth believe bipedal females had to go against what must have been a deeply ingrained instinct and seek assistance before the birth process began. Women sought a supportive, familiar individual at this critical time.[13] They may have asked for help from a neighboring female who might need the same assistance herself someday. We can only imagine how they asked, whether through facial expression or hand gestures or distinctive sounds—perhaps a stimulus to the invention of language itself.

Birth assistance was all the more helpful because in hominids, and eventually human beings, hands never used for walking were developing increasingly opposable thumbs and thus became well adapted to securely cradling the small round skull of an emerging infant. Some females may have found that their growing proficiency at assisting births earned them status or other benefits. We could call these females *midwives*, an ancient word derived from Old English for "with woman."

Could these midwives have been male partners or other men? We can't rule it out, but the history of human childbirth up to the days of modern medicine offers no basis for assuming such a male role. Midwives in nearly all cultures have been almost exclusively female, and the delivery room a female realm—a point made especially clear in scenes of childbirth in Renaissance European painting.[14]

For hominid mothers, assisted birth was no small behavior change. Most animals not only give birth unaided, they go to great effort to find solitude before the critical moment. Domestic dogs and cats find havens of privacy behind boxes in a cluttered basement or garage. Most mammal mothers will not tolerate attention when caring for newborns. Baboons are so protective of their infants that any nearby female must first groom the new mother's coat just to sneak a peek at the new arrival. The fewer babies in a troop, in a nice example of primate supply-and-demand economics, the longer the required "pay-per-view" grooming time.[15] For anatomical reasons, our foremothers took a different route. We can guess that their reliance on birth assistance also made it easier to accept help throughout the long process of raising a child. This, too, likely made all the difference in child survival.

While there's no way to be certain that assisted birth and midwifery itself are as old as bipedalism in humans, the hypothesis is not widely challenged. My own conversations with skilled and traditional birth attendants in developing countries support the universality of rear-facing birth as "normal" in those countries, just as it is in industrialized countries. True, unassisted births are hardly unknown today. Djenaba, a Malian teenager whose story I tell later in this book, related to me that she considered it shameful to ask for help at a birth. There's something of a myth that rural women in developing countries routinely set their work aside and give birth alone as if it were the most normal thing to do in the world. In reality, however, unassisted birth is a hazardous aberration occurring mostly in those countries with the least developed health care delivery systems. One recent study of childbirth in a rural district in Nepal found that 89 percent of births there were assisted.[16]

Assisted birth may have become the norm soon after the lineage of humans and chimpanzees permanently forked. Or it may have emerged more gradually, becoming truly essential only as large infant skulls made deliveries even more dangerous. At some point in the distant past, at least, midwives gained their unique expertise, and obstetrics—the true "oldest profession"—was born.

Why is this so momentous? For the simple reason that midwives guide infants through the most dangerous moment in all of life. Even in wealthy countries today, where fewer than one child in a hundred dies before his or her first birthday, there's no other half hour in a human life span that claims so much life as the very first. Not the tenth hour or the thousandth or seven hundred thousandth. The changes in pelvic structure that allowed hominids to walk on two feet actually *accentuated* the dangers of childbirth, yet bipedal species did not die out, but rather started to grow. If the hazards of bipedal childbirth forced women to go against eons of instinct and ask for help, such a master stroke of cultural evolution may well have more than compensated for the dangers of the biological kind. Midwifery, in short, may have dramatically elevated child survival rates, the essential ingredient of species-wide population growth. The tools and cooperative hunting strategies so long celebrated in earlier accounts of human evolution undoubtedly played a role, but without new adaptations that made birth safer and helped females nurture helpless and slow-growing infants, the gradual demographic expansion of ancient hominids and modern humans never would have occurred.

We will see more of midwives in this book. Their expertise encompasses not only safe delivery, but safe pregnancy before birth and safe infant and child care afterward. At some point, midwives' wisdom also came to include how to prevent pregnancy, how to avoid a birth once pregnancy had begun, and—in some cases and as a last resort—how to end motherhood by ending the life of the infant. The ongoing balancing act of sex, birth, maternal investment, and offspring survival is something females have lived with since before humanity began, and it is intimately connected to the path human population has taken from prehistory to the present.

Survival Strategies

Enough human babies survived to expand our numbers. This is one difference between hominids and our great-ape relatives, whose populations probably never exceeded the single-digit millions. Chimpanzee females, for example, typically give birth to four offspring, of which two survive, leaving chimp populations roughly stable at low levels.[17] We know little about the demographic careers of most hominid species, except that those of every species but *Homo sapiens* ended. But as we'll see, at least some species of the genus *Homo* eventually burst out of Africa to occupy other continents. At key points over the past 2 million years, third surviving children were more the rule than the exception.

To understand why hominid numbers grew while those of related species remained constant or dwindled, it's helpful to look at the connections between reproduction, survival strategies, and evolution. We'll see later that the nineteenth-century pioneers of the concept of natural selection, Charles Darwin and Alfred Wallace, were inspired by Thomas Robert Malthus's work on human population. Evolutionary biology and demography also share an obvious and overwhelming interest in reproduction and its failures and successes.

Like all species, ours is the product of unplanned parenthood—random genetic shifts and natural selection interacting with environmental changes and perhaps the occasional catastrophe. The idea of *reproductive success* lies at the heart of the evolutionary theory that explains this process. Survival of

the fittest isn't really the point; what matters is that the fittest reproduce successfully. It's not even enough just to become a parent. What you really want
to do is become an *ancestor*. The daunting feat of hurling your genes into the
distant future requires that your reproduction "takes" for generations to
come. Your young must survive to their own reproductive ages and accomplish the same feat with their young.

This survival challenge is shared by every species that reproduces sexually.
Mrs. and Mr. Mole, Magpie, or Mayfly need at least two offspring that make it
well into their own age of reproduction, and having more improves the chance
that generational replacement will continue. The Law of the Third Child—
without some third children, your population disappears—applies to all sexual
reproducers. Frogs, turtles, and any number of fish and insect species lay eggs
by the hundreds and thousands, all in the hope (speaking biologically) that at
least two will make it to adulthood. In a stable population, on average, over time,
only that many succeed. One frog couple may produce three frogs that make it
to adulthood, but another frog couple will produce only one—unless environmental checks on population growth are overcome. If many third, fourth, and
fifth offspring can survive those checks, the population will begin to grow.

Ecologists identify two broad strategies for getting sufficient numbers of
children to survive to adulthood. One, called the *r* strategy (originally for
"rate of growth"), is to produce as many little zygotes as you can, as quickly
as possible, and then ignore them once they're born. Surviving is their problem. You hope that at least two and maybe three or more out of the myriad
to which you've given birth ultimately will make it through the perils of life
long enough to provide you with grandzygotes. But you offer no help, not
even an allowance or the keys to the family car. Frogs, turtles, reptiles, and
insects are all *r* strategists.

The second strategy is called *K*, for carrying capacity. *K*-selected parents
are all about their children. The females are soccer moms. They have few offspring and grow each one within their bodies for a long time. Then they actually *care* for their offspring in life, feeding, protecting, and guiding them a

good bit of the way to adulthood. This was an evolutionary revolution whenever it first arose, and it is now common among mammals, birds, fishes, and some reptiles. Some dinosaurs appear to have cared for their young.[18]

K and r are really opposite poles on a continuum of reproductive strategies. Few species occupy the extreme ends. Most species are identified with one or the other strategy relative to what is done by some other species or under some other circumstance. Compared to reptiles, mammals are very much K-selected. Mammals in fact gained their name from organs (mammaries) that evolved to allow mothers to feed their dependent newborn on demand. Other characteristics—fur, live birth, and four-chambered hearts, for example—also distinguish this class of animals. But Carolus Linnaeus, the mid-eighteenth-century Swedish naturalist who invented modern biological taxonomy, named mammals for their teats. We'll revisit him and his fixation with breasts, sex, and population later.

Human beings are in most ways an extreme example of K-selection. In no other species do offspring return to their parents for shelter and feeding after adolescence. Everything is relative, however, and in various places and at various times humans tilted slightly toward r-selection, with relatively high fertility in comparison with our great-ape relatives, who are notoriously slow reproducers and whose populations rarely grow. This modest boost in the number of births helped guarantee our survival in a dangerous natural world. It seems less adaptive today, as parents struggle to provide each child with the best health care and education their money can buy.

Men Are r, Women Are K

From Darwin's time onward, evolutionary biologists have understood that males and females have differing strategies for reproducing and passing on their genes. By nature, males tend to behave more like r-selected organisms, even in a finely honed K-selected species like our own. Producing 100 million sperm each day and capable—or so we males like to think—of copulating whenever an opportunity arises, men physically are able to conceive children with hundreds of women. A few may have done so. Moulay Ismail the Bloodthirsty, an early eighteenth-century Moroccan ruler, reportedly enjoyed a harem of 500 women and fathered 888 children. (By contrast the fertility record for women may be 64 children, given the more exigent female reproductive role.[19]) Psychologist Dorothy Einon and several colleagues argue that such high male fertility is exaggerated and that unauthorized harem visitors probably fathered many of Ismail's children.[20]

Through DNA analysis, scientists can identify the descendants of prolific fathers who lived centuries ago. Genetic analysis has suggested that some 16 million men living today in and around central Asia can trace a direct patrilineage to a single ancestor of Genghis Khan. Researchers figure that the great marauder's brothers and perhaps even his uncles were reproductively active as well, making the most likely common male ancestor of these 16 million men the father or grandfather of the historic Khan.[21] It's a safe bet, to say the least, that men like Moulay Ismail and Genghis Khan adhered to the other key aspect of the *r* strategy as well: offering zero care to any but a favored few of their offspring. When you sire dozens or hundreds of children, you can be confident that some of them will secure a perch for your genes in future populations. The kids' mothers, whatever their names were, will see to that.

Few men, of course, are as reproductively successful as these paragons of the *r* strategy. And to be fair, today and in the past many men contribute significantly to their children's survival and well-being. The male *r* strategy was nonetheless probably common among our hominid ancestors, as it is in many human cultures and among many of our primate relatives. In any species, behavioral ecologists note, it is the sex (usually female) that invests more in care of offspring that most determines whether reproduction will succeed—by producing young that go on themselves to reproduce. For the sex (usually male) that invests less in offspring care, the best reproductive strategy is to maximize mating opportunities, since any investment in parenting is likely to matter less to long-term reproductive success.[22]

Natural selection encouraged adaptations among males that helped them hurl their genes into the future like a message in a bottle. Among these adaptations were large overall size in gorillas and prodigious testicles among chimpanzees. Deadly accurate throwing arms among early men may have played a similar role by demonstrating hunting prowess to potential mates. One implication of female and male reproductive traits is that most females will end up producing long-lived offspring, but only the successful competitors among males will do so. That, in turn, may influence how much care mothers invest in sons compared to daughters, based on maternal assessments of sons' reproductive potential.[23] High-status females may consciously or unconsciously favor male offspring, who will presumably inherit their status and thus be likely to extend their genetic legacy through prolific reproduction. Low-status females may prefer daughters, since—assuming status is largely inherited—the daughters are more likely than any sons to produce at least two or three offspring who will survive to adulthood.

Since frequency of sexual intercourse is an important factor in the probability of conception, an energetic male whose partner at least tolerated his attentions could improve his odds of becoming an ancestor with that partner. But without a role in childbirth and not much of one in child care, a male's best shot at producing a little bundle of reproductive success came from outcompeting other males for mating opportunities. No matter how healthy or attractive an impregnated female, however, she could be an unwilling or incompetent mother and hence might lose or abandon her child.

A Mother's Love

The lack of more direct influence on child survival complicates male reproductive strategy. Until recently, one typical hypothesis was that violent and hypersexed males naturally succeeded in passing on their genes, thus winning the selection game and becoming, in effect, *us*, dude. Evolutionary biologist Randy Thornhill and evolutionary anthropologist Craig Palmer contended that rape is adaptive, because males find it an "efficient" route to reproductive success. Rapists actually choose the most nubile targets and avoid unnecessary violence, the two argued, in the interest of maximizing the probability of the act resulting in successful conception and birth.[24] This idea, however, seems to ignore the role of parental investment and nurture in long-term reproductive success. That success depends critically on the commitment of mothers and their chosen helpers to invest in infant and child survival for fifteen years or more. If at any point a mother stops investing in her child—perhaps because she did not choose or welcome either the father's sexual attention or the resulting conception—that child is very likely to die, and the father's genes with it.

The recent few decades of research on nonhuman primates and human societies—by anthropologists Sarah Blaffer Hrdy, Barbara Smuts, and others who have followed in their path—make clear that "mother love" is not so powerful and undiscriminating that any child born alive is guaranteed unlimited maternal care. Mothers can favor certain offspring while caring indifferently for others. Or they can neglect, abandon, or even kill their young. However abhorrent to us, such behavior is not necessarily patholog-ical but may instead result from a subconscious calculation of reproductive self-interest. Pregnancy, birth, breastfeeding, and basic infant care demand a staggering and almost unceasing outpouring of maternal energy and resources. As we'll see in more detail, breastfeeding intensively and on demand acts as a fairly effective contraceptive. A mother who commits to raising a child who dies young has squandered time and resources that might otherwise have gone to a child who would survive and reproduce successfully in turn. This is a main reason, Hrdy notes, that "quantity [of children] has rarely been the top priority for a mother."[25]

At some point in human evolution, such subconscious calculations of reproductive self-interest transformed into consciousness and reproduc-tive strategy. Women didn't simply wake up in some recent century and realize it might be possible to prevent an unwanted pregnancy or birth. Documentation of that realization goes back thousands of years, as we'll see, and anthropological evidence suggests it has been common all over the world. The animal comparisons noted by anthropologists such as Hrdy and Smuts suggest that the roots of the urge to avoid conception may be truly ancient indeed.

At first glance it may seem that male reproductive success is at odds with the female interest in rationing maternal care to produce the best long-term outcomes. If males are making little investment in birth and childrearing, it seems logical that their best bet is to father as many children as possible. But this isn't the whole picture. It turns out that to really win the sexual selection game—and also to contribute to the growth of one's group—primate males need to mate with females who will be "good mothers." From an evolutionary perspective, these are mothers who make their own reproductive calculations successfully and who strategically nurture to adulthood any child in whom they "invest" their own energy and resources.

Males might also help out the females with nurturing. That may mean little more than sharing food with females. Some male chimpanzees do this, and females who receive these food gifts appear to do a bit better reproductively. But that's not the same as true offspring care. A few primate dads have evolved to specialize in infant and child survival. Tamarin and marmoset males sometimes help deliver their mates' offspring, apparently the only examples of assisted birth among nonhuman primates. And some fathers among indris, the largest species of lemur, nest with older offspring while the mothers cuddle in a nearby tree with the latest arrival.[26] Care of older offspring is especially important to population growth, because adolescence is the stage just before reproduction, so indri dads are making a real contribution to their own reproductive success.

There's no way to know when hominid or human father care—direct male investment in their children's survival—began. And what actually constitutes male care is another issue—more than simply bringing home the bacon, whether a rib of mastodon or a big bonus from the boss. Some male apes engage in occasional physical play with young individuals. A few even foster orphans. Among humans, one indicator of paternal involvement in childraising is the extent to which men carry infants and young children. Assessing this in hunter-gatherer societies is akin to a modern woman asking about another's husband, Does he change the diapers? How often?

Among the !Kung San people of the Kalahari Desert in southern Africa, researchers have credited men with carrying infants under six months old only about 2 percent of the time these children are carried. Among the Aka Pygmies of central Africa this proportion approaches 20 percent.[27] It's hard to know how typical these time values are, but in no known group are children carried more often by their fathers than by their mothers. Similarly, in all the groups studied on these points, men tend quickly to hand finicky or crying infants and toddlers back to women, as if only women knew the secrets of soothing troubled children.

One indication that fathers' contributions to raising children don't matter much, at least as far as natural selection is concerned, is the lack of menopause in men. From an evolutionary perspective, the survival of females well past the age at which they can reproduce is puzzling. Some scholars connect postmenopausal survival to the so-called grandmother hypothesis, which says that women contribute to the survival of their children's children. If females gave birth near the end of their lives in a species such as ours, where so much depends on mothers "being there" for offspring during a long dependent childhood, what would become of the children orphaned after their mothers' deaths, including emotionally needy teenagers? By contrast, if women stop reproducing in their late forties and give care instead to grandchildren, reproductive success takes on a meaning unknown to any other K-selected species, with females directly ensuring their own status as ancestors.[28]

Nothing comparable to menopause developed in older men. This is unlikely to be because they were needed to father more children—sperm is perpetually a glut on the market—but because male care was rarely critical to the survival of children they conceived at any age. "If the father is dead, the family suffers," a nineteenth-century Sicilian proverb suggests. "If the mother dies, the family cannot exist." Researchers found that in nineteenth-century Sweden only 1 in 50 children whose mothers died within a year of the birth survived to age five. A 1974 study in Matlab, Bangladesh, found that only 1 in 20 infants who survived a mother's death at delivery reached their first birthdays. Some Eskimo groups customarily abandoned to the open Arctic air any infants and one-year-olds whose mothers had died.[29]

The Mating Game

For most apes and probably for early hominids, we wouldn't expect much dadlike behavior. How would a male know he was the dad? Establishing paternity is an age-old dilemma, and the inevitable uncertainty has influenced male-female relations and the many sexual and parenting arrangements observed in primates and human societies. Female chimpanzees, bonobos, and orangutans tend to have multiple partners during any sexually receptive period, sometimes as a result of coercion by larger, overpowering males. Even gorilla females may have multiple mates despite spending much of their time in a group of one alpha male and several submissive females. There's no consistent pattern and often considerable diversity within species, so there's not much to go on in speculating about male-female sexual and social relations among our hominid ancestors. Such relations don't fossilize. Even the remains of stone tools are silent on gender, since there's no way to be certain who shaped them.

Bodies tell tales, however—even about gender relations. After the anatomical specialization for reproduction, average body size and shape present the next most obvious difference between the sexes. Most primates are at least moderately dimorphic, meaning "of two shapes." Among our great-ape relatives, males average anywhere from a few pounds heavier than females to nearly twice their size. Why these differences among the sexes, and why the variation among species? It's likely that males competing to control multiple female mating partners gained an advantage with larger bodies—assuming they were spending more time stable on the ground than precariously in the treetops. With less need to overwhelm rivals, monogamous males—gibbons and indris, for example—tend to be closer in size to their mating partners.

The variation in gender size ratios among nonhuman primates was echoed among the hominids. Males in such early species as *Australopithecus afarensis* (to which the famous fossil Lucy belonged) were around 50 percent larger than females. Men today, by contrast, have an edge on women of only around 15 to 20 percent.[30] Since these dimorphic differences seem to be related to mating arrangements, they ought to tell us something about our own in prehistory. Based on male genital differences between humans and great apes—humans fall midway between gorillas and chimpanzees, for example, in testicular endowment—Hrdy concludes that today's humans come from a legacy that was either polygynous or that combined both polygyny and monogamy. She thinks solitary males mated opportunistically, only sometimes committing to specific partners and their offspring. Considering today's mating spectrum, from the multiple wives of some Muslim cultures to big-city singles bars from New York to Nairobi, the picture has a certain familiarity.

To add to the mystery of sex lives past, humans are in most ways more flexible in their approach to intercourse than their primate relatives. In most species females will tolerate sex only around the time they ovulate and can conceive, a behavior called estrus. During this period, females signal their sexual receptiveness with obvious physical and color changes in their rumps and genitals. Human females are unusual in being able to choose sex at any time. That's not to say that they will do so at any particular time, a point some male scholars have embarrassed themselves by confusing. When anthropologist Owen Lovejoy published his hypothesis about the origins of bipedalism in 1981 in the journal *Science,* the editors failed to notice and excise an adolescent inside joke Lovejoy included. "Human females are continuously sexually receptive," he wrote, appending the endnote, "D. C. Johanson, personal communication." The communicator of this "finding" was Donald Johanson, a friend of Lovejoy's and the discoverer of the Lucy fossil. "Any male who entertains this illusion" of continuous human female sexual receptivity, psychobiologist Frank Beach famously commented, "must be a very old man with a short memory or very young man due for bitter disappointment."[31]

Hypotheses to explain the lack of estrus in women are as numerous as those who come up with them. No one really knows when or why human females discarded this basic primate behavior. One of the benefits of women's time-flexible openness to sex, suggests physician and family planning specialist Malcolm Potts, may be the male-female bonding that ongoing and frequent sexual intercourse can promote. Such bonding (and the frequency of sex itself) boosts men's confidence in paternity and their interest in the survival of offspring. Even if women continued to provide the primary child care, paternal involvement with children through food provision and family defense would have promoted reproductive success.[32]

The evolution of pair bonding—marriage, essentially, before licenses and joint income taxes—is an almost comically contentious topic in the gender-sensitive discipline of paleoanthropology. In 1968, male anthropologists Sherwood Washburn and C. S. Lancaster speculated that as hunting skills improved in early *Homo* species, females began to trade sexual favors with males willing and able to offer them and their offspring protein-packed meat in exchange.[33] A few years later, anthropologists Nancy Tanner and Adrienne Zihlman made a feminist-tinged counterproposal. Males in prehistory were essentially bumptious oafs, they argued, useful mainly for reproduction. Hunting large animals was less dependable and much less important to group food security than the gathering and collecting that females performed. Hence there was no real need for the food contributions of males. True, men did form what the anthropologists called coalitionary groups to help each other hunt, but women did the same thing to improve their foraging, and they were by far the more dependable providers of food.

The cooperative arrangements women developed while foraging, Tanner and Zihlman suggested importantly, were also useful in *alloparent-ing*, a term that means acting as a short-term surrogate mother ("other parent") as a favor to a relative or comrade in need of a babysitter.[34] We might guess that midwives were among the first alloparents, having already bonded in their own way with the newborns of other women. Researchers who followed Tanner and Zihlman developed the thesis that human alloparenting itself may have been among the most important behavioral advances for ensuring the survival of third children and the species itself.[35]

But back to mating. Another popular paradigm among scholars was the "bodyguard" model, with pair bonds emerging as females strategically traded sexual favors to selected males in exchange for protection from aggression and sexual coercion threatened by unfavored males.[36] While hardly an attractive antecedent for modern matrimony, this model does have the advantage of contemporary illustration. An anonymous German woman, for example, wrote about the rapes she endured in Berlin in 1945 by occupying Red Army soldiers. She soon developed an exclusive sexual relationship with one rapist willing to protect her from other attackers and provide her with food. "The spoils [women] are now in short supply," she wrote. "I hear that other women have done the same thing I have and that they're now spoken for [and] for officers only, who don't take kindly to low-ranking poachers trespassing on their private reserve."[37]

In 1999, Richard Wrangham and several colleagues stirred the pot (and inspired a bouillabaisse of similarly bad culinary puns) by proposing that the invention of cooking occurred at the dawn of *Homo erectus* 1.9 million years ago.[38] They argued that the innovation of applying heat to food launched not only the pair bond but also radical shifts in the head and body that made this hominid the first to closely resemble modern human beings. Foremost among these shifts was the near closing of the gender gap in body size due to the sudden leap in the availability of nutritious food that cooking provided. Male bodies seem to have already arrived at the optimal size for bipedal scavengers and hunters. Female body size, however, had been held to a proportionally smaller frame by the huge energy demands of pregnancy and lactation, until the new source of more abundant food energy—cooking—allowed them to burst the shackles of these constraints. The differences between male and female bodies correspondingly grew less noticeable. Some other experts also attribute the reduction of dimorphism that occurred at this time to better food, but rather than cooking they suspect improvements in hunting skill and hence meat consumption as the basis for the nutritional leap.[39]

Whatever its cause, this dietary shift and the fact that women became closer in size to men had important implications both for female standing relative to males and for population outcomes. Wrangham's logic is that savory heaps of just-cooked food would draw hungry free-riding male scroungers like lumberjacks to a logging-camp kitchen. The scroungers could easily overwhelm female cooks unless the latter had the benefit of vigilant male protectors. Sex, as usual in these scenarios, was the currency of the exchange.

Anthropologist C. Loring Brace took the authors to task for offering "a stereotype that is guaranteed to grate on feminist sensibilities, the archetypal picture of the female as defined by the role of provider of food and sexual gratification." Brace suggested a simple alternative hypothesis: that the dawning awareness by males that sex leads to pregnancy and childbirth could have spurred pair bonding "as a kind of kin selection."[40]

Clearly there's not much certainty about when, why, or how the pair bond originated—and no strong case that it gave human reproduction and populations their early boost. Indeed, Wrangham and his colleagues suggested in their 1999 paper that *Australopithecus*, a genus of hominids found from Ethiopia and Chad to South Africa until the last of their species went extinct about 1 million years ago, "may have lived at higher population densities than forest-living apes." The considerable difference between male and female size among australopithecines makes monogamy an unlikely pattern among them.

Surviving Helplessness

Another scenario makes more sense than pair bonding in explaining why the number of births, in addition to child survival rates, first increased.

As we've seen, *Homo erectus* females gained on males in size, half closing the dimorphic gap. While females were a mere three or four feet tall among the australopithecines, they grew to be about five feet in *Homo erectus*, not much less than the average height of women today. The relative increase in female size implies other changes. Females that approached their mating partners in height and weight probably gained a certain social standing, no pun intended, given the common association of size and status in the animal world. Females were obviously eating more and better as well, and sending more of this ingested energy to feed their larger brains at the expense of proportionally smaller chests and guts. The *erectus* body appears to have been an improvement over previous models in its capacity to store fat, an important asset in conceiving and bearing young.

These changes may have allowed *Homo erectus* females to give birth more often than any hominid species before them. The reasoning runs along these lines: Large females in less dimorphic species give birth to large babies, which can be draining—literally—to breastfeed for several years. Better access to more nutritious food may have allowed mothers to wean babies earlier and bear more children in quicker succession, which is more efficient in terms of both energy and reproduction. This weaning food may have been Wrangham's cooked dishes, or meat produced by increasingly successful male scavengers and hunters, or simply a greater variety of every kind of food that both sexes were bringing home.[41]

Pregnancy, too, underwent changes to accommodate larger babies with proportionally even larger skulls. Despite the longer life phases

Homo erectus enjoyed, pregnancy failed to lengthen a commensurate amount. Instead, evolution produced an elegant adaptation—early births of smaller, less developed babies in comparison with other primates—to spare women greater hazards than they already faced in childbirth. In any other species, human infants would be considered fetuses cast out of the womb before they were ready. By giving birth when their babies were effectively still fetal, women didn't need pelvises so wide that bipedal running would have become impossibly awkward.

As it is, many women's hips are wide enough to handicap them as runners relative to men, whose generally more vertically positioned legs may allow them to run faster and to suffer fewer knee injuries.[42] For our ancestors, though, being able to run was a matter of more than just athletic pride or physical comfort. In environments in which predators or human enemies were among the biggest threats, a mother's running speed and endurance sometimes may have made the difference between life and death for her and her baby. As University of Wisconsin biological anthropologist Cara Wall-Scheffler and colleagues note, "Among the costs of reproduction, carrying one's infant incurs one of the greatest drains on maternal energy, simply because of the added mass alone."[43]

Wide as they are on average today, the hips of human females allow next to no extra room for the typical skull diameter of a baby at birth, an important reason the process is so perilous. Being born unusually helpless is the compromise that large-brained babies make with their mothers to avoid pushing them farther toward the extremes of either compromised two-leggedness or death-defying childbirth. This compromise probably took shape among *Homo erectus*, though the process no doubt continued its evolution as brains grew even larger among the later Neanderthals and *Homo sapiens*.

Principal reasons for human demographic exceptionalism—why did we grow unlike any other species before us?—thus appear to lie in a series of evolutionary changes already evident in *Homo erectus*: more protein- and calorie-rich food, less time spent breastfeeding, and probably a longer period of fecundity over an individual's lifetime. These changes led to more births in less time per female than in any other hominid. But births, as we know, are only the beginning of the population-change story.

In evolutionary terms, a shift toward newborn helplessness should have pushed new human species into the brick walls of extinction. Instead, there had to have been compensating adaptations to allow babies to survive to their own parenting age *despite* being born helpless. Parents—and especially mothers—had to rise to the challenge. Without the emergence of midwives and cooperative childrearing arrangements, more children may have been born, but more children would likely not have survived. Here again, a possible synergy arises between women's adaptations and those of human species as a whole. Big-brained babies made human birth even more dangerous than the much earlier shift to bipedalism had, requiring even more skill—and perhaps even verbal communication?—from those who assisted the process. And the large-brained adults who survived these hazardous births were on average better able than their smaller-brained forebears to apply intelligence to the challenge of fitting into new and diverse ecological niches.

As noted earlier, tens of thousands of years ago the population of our *Homo sapiens* ancestors was for a time as low as 20,000 or so individuals. We don't know why our population passed through this early bottleneck. Perhaps, as University of Illinois anthropologist Stanley Ambrose has proposed, the Toba crater's eruption in northern Sumatra around 72,000 years ago unleashed a thousand-year-long volcanic winter upon the world—and thus killed off all but a few thousand members of *Homo sapiens* thousands of miles away in Africa.[44] We can at least be confident that by that time the capacities that led to our later population growth were already in place. Never again, once the mystery peril had passed, would modern human beings live in small numbers isolated on one continent. We had already evolved spectacularly successful ways to consistently raise more than two children to mature adulthood. In so doing we changed the vast planet and made it our own little ball.

THREE

Outbound

Our land's too small to serve us all, so some of us must roam.
  —*Traditional Irish song*

S ometime around 1.8 million years ago, a group of erect, two-footed creatures walked from Africa into the Middle East. The trek may have taken
them across the northern plain of the Sinai Peninsula in Egypt, or perhaps
they crossed into Arabia at the Bab el Mandeb Strait at the southern end of
the Red Sea. Both areas were even drier and harsher at that time than they are
today. With arms swinging free, the travelers may have drawn the attention
of curious animals along the way. Outside of Africa nothing quite like them
had ever moved before.

Homo erectus, as anthropologist William Leonard puts it, "hit the
ground running." Fossil finds suggest that the species reached eastern Asia
a mere 100,000 years or so after it first appeared in eastern Africa.[1] It's
probably no coincidence that the first hominid species to leave Africa and
colonize a new continent was also the earliest among which babies were
helpless for months after birth and women lived past their own reproductive ages. As I discussed in the last chapter, those changes contributed
to the development of assisted birth and cooperative female caregiving,

which in turned allowed enough babies to survive to give population an early boost. *Homo erectus* populations must have been minuscule compared to our own, and it's not easy to imagine the giant continent of Africa being too small to serve them all, as in the Irish song quoted above. But given the increasingly meat-based diet and possible use of fire among *erectus*, the steady accumulation of modest reproductive success likely would have strained local resources, prompting hominids to roam widely in search of new lands. During much of the past, migration was likely spurred by population growth that could not be sustained without the release valve of dispersal. Once again we see the distinctive influence of child survival in making humanity the globe-straddling species it has been for the last few thousand years.

Standing on Her Own Two Feet

The evolutionary changes that triggered the emergence of midwifery and alloparenting also made migration physically possible. The *Australopithecus* hominids of 4 million to 1 million years ago probably spent time in trees and may at best have been awkward bipedal runners, easily tired. In *Homo erectus*, bipedalism flowered into a fully modern, energy-efficient stride that facilitated far-flung wandering. That improvement in gait was well-timed to an overall drying trend in eastern Africa. Rains that had once fallen throughout the year were now seasonal, the once-thick blanket of forests was patchy, and hominids needed to forage farther afield than ever before.

It may have been at this time that humans exchanged primate fur for bare skin, though no explanation for this has ever gained scientific consensus.[2] Whenever it occurred, the loss of fur assured there would be no return to the trees and to four-legged locomotion. Infants lost forever any option of clinging to their mothers' body hair and had to be carried— unless, as in the charming vision of marine biologist Alister Hardy and writer Elaine Morgan, an ancestral hominid species at some point lived in flooded or other aquatic environments and was swimming. In that case, infants may have been riding half afloat on their mothers' backs, holding the long hair like reins.[3] Hominid infants, in any event, would have been poor clingers, since their foot thumbs had turned into big toes, useless for grabbing tufts of Mom's fur. And an upright mother is a lot harder to ride on or cling to than one moving horizontally on all fours. When the tufts of fur thinned out and disappeared, so did any remaining infant clinging, and mothers' arms wrapped around babies were useless for grabbing tree branches, climbing, or walking. It's hard not to see the evolution of bare skin as a setback for females, at least at first, as mothers lost most of the use of one arm for food gathering and other purposes.

In fact, the evolution that produced *Homo erectus* offered a mixed bag of benefits to females. In addition to losing a convenient way to carry off-spring, females may have lost some running ability, and hence autonomy, as their pelvises widened to accommodate large-headed babies. On the flip side, females were closer in size to males than was the case in earlier hominid species, which, as we've seen, likely would have brought with it more equal status. And walking on two feet may have allowed hominid females to use their newly free hands to fashion weapons and other tools, which would have proved helpful to group livelihood and their own position. When it comes to gender status, food production seems to trump reproduction, at least in recent times. Women fare better in hunter-gatherer societies in which the roots, tubers, and small animals they collect provide most of a group's food than in those in which the contributions of male hunters do.

Even the loss of fur had an upside. When children could no longer cling to their mothers, the furless females improvised, creating devices to carry both their kids and their kits, the supplies that made long-distance travel possible. This equipment—including sturdy containers for gathered plants, small hunted animals and, critically, water—was essential to the long-ago dispersal of hominid populations.

For their most precious cargo, women may have invented slings. In 2006 Cara Wall-Scheffler and her colleagues observed college women at the University of Wisconsin as they strode on treadmills carrying sacks of sand with the shape and weight of six-month-old infants. The experiment was designed to measure how much energy the women expended carrying the simulated babies in their arms or secured to their bodies in various positions with belts or slings. Carrying the "babies" in their arms required the women to expend 16 percent more effort than using slings. Wall-Scheffler and her colleagues speculate that *Homo erectus* females would have been unlikely to have left Africa before someone put a sling together and discovered how much energy she gained to go the distance. How else but with slings could mothers keep up with the rest of the band?[4] The earliest carrying devices may have been baskets made of branches, dried gourds, or animal skins or organs. Eventually, inventors and artisans perfected the use of fibrous cords, netting, and at some point textiles—which went on to become the first clothing.[5] Such materials deteriorate in mere months, compared to the millennia that stone tools can endure, so experiments and imaginative thinking like Wall-Scheffler's most likely offer us the best window on these early women's tools and crafts.

It's a well-worn cliché in the interpretation of early human art and artifacts that projectiles and points reside in the male realm and containers in the female. As we've seen, this gender association doesn't seem to apply to chimpanzees, so we should be humble about assuming how ancient it is. With almost all modern human cultures, however, Freudians have a field day in associating craftmaking with the genitalia of the crafters. Women indeed are the predominant producers and users of containers among hunters and gatherers. They tote the water and food in much of Africa and in many cultures outside it. On most of the road trips I've taken, for what the personal observation is worth, women have been the ones who prepare and remember the cooler before the car rolls down the driveway.

Carrying water probably would have been essential to any food-gathering forays far from streams or watering holes. Fur-free humans release moisture through millions of pores in their exposed skin. That enables us to shed heat rapidly, which facilitates bursts of speed. But it also increases the body's loss of water, thus making *erectus* and the modern humans who followed "more than usually water-dependent animals," in the words of paleontologist Richard Leakey and science writer Roger Lewin.[6] This was yet another precarious evolutionary development at precisely the time these creatures were wandering ever more widely across progressively drier landscapes. As any modern marathon or bicycle race demonstrates, our dependence on frequent water intake challenges us still.

The invention of containers for food and water thus must have preceded long-distance travel. In just a few centuries after the first crossing of Sinai, it appears, hominids were living in China and on the island of Java in Indonesia, six thousand miles away from eastern Africa. Intriguingly, this migration occurred *before* the invention of *erectus*'s distinctive Acheulean tool kit of hand axes, cleavers, and other double-sided blades. The new tool kit may have contributed to the species' later hunting successes in Africa, but it played no role in the trek of some subpopulations to new continents. Rather, the technological innovations that allowed transcontinental travel were those that women more likely than men invented, like food baskets, water sacks, and baby slings.

Discomforts of Home

Members of *Homo erectus* may have been well equipped to migrate, but it's not likely they did so merely because they had a yen for travel. "Most mammals," biologist John Christian writes, "are reluctant to go beyond the limits of familiar territory—their home range—and generally must be forced to do so."[7] Leaving aside the sheer effort of travel itself, who knew what lay far downstream along the local river or beyond the visible mountains? Would there be predators? Water? Food? *Mates*? In prehistoric unpeopled landscapes, emigrant teenagers would have faced the prospect of pairing for life with close relations and playmates they had known their entire lives. If they were anything like the teenagers I've known, they would have much preferred meeting new members of the opposite sex.

The few paleoanthropologists who speculate about ancient migration tend to see it as an expression of our intelligence, social skills, planning capacity, and curiosity. Clive Gamble, whose book *Timewalkers* addresses the mystery of first dispersals, suggests that the earliest migrants had *purpose*. He defines this as an intent to accomplish an objective through deliberate action, despite any risks and obstacles involved. Gamble believes most migration was preceded by short forays into unknown lands. Explorers gained status by returning to the larger group with reports and evidence of new and promising territory. Then they exploited their new status to become leaders of new groups that fissioned off and wandered away.[8]

Such explanations are at best partial, implying that necessity played no role and migration was merely an option chosen by the curious and the brave. It's worth recalling that the earliest emigrants had to move in groups large enough to sustain their populations genetically, unless others quickly followed them. Either way, something had to exert the *force* that Christian mentions to convince significant people of both sexes and multiple ages to give up the only home they had ever known. Scholars who study migration today write about the push and pull factors behind the drive to settle in a new land. But when the land ahead had never felt a human footstep, the only factors at work were pushes.

Abrupt changes in climate may have been one such push. The 1.5-million-year reign of *Homo erectus* was a time of frequent climatic shifts. A brief warm phase sandwiched between cold spells may have allowed these tropical hominids to make themselves at home on a lakeside near

Beijing, China, roughly 1.7 million years ago.[9] But such climate changes were at best prods for *some* emigrants, at *some* times, since the descendants of those who remained behind in tropical Africa thrived long after the migrations began.

Rather, the most likely hypothesis for what sent the first bipedal primates out of Africa is a prehistoric version of crowding. *Erectus* was never "thick on the ground," as writer Ronald Wright puts it.[10] Yet the consistent survival of third children pushed populations beyond what local animal prey and food plants could support. William Leonard suggests that *erectus* was the first successful large-game hunter and needed nearly the same vastness of land per individual as top predators like grizzly bears and lions.[11] We might have a hard time imagining that there was population pressure at such low human densities, but we're not thinking like a grizzly. Without agriculture, thin populations of hominids that barely ran into each other on the landscape would nonetheless have been faced with scarcity. To maintain the low population-to-land ratios their survival required, the groups had no choice but to spread out.

"Such an expansion implies population growth," write Leakey and Lewin of the *erectus* migration out of Africa.[12] But all the way to China? It may be that over a few tens of thousands of years, population after population expanded quickly to take advantage of rich resource bases in previously unpeopled ecosystems. Then these populations grew in turn, only to propel yet more subgroups farther eastward until they found the next hospitable landscape, eventually near what is now Beijing. It wouldn't have seemed a sprint to them, but to us it's as though Asia was peopled in a mere instant.

While hominids ventured farther and farther afield, they couldn't always outrun scarcity. Many demographers see resource shortages as the major check on population growth throughout prehistory. The low *carrying capacity* of the landscape—the theorized highest population of organisms that a unit of land can support—set limits on human density. When these limits were reached or exceeded, death set in, with a merciless predilection for carrying off young children.

Cultures with roots in Christianity long have known the most common causes of such demographic retreat as the Four Horsemen of the Apocalypse. Actually, there were only three: war, famine, and pestilence.[13] The fourth horseman—death—was simply the body collector for the other three. The apocalyptic riders provided the culling mechanism, as early people struggled to find or fought over food and other resources made scarce by their own growth. Yet at key points in the past, groups of hominids escaped this deadly cycle through migration, until eventually *Homo sapiens* filled the continents and then the islands of the world.

Far from the Madding Crowd?

Over the last few decades, there has been intense debate about hominids'—and ultimately humans'—response to crowding. Did they, and do we, react by migrating to unoccupied territory, as I've argued was the case with *Homo erectus*? By self-regulating population? Or by simply learning to adapt?

Some archeologists in the 1970s and 1980s contended that small groups of hominids were able to cap their own populations over long periods of time in balance with what the land could support. Modern ecologists tend to doubt this, however—they can't even quantify the carrying capacity of any particular place. Often it's not clear that people or animals have exceeded that capacity until critical systems are in full collapse. The idea that early human groups successfully controlled their population through some sort of collective strategy strikes many scholars as quaint, like the view that things only began to go wrong in human societies when European exploration and colonialism began in the 1400s.

In the 1960s and 1970s, researchers figured that studying how animals respond to their own rising population density might provide some clues to the future of human population. Experimenters in white coats filled laboratories with rodents while field researchers went forth, notebooks in hand, and tracked voles, squirrels, and rhesus monkeys to see what happened as animal populations crowded cages and landscapes. The Norway lemming, *Lemmus lemmus*, gained a cartoonish fame for its quadrennial population explosions, in which teeming shoals of swimming animals crammed Norwegian fjords. Steamer operators reported that their vessels knifed through waving carpets of lemmings for fifteen minutes at a stretch.[14] Most of these small mammals nonetheless seemed to regulate their populations at levels that supported their long-term survival. They suppressed various essential reproductive mechanisms as crowding became oppressive and then liberated them again when populations thinned out.

But comparable human studies of crammed urban neighborhoods found nothing like this effect. Crowding didn't seem to make much difference to people or to directly dampen their reproduction. Researchers took humans' apparent resilience in the face of population growth as support for *human exceptionalism*, the idea that we are so different from the rest of the animal kingdom that its rules don't apply to us. The animal population-density studies were dismissed—until recently—as "rats in a cage," irrelevant to human beings.[15]

So what could it be about our humanity that allows us to tolerate larger groups than other animals can? One likely candidate: language and the social adaptability it confers. Liverpool University evolutionary psychologist Robin Dunbar hypothesizes that music and eventually language grew out of adjustments that hominids made in order to sustain group cohesion and close social relations as the size of their groups grew. Monkeys and apes maintain the social bonds they need for daily life in their groups of fifty or fewer animals by grooming each other's bug-infested fur. Once human groups began to outgrow that size, Dunbar suggests, group singing may have replaced grooming as a social glue. He claims as evidence the production of endorphins, a hormone critical to bonding, among people singing together in church. Eventually, he thinks, musical vocalization merged with distinctive nonpitched adjustments of the voice and mouth to produce communicative speech.[16] Chris Knight, a Marxist sociologist and writer, offers an observation to support the argument that women were the more likely sex to come up with the supremely human innovation of language: they are on average more verbal than men and more active in developing and maintaining social alliances.[17]

The birth of spoken language allowed human group size to settle at around 150, three times larger than the most frequently observed social groups of other primates. This is a social size, Dunbar and colleagues have found, that is characteristic of cohesive human groups with minimal social hierarchy, groups in which everyone knows everyone and understands their relationships. This clanlike size in fact tends to characterize many human groups today, from villages to small businesses to military companies, in which personal relationships more than hierarchy and bureaucracy govern affairs.[18] (Don't even *think* about social Web sites like My Space and Facebook, where you can "friend" thousands of people and "virtually" know them—without trusting more than a few to take care of your dog.) An important difference between clan-size villages and populous cities is captured by the story of the small-town sheriff who asks a witness if he can describe the perpetrator of an assault. "Sure, I can," the witness responds: "Dwayne."

Of course, today many human groups are much larger than 150 people. The development of cultural identity and organizing institutions allows us to be part of groups in which it's impossible to know everyone. In the hive of a major city, most people manage actual relationships with at most 100 to 200 people while negotiating the hubbub of tens of thousands of strangers as a normal aspect of the external environment. In the past few thousand years of growing populations, humans learned to tolerate crowds of anonymous others far bigger than we could ever manage in an active social circle.

Recent research suggests, however, that our unique ability to cope with continuous increases in population size and density may have its limits. In 2007, German demographer Wolfgang Lutz and colleagues compared data on population density and fertility records in 143 countries from 1960 to the present—and found "consistently strong and negative correlations between density and family size." Turning the earlier research on its head, these authors hypothesized that crowding might dampen reproduction in humans just as it does in animals—through "endocrine responses to crowding"—but also perhaps through calculations of the costs of additional children and reasonable access to contraception in densely populated urban areas.[19]

If modern humans can't learn to live with unlimited crowding, as popular wisdom once suggested we could, it's even less likely our hominid ancestors were able to do so. *Homo erectus*, after all, lived in some transitional realm between nonhuman animals and us. Maybe the adaptation to high population density evolved after *erectus* moved to Asia nearly 2 million years ago. That human beings, ancient or modern, might react similarly to animals in response to the press of other members of their species is perhaps easier to accept today than it once was. Evidence is emerging that certain animals share emotional states and behavioral learning capacities with humans in ways few researchers would have dared suggest three or four decades ago.[20] The suggestion that animal research has nothing to tell us about human behavior is less tenable than ever.

Most animals, of course, don't live in cages like laboratory rats, but in open nature. When mammals and birds succeed for several generations at raising third offspring to maturity, they typically regulate their population density through dispersal. Sometimes animals leave their home territory before its carrying capacity is reached, sometimes after. Relative status—as important in the animal world as in human society—is an important factor in such dispersal mechanisms.[21] High-status individuals tend to stand their ground, while lower-status ones leave. If nearby habitats are already fully occupied, ecologically speaking, most of the dispersing animals die or fail to find mates. It's a brutally effective way to cull excess population.

If suitable habitat is available to the migrants, new colonies form. These groups tend to vary genetically from the home colony and can eventually evolve into new subspecies and species. The emigrant population, already drawn from a subset of the larger group's genes, is small and especially susceptible to *genetic drift*. (This important mechanism of evolution changes genetic makeup based on chance rather than on selection. One family may drown in a flood, for example, while another nearby survives on higher ground—and thus passes on its genes.) Over time, dispersal is an important driver of animal speciation, an intriguing thought given the possibility that at times there were a dozen or more separate hominid species in Africa and elsewhere.[22]

Young and in the Way

Two other findings from animal research have significant implications for human migration. One is that, for some animals, aggression may have little to do with reproductive success and a lot to do with regulating population through dispersal. Aggressive males of some species don't seem to have more offspring than their meeker cohorts, but they do have higher status and are more likely to hold the home territory and drive competing males away.[23] It's as though aggression evolved, at least among some studied animals, more as a way of telling other individuals to "get out of my face" than as a means of scaring them away from potential mates. Aggression plays this role, researchers found, not only among rodents and wolves, but among at least one primate species, rhesus monkeys.[24] (Among prehistoric humans, females probably routinely dispersed from their home groups, as they do in many hunter-gather cultures. But this mechanism tends more to redistribute females among existing communities than to drive outward migration to new lands.)

Male physical aggression shows at best an uncertain connection to reproductive success among humans. Aggressive men may well impregnate more mates than timid ones. But in some ape and monkey species researchers have observed that male cleverness is a more effective strategy than aggressiveness in winning mating opportunities. How many women really prefer men prone to violent outbreaks—and seek to bear and raise their offspring? Extreme physical aggression doesn't seem adaptive in terms of reproductive success. And it may not be generally adaptive either. "A species that insists on settling disputes violently reduces its overall fitness to thrive in a world that offers enough environmental challenges anyway," Leakey and Lewin suggest.[25]

It's possible that hominids did not use aggression to win mates so much as to chase away competitors. Aggressive behavior may often express the need for space, free of competing individuals. If so, this behavioral trait would have become increasingly dangerous to others as humans gained destructive power through the development of weapons and experience in killing large prey. But those who could scatter competing males may have condemned many of the latter to oblivion while securing a niche in the landscape for their own offspring.

This idea differs both from the man-as-killer-ape model, developed by anthropologist Raymond Dart, ethologist Konrad Lorenz, and writer Robert Ardrey in the 1950s and 1960s, and from the later model of man as inherently peaceable until made bellicose by structured societies, promoted by anthropologist Ashley Montagu.[26] Aggression as a dispersal mechanism suggests instead that violent behavior was a capacity held in reserve among early humans, as among our primate relatives, to be used against wandering strangers who competed for space and critical natural resources and occasionally against kin when those resources were especially scarce. This behavior logically would come into play when the local home territory grew too crowded, a result of so many third and fourth children growing to maturity and starting their own families. Again, *crowded* and *dense populations* are relative terms. If *Homo erectus* was relying increasingly on large animals as a source of protein, a few groups of bipeds along a short stretch of a river valley might overtax local resources.

A second intriguing finding of animal research on dispersal is that juveniles are the most likely to leave home. On average, the young in any group are physically smaller and they've had less time to develop a network of allies. With less status than their older siblings and cousins, the young are more likely to be forced from home if their elders need to bare their teeth and monopolize a limited food supply.[27] The "juvenile migrant" effect has operated among humans as well, most dramatically in the routine dispersal in many cultures of young women to mates in outside groups.

In larger and more socially complex groups, custom and the rules of inheritance often favor first sons in large families and leave younger sons to fend for themselves. In the seventeenth and eighteenth centuries, the British colonies in North America became the destination of thousands of second and third sons of English and Scottish men of means, who by the custom of primogeniture bequeathed their position, land, and effects only to one high-status, firstborn son. Alexander Hamilton, for example, was the son of the younger son of a Scots laird who had left home for the Caribbean. The Spaniards had a term for such aristocratic colonizers and conquerors: *segundones*, or noninheriting "seconds." In today's globalized society, birth order seems less strongly correlated with most decisions to leave home, but in China it has often been second and third sons who must leave the parents' farming village to find work in the cities.[28]

Two thousand years ago, younger sons in southeast Asia and Melanesia pushed off with their own large families in boats for known or unknown islands hundreds or thousands of miles away in the great Polynesian migration, the last to bring humans to previously unpeopled land. "They were descendants of settlers who were junior siblings," University of California–Berkeley archaeologist Patrick Kirch told the *New York Times*. Migrants had earlier settled southeast Asia and Melanisia as well, he noted, "and their own explorations were very often conducted by junior siblings." Polynesian societies generally rank status by family birth order, Kirch added, so that younger siblings "were the ones with a reason to explore, to find new land and claim that for themselves."[29]

Populations that routinely produced second surviving sons also brought daughters to adulthood. Even if two parents raised no more than three children to adulthood on average, each generation would have been at least 50 percent larger than the preceding one. Without an ongoing series of new technologies or land-management innovations, generational growth on that scale would have stoked consistent pressure for population dispersal.

At times even larger families must have been common. The folk traditions of Easter Island, among the last of the Pacific Islands the Polynesians colonized, tell of the chieftain Hotu Matu'a (whose name means "the great parent"), who settled the island with his six sons and extended family.[30] It seems reasonable to conclude what logic suggests: that from earliest times human migration has been a necessary consequence of success in consistently bringing more than two children to maturity over time. In most places and at most times in the human past, population growth could only be sustained when new generations broke up through fission and found new and often distant homes—or died trying.

Wise Man Wandering

Homo erectus, then, most likely succeeded at various times in establishing populations in suitable ecosystems along networks of trails that led from Africa to eastern Asia. These would have been areas where the large animals on which *erectus* depended for prey were relatively abundant. If this hypothesis is correct, more remains of *Homo erectus* should turn up along the route, as some 1.75-million-year-old ones did in 2000 in Dmanisi, Georgia.[31]

A similar process probably explains our own species' much later departure from Africa and eventual appearance not only from Australia to Britain, but also in the Americas and Polynesia. *Homo sapiens*—with the high foreheads, prominent chins, and relatively flat faces we see all around us today—probably evolved into our modern form some 200,000 years ago from an *erectus* population that never left Africa. All 6.7 billion of us today are the progeny of an isolated population that, as we saw in the last chapter, may never have exceeded 20,000 for a thousand years or more. The ancestral homeland, somewhere in East Africa, might have been no larger than Rhode Island.[32]

Then, sometime between about 80,000 and 50,000 years ago, members of *Homo sapiens* began venturing to new continents. Their routes may have differed from those of *Homo erectus*, but their reasons for leaving logically traced back to the same force, a demographic one stemming from consistent success in raising more than two children per woman to adulthood. In fact, this population of *Homo sapiens* grew more rapidly and steadily and for a longer time than any group of large mammals before.

Innovations in assisted childbirth and care likely played an important role in this growth, just as they did in the growth of *Homo erectus*. So too did crafty new tools. "Expansions are frequently the result of innovations, biological and technical, that increase the availability of food and thus determine local growth," geneticist Luigi Cavalli-Sforza and two colleagues wrote in 1993. "Out-migration to relieve population pressure follows, and when this cycle repeats, expansion proceeds in all directions until insurmountable barriers are reached. Innovations that favor transport and settlement in new environmental niches can also spark new expansions."[33] In other words, innovation leads to growth, which leads to scarcity, which leads to further innovation, which leads to yet more growth. (This pattern has played out countless times throughout our past, and we'll explore it in more detail in the next chapter.)

One key innovation was fishing. In the Blombos Cave at the southern tip of South Africa, archaeologists found finely crafted stone points along with awls and tools made from bone around 75,000 years old. Both the age and the tools suggested that these were made by *people like us*, "wise man," as we named our species in a self-congratulatory Latin fragment. Among the artifacts were the bones of black musselcrackers, a dogged twenty-five-pound fighter of a fish that still challenges coastal anglers in the area. Possibly the early fishers somehow lured musselcrackers close to shore and speared them.[34] Archaeologists eighteen hundred miles to the north in what is now the Republic of the Congo found bone harpoons and the bones of six-foot-long catfish among the remains of people who they believe lived around 90,000 years ago.[35]

Such new approaches to making a living coincide with the beginnings of ornament and symbolic art, including perforated shell beads at Blombos Cave and perhaps even a bit earlier in what is now Israel.[36] Together these innovations suggest that humans were approaching a breakout point, a quantum leap in capacities that made us something truly new under the sun. The timing of this "creative explosion" is often thought to have occurred about 40,000 years ago, just before art of breathtaking skill and beauty began appearing on cave walls in Europe. The apparently early dates of fishing, refined weapons, and ornament in Africa and the Middle East, however, undermine the idea of a sudden human leap occurring so late. Somewhere between about 60,000 and 45,000 years ago, *Homo sapiens* had arrived by boat in Australia, where artistic expression developed even earlier than in Europe.[37] Within a few millennia, our species occupied much of Asia and Europe and had pulled together a vast biological potential—for language in multiple tenses, for complex analytical thought, for exquisite handwork—that had lain dormant in human bodies and brains for tens of thousands of years.

What stimulated the firecracker blasts of artistry and technology that punctuated thousands of years of stasis? An increasingly appealing answer— drum roll here—is population growth. "The presence of more people put more pressure on resources, forcing our ancestors to devise cleverer ways to obtain food and materials for toolmaking," writes Kate Wong, an editor of *Scientific American*. "More people also raised the chances of encounters among groups. Beads, body paint and even stylized tool manufacture may have functioned as indicators of an individual's membership and status in a clan, which would have been especially important when laying claim to resources in short supply. Symbolic objects may have also served as a social lubricant during stressful times . . . Conversely, when the population dwindled, these advanced practices subsided."[38]

Archaeologist Stephen Shennan, of University College London, went so far as to try to model the extent prehistoric population size mattered to the cultural transmission of skills—for example, in the craftmaking that young people tended to learn from a parent or similar adult of the same sex. He applied a set of equations developed for genetic analysis, using in his calculations the more flexible adult-to-child transmission that occurs when any nearby adult might convey how to sharpen a stone's edge or turn an animal bladder into a sack for carrying water. The population size of any group, he concluded, was critical to determining if new and useful innovations would "take"—and thus contribute to a group's reproductive success—by being passed on to successive generations. Higher numbers of young people and old people, and hence more interactions between the generations, made chance technological or artistic improvements more likely to be passed on. Only after humanity passed through its demographic bottleneck of 70,000 years ago, Shennan concluded, was its size sufficient for the cultural explosion that led to modern humanity and civilization.

"Demographic fluctuations may be the single most important factor in explaining how and why the emergence of modern human culture occurred when it did," Shennan wrote. "Rates of successful technological innovation may have been correlated with population sizes and densities from the origins of [hominid] culture to the present."[39]

None of this means that the demographic path for *Homo sapiens* kept climbing forever after. Sometimes population size was stable. Sometimes it crashed. The Tasmanians are a classic example of dwindling population leading to subsiding art and technology. These people once wielded bone tools, bows and arrows, and fishing nets—before rising sea levels cut off their island home from Aborigine-populated Australia. Adapting to their isolated habitat by maintaining a small population size, the Tasmanians literally moved backward technologically. When Europeans landed on their island in the seventeenth century, the Tasmanian tool kit consisted mostly of flakes of stone. Who knows how often this happened in remote and cutoff corners of the world?

Among the advanced practices that thrived in the more frequent periods of demographic expansion were those that facilitated walking, rafting, and boating to every ice-free land on the planet. Every step or paddle of the way, to assure that *Homo sapiens* circumnavigated the planet, it was essential that the critical number of babies per woman were born safely and that these children grew to adulthood. The babies were. The children did. And here we are.

The Others, and What Became of Them

When anatomically modern humans reached the Middle East and Europe, they encountered slightly different human beings who had occupied the same regions for some 200,000 years previously. These were Neanderthals— cold-adapted, powerfully built people so much like ourselves that they have preoccupied paleoanthropology for decades and inspired a steady stream of fiction, from *The Quest for Fire* to the ice age novels of Jean Auel.[40]

The most interesting questions about Neanderthals involve sex and violence. Did we mate with them, and do we now carry their genes? Did we kill them off? A single species by definition embraces all populations that can and do mix reproductively to produce fertile descendants. Though some ancient human skeletons are interpreted as possible *sapiens*-Neanderthal hybrids, there's no compelling genetic evidence that these two kinds of human beings succeeded in mixing permanently. Neanderthals did disappear, however, at just about the time of their first encounters with *Homo sapiens* in Europe. Why this happened is relevant to other sibling species our ancestors may have met along the way as they moved through Africa and on to the far reaches of Asia. Only because we know so little about these other dramas does the focus of the story shift at this point to Europe.

"You can't imagine one human population replacing another except through violence," notes paleoanthropologist Milford Wolpoff of the popular view that modern humans killed off the Neanderthals. He is the spokesman for "multiregionalism," the thesis that Neanderthals, *sapiens*, and perhaps other human populations all descended from pancontinental *Homo erectus*. According to this thinking, human subspecies that traded genes through frequent interbreeding all over the Old World evolved in multiple locations to produce modern humans.[41]

Based on recorded history, Wolpoff has a point about the violence. A demographer, however, easily imagines the extinction of a human species as the nonviolent outcome of many generations of below-replacement fertility, in this case perhaps due to resource competition from a more reproductively successful species—us.

Suppose that modern humans 35,000 years ago were slightly better at exploiting their surroundings and keeping their children alive than Neanderthals were. The probabilities of survival for Neanderthal children would have declined due to an unprecedented competition for food and shelter by newcomers increasing in number. Among the *sapiens*, let's say that 104 daughters for every 100 women survived to become mothers, but only 96 daughters per 100 women made it that far among the Neanderthals. (As always, it's the number of survivors rather than of births that matter.) Not a huge difference, but decisive over just two millennia. The result would have been a population of 100,000 modern humans growing to nearly 3.4 million, assuming twenty-two years between generations, while an identical number of Neanderthals would have shrunk to 2,500 genetically stressed individuals, barely clinging to survival in isolated pockets of southern Europe. A few dozen generations more, and the species would have sputtered into oblivion, as it eventually did.

Were modern humans simply better hunters than Neanderthals? Did they shoulder them out of their longstanding predator niche in Europe by engaging in sophisticated weapons trading, strategic planning, and teamwork lifted to new levels by complex language? "*If* the weather stays cold, *then* the mammoth herds will come our way in eight days; *otherwise*, we'll have to move north up the river valley to find them." Maybe. Stone Age *Homo sapiens* moved around for a living more than Neanderthals did and used spears to kill from a distance. Neanderthals, by contrast, moved in for close kills. "They must have literally come to grips with the family dinner," C. Loring Brace once noted.[42] Many excavated Neanderthals skeletons bear the kinds of bone breaks seen today in rodeo riders. Yet the two species appear to have used many of the same stone tools. And compared to the lithe newcomers from the tropics, Neanderthals had evolved a superb stocky physique for weathering the frigid European climates. They had survived several earlier climatic vicissitudes at least as dramatic as those rocking Europe 35,000 years ago, at the peak of the Pleistocene.

Three explanations for the triumph of *Homo sapiens* over *Homo neandertalensis* support the argument for nonviolent demographic competition, and all feature important roles for women. The newest and perhaps most intriguing is a proposal from anthropologists Steven Kuhn and Mary Stiner of the

University of Arizona that, unlike *Homo sapiens*, the Neanderthals had no division of labor in food collection. Kuhn and Stiner find that Neanderthal sites offer no evidence of tools for plant food processing, no bone sewing needles, no small-animal remains—all of which are evident in *sapiens* sites from 45,000 to the dawn of agriculture 10,000 years ago. Yet Neanderthal women were clearly not simply sitting in caves tending to children and waiting for their men to arrive with the groceries. Women appear to have been nearly as heavily muscled as men, and their skeletons, too, show evidence of trauma. Quite probably, the two researchers reason, they were helping men bring down large game.[43]

If this is true, Neanderthals had a critical livelihood handicap relative to their modern human neighbors. With all their adult resources focused on hunting the big game on which they depended for food and other resources, Neanderthals lacked flexibility for surviving and thriving when these creatures were keeping their distance. With their gender-based division of labor, by contrast, members of *Homo sapiens* could get by on the small animals and plant foods that women collected when no large game was to be found. Such differences in livelihood between the two human species could by itself explain the demographic victory of modern humans over the Neanderthals. But *Homo sapiens* had still more advantages.

In all probability, *Homo sapiens* included grandmothers, whose alloparenting of their children's children may best explain the quantum leaps in child survival behind prehistoric human population growth. In 2006, researchers in Austria announced that they had uncovered the remains of three infant burials from nearly 30,000 years ago, shortly after the Neanderthals' demise. The careful burials suggest that these anatomically modern people accorded babies full status as human beings, rather than waiting for a year or two to see if newborns would survive to justify such an investment by their parents and the group. And that hints at relatively high rates of infant survival to adulthood.[44] Over time, elevated child survival produced more grandmothers per 100 children born. *Sapiens* indeed must have had higher proportions of grandmothers in its populations than did Neanderthals, whose skeletal remains suggest that most women died in their childbearing years.

The third idea combines women's longstanding role as gatherers of plant foods with a bold hypothesis offered by science essayist Colin Tudge. He argues that even the first modern human migrants to arrive in Europe brought with them rudimentary knowledge of how to coax food out of the ground. In a word, they gardened. Contemporary scholars agree that women probably invented horticulture, a word that means "garden tilling." It's logical to presume that in carrying food-bearing plants women unintentionally spread seeds along the paths they traveled, noticing later that their favorite plants had taken root there. Or maybe they stuck branches into the ground as fences to keep predators away from food caches or fruiting trees—and later noticed that the fence posts were sprouting leaves and then fruit.[45]

There's no evidence of horticulture prior to about 18,000 years ago, but Tudge makes the case that inventive modern humans in verdant tropical Africa would have developed basic techniques for manipulating plant growth there—and then would have brought this skill to Asia and Europe when they migrated. To the Neanderthals, adapted to the cold and dim north of the world, the idea of manipulating plant growth for food might well have been as novel as the new arrivals' rapid-fire babble and highbrow art.

These "gardening" manipulations were not farming in today's sense of clearing land and planting crops. They may have simply involved protecting favored plants. Some plants women may have dead-headed, clipping blooms to encourage growth; others they maybe coppiced, cutting main trunks to encourage sprouting. In some cases they may have pressed fruit pits a few inches into soft soil, maybe with a prayer or incantation, to see what emerged later. By women's modest alterations of the nature around them, some human groups would have gained a crucial survival edge over those whose population size necessarily waxed and waned along with the fortunes of wild plants and game animals.[46]

It seems counterintuitive, but supplementing traditional hunting and gathering with a little management of the local plant life may well have facilitated the extinction of local animals, which seems to have occurred in most of the places to which ancient *Homo sapiens* migrated. Once "highly controversial, . . . the general thesis that humans played a significant role [in these extinctions] is now widely accepted," writes Cornell University evolutionary biologist C. Josh Donlan.[47]

Tudge points out that successful "protofarming" could have allowed human populations to grow even when animal prey grew scarce or went extinct. Such an effect would have been ecologically unusual. Loss of prey usually shrinks predator populations. In relying on a limited suite of animal prey, Neanderthals would have been less likely to drive Pleistocene mammals or birds to extinction. Like other specialized animal predators, their populations would have more consistently dwindled along with those of their prey—hence assuring the long-term survival of the latter. Members of *Homo sapiens*, by contrast, sustained themselves by hunting, fishing, and plant gathering—all possibly supplemented by rudimentary gardening.

Through these alternative livelihoods, modern humans could thrive even while delivering the *coup de grace* to countless large-animal species around them. All our species needed was a slight advantage in reproductive survival to send the Neanderthals into extinction. Along with caring grandmothers, our ancestors' flexible livelihoods—perhaps sustained at key moments by women gardeners—could have provided exactly such an advantage. Our *Homo sapiens* ancestors literally ate the Neanderthals' lunch, little knowing where the meal would lead them as they—we—gained uncontested human dominion of the world.

FOUR

The Grandmother of Invention

. . . and the people multiplied.
The land was bellowing like a bull;
The god got disturbed with their uproar.
   —The Atrahasis Epic

In 1978, traveling as a journalist in southern Mexico, I took a day off to find my way to a lake near the Guatemalan border and spent a day hiking and swimming in a forested landscape that was little short of paradise. Between the times one bus dropped me off in the morning and another picked me up in the late afternoon, I saw no human being. In 2002 I revisited the area, and the forest I had explored was gone, replaced by farms and cattle pasture and, in a few places, the still-charred stumps of trees. Humanity had arrived and was getting down to business.

As a wealthy foreigner, of course, I had made my own touristic use of the forest. I could hardly resent the more urgent needs of the Mexicans who altered the landscape to feed their families. People need food and shelter. How many news accounts quote someone who justifies an environmentally destructive livelihood—maybe buzz-sawing primary forest or slicing off the fins of captured sharks—by explaining that "I have to feed my family"? And as the families and the populations grow, those needs press harder. Sometimes the needs wipe out natural landscapes and ecosystems.

I'm hardly the first or last to witness this process of humanizing nature and to be struck by how rapid and dramatic it can be. Ecologist Thomas Lovejoy first visited the Amazon River basin at age twenty-three and found, in the words of *Washington Post* columnist David Ignatius, "a boundless wilderness, the size of the continental United States [with] just 2 million people and one main road." Four decades and a hundred of Lovejoy's visits later, the basin has ten times the population and is laced "with roads, new settlements and economic progress." For the first time in centuries, the forest is prone to drought and forest fires. The early manifestations of global warming combine with other environmental stresses to increase the deaths of trees sixfold.[1]

Human beings alter nature for our own ends and only learn later that we have unleashed forces that undermine our own survival. The alteration often begins modestly, when human numbers are negligible relative to the local landscape. Then the change accelerates as human population grows, until unintended side effects begin to appear, bearing the increasingly insistent message that all is not well as before. This process has been occurring, on one scale or another, at least since *Homo sapiens* learned how to kill large mammals. It reached new heights of intensity, first with the adoption of extensive agriculture 10,000 years ago and then with the dawn of the industrial age 250 years ago.[2]

We could call most of the inventions that led to these shifts win-lose innovations, because they seem to work that way in sequence. Revolutions in chemistry, genetics and nanotechnology are among the win-lose developments of our era. We win at first, but—*oops!*—we lose later, as little bits of nature start to get strange. The eggshells of birds become too fragile to keep chicks alive. An engineered gene that was supposed to stay in a strain of cultivated grass slips into the wild. Nanoparticles of titanium dioxide engineered into sunscreens to help protect against skin cancer may themselves damage cellular DNA. Amphibians that are supposed to be males or females appear to be both at the same time.

Win-lose innovations may be as old as the spear. (Those with an especially dark view of humanity might put assisted birth in this category.) What these innovations share is that they work brilliantly for their purpose on small scales, but surprise their creators with unintended, indirect, and risky side effects when the scale is large. The process of innovating until we win and then lose has accelerated to warp speed since our numbers crossed into the billions. Scale matters incredibly to nature, because the interplay of the size and quantity of forces, materials, and beings are what determine nature's state. This is true of climate, the makeup of soils and atmosphere, the presence or absence of water, what can live here, and what can live there.

The Extinctionists

With a critical mass of *Homo sapiens* roaming the landscape from about 35,000 years ago onward, individuals of other human species couldn't live anywhere. Once we had eliminated the Neanderthals the whole world opened up to us like a well-earned prize.

The people who first entered new lands, perhaps low-status outcasts from groups experiencing too-rapid growth, were probably not numerous themselves. One recent genetic study suggests that the founding population of the Americas consisted of no more than seventy reproducing adults, who broke away as long as 14,000 years ago from an Asian community of about nine thousand people.[3]

But hunting groups could grow rapidly once they encountered animals that had never felt the sting of human predation. When the hypothesis that humans had caused the great American Pleistocene extinctions arose in the late 1960s, skeptics doubted that a few bands of Stone Age hunters could possibly wipe out whole genera (groups of related species) of large animals.[4] But, as paleoecologist John Alroy demonstrated in 2001, the same mathematics of reproductive survival that probably doomed the Neanderthals would have proved even more destructive to the slow-breeding big mammals that humans were slaughtering for dinner.[5]

A similar loss of giant marsupials, tortoises, and flightless birds has been documented in Australia after people arrived there, tens of thousands of years earlier than the passage took place to the Americas. Much more recently, only 800 to 2,000 years ago, similar extinction waves washed away giant birds and other large animal species in the islands of the Indian and Pacific oceans shortly after humans first stepped ashore. In Madagascar, carbon-14 dating has indicated that twelve species of lemurs, a dwarf hippopotamus, and the half-ton elephant bird disappeared not long after humans arrived by boat from Indonesia. (Small hippopotamuses must have been popular meals for early humans. A "pygmy hippopotamus" disappeared from Cyprus in about 8000 BC, around the time humans arrived there.) In New Zealand, first settled just 800 years ago, a giant moa more than nine feet in height and twenty-six other species of flightless birds went extinct in a matter of a few centuries.[6]

Overhunting is a logical suspect in all these disappearances, and some scholars have long pointed to climate change as a likely perpetrator in species extinctions. Almost every other likely culprit, however, can be traced to our own migrations and settlements. Infectious diseases spread by people or their domestic animals may have been species killers. Habitat change almost certainly was, as it is today. Early Australians burned vegetation across the continent to draw animals to the tender green shoots that grew out of the ashes. This "firestick farming," as anthropologist Rhys Jones calls it, reduced the continent's rainfall and hence its greenery by as much as half. Some animals long adapted to the prehuman environment could no longer survive.[7] Humans are the only logical suspects in the Australian extinctions, as no significant climate changes were occurring at the time.[8]

In Eurasia, climate change no doubt took its toll on populations of Irish elk, an animal with twelve-foot-wide antlers, and similar large mammals. But here as elsewhere it was most likely members of *Homo sapiens* who in every case delivered the final blow, as they probably had to the Neanderthals. They did this in various ways, but the common denominator was probably that their proliferation across the landscape made survival impossible for genera that had muddled through rough times and hardship rations during several shifts in climate prior to the times modern humans arrived on the scene.[9]

A population of giant elk, for example, appear to have survived in the southern Ural Mountains fully 3,000 years after the species disappeared elsewhere in Europe, according to Anthony Barnosky of the University of California–Berkeley. "They lingered on, but why couldn't those populations once again expand" as they had done before once climatic conditions for them improved? he asks. The answer, Barnosky suggests, is that by this time hunters and gatherers in the area had stopped their wandering and settled down, "and there were many more of them." By 5000 BC, even the Irish elk of the Urals were gone and the species globally extinct.[10]

The loss of so many massive prey animals no doubt set early groups back. But no human extinctions followed the animal ones; quite the reverse. As we saw in the last chapter, people supplemented animal food with gathered plants—and possibly a few cultivated ones. For animal protein they dropped to lower links in the food chain, preying on smaller creatures—until many of these, too, disappeared. At which point, the bipedal predators adjusted again.

Archaeologists are now learning how to judge, by reading bones in buried middens, when early human populations were small and when they had grown larger. In the Mediterranean, the tale is literally about the tortoise and the hare. People ate the former—slow-moving, easy to catch, and baked delectably between its shells—when the reptiles were abundant. But tortoises don't tolerate much predation, and once human numbers started to grow the number of tortoises quickly diminished. Then, the excavated middens make clear, people switched to hares—fast-moving, hard to catch, but worth the effort to the hungry. (Thanks to their own well-known reproductive habits, hares were also less likely to go locally extinct). Using ratios of unearthed tortoise and hare bones, archaeologists have dated spurts of population growth at one Israeli site to 44,000 years ago, while the population at an Italian study site first jumped 23,000 years ago.[11]

Similar population increases may be traced in the Channel Islands off the southern California coast, where shell middens indicate a Russian-doll-like succession of smaller and harder-to-catch shellfish harvested over time by Native Americans. A flightless sea duck disappeared altogether soon after the islands were first occupied. At what is now Emeryville, near San Francisco, a similar succession of progressively smaller mammals, fishes, and birds was harvested between 600 BC and AD 1300. Clearly, growing populations were exploiting the largest and most attractive species until each one blinked out, at which point people moved on to the next most attractive prey, until it too was overharvested into extinction.[12]

And so it went in most of the world, to greater or lesser degrees, as the wild bounty at different times and in different places withdrew, held back, and forced people to find new ways to live. Even the sluggish growth of small groups of successful childraisers over time could turn what had long been a sustainable livelihood—the taking of wild animals and the gathering of wild plants—into an overexploitation of nature. It wasn't anyone's "fault," or the product of carelessness or miscalculation. It is simply how population growth works, then as now: it amplifies the scale of human activities and pushes them past tipping points, at which time conditions shift irrevocably toward greater scarcity, complexity, and risk.

Mysteries of Venus

One way to deal with the increasing scarcity of game was to turn to other sources of food. As we saw in the last chapter, dietary flexibility may have been the major reason that we survived and *Homo neandertalensis* did not. *Homo sapiens* thrived by relying on both hunting by men and gardening by women. It was a Paleolithic version of the two-income family, and it suggests that gaps in gender status at this time were minimal. Sociologist Elise Boulding, penning a history of women in the Western world, speculated that *sapiens* women's early development of improved seed technologies, containers, and the preservation and processing of food would have secured a high status for them, perhaps equal to that of males.[13]

Some archaeological findings from later eras lend credence to this reasoning. So does a common artistic image that spans tens of thousands of years. Archaeologists have spaded up small figurines of limestone and ivory depicting women's ample but faceless bodies across Europe and in the Indian subcontinent. The oldest date back 30,000 years, close to the demise of the Neanderthals. The youngest found are 5,500 years old.[14] Naked, wide-hipped, round-bellied, and distinguished by what chroniclers describe as "pendulous breasts," the figurines came to be called Venuses and have been associated (though no evidence supports this) with the worship of fertility goddesses.

The figurines became especially iconic for some feminist interpreters of prehistory, who advanced the hypothesis that Europe and the Mediterranean were home for millennia to matriarchal societies that worshipped a supreme female deity. Some proponents of this basic view clarified that these societies were not so much matriarchal, with women ruling over men, but egalitarian, with men and women equal to one another.[15] These hypothesized cultures thrived from India to western Europe until warrior herders from the steppes of eastern Europe and northwestern Asia overthrew them, beginning around 4000 BC. The conquerors installed patriarchal cultures based on muscular sky gods whose legacy survives today.

To be fair, these arguments are rarely heard any more. Most archaeologists and paleoanthropologists rejected the concept of a unified, truly matriarchal "goddess culture." The mystery of the fat figurines, however, remains.

Archaeologists seem to lean toward the view that women carved them, though there's no certainty of this. Maybe they were amulets. Maybe they stemmed from a pervasive, long-lasting female mythology and set of rituals, perhaps related to ancestors or to nature and the earth as "mother."[16] Maybe they served some kind of erotic purpose for lonely hunters. Or they were idealized self-portraits. There's no way to know.

It strikes me, however, that these figurines must have had *models* in the real world. They realistically represent the substantial thighs, bellies, buttocks, and breasts of what modern marketers call full-bodied women. The sculptors had carefully studied such bodies. For thousands of years, from what is now France to India, some women apparently filled their bellies with consistently high-calorie food and were excused from the occupation of food gathering that kept their sisters slim. This suggests that women were valued members of their communities and that the combination of hunting, gathering, and gardening allowed humanity to eat quite well. It also suggests that certain women were granted especially high status, maybe leadership status, during the era of hunting and gathering.

Sweating It

Eventually, success caught up. Third children continued to survive and populations continued to grow, pressuring the local supply of wild food and other essential natural resources to which any one person could gain access. And as suitable ecological niches filled, migration became a less reliable safety valve. Then there was no choice but to wrestle with scarcity through yet more ingenuity and inventions. Among the most influential such innovations in human history—right up there with assisted birth—was intensive farming, a surprisingly mixed blessing.

The origins of agriculture remain shrouded in mystery, but it was almost certainly born of necessity. After gradually learning how to grow food-producing plants from seeds and cuttings, it seems unlikely that people would have shifted abruptly to full-scale farming if the environment had been providing the nutritious bounty it once had. Colin Tudge expresses the increasingly widespread view that changing climate, rising seas, and growing human population combined to undermine subsistence lifestyles that had supported humanity for tens of thousands of years, forcing people to find new way to feed themselves. The shift to full-time cultivation of crops and tending of animals probably occurred independently in several places around the planet—from 10,000 years ago in the Middle East to less than 1,000 years ago in parts of the Americas and the islands of the Pacific. Continuing the cycle of growth, scarcity, innovation, and more growth, agriculture led to leaps in population that forever foreclosed a widespread return to hunting and gathering.

Some experts on the origins of agriculture have failed to see population growth as a *cause*, because it was so obviously an *effect* of adopting farming, with its bulging bins of grain and other surpluses. But the demographic interactions with the natural world and with human relations invariably are more circular, coevolutionary, and subtle than are single causes that produce single effects. A pace of growth that in today's world would hardly merit notice nonetheless led to a several-hundredfold population explosion of *Homo sapiens* from the time the species emerged to the beginnings of full-time farming.

Despite the frequent depiction of agriculture as a human triumph over the whims of nature, scholars recognize that the beginnings of full-time farming were initially no great bargain. Breaking up soil, cultivating and irrigating crops, and grinding grain required much harder work and longer hours than hunting and gathering had. "A few million years of nomadism had not prepared the human body for the literally backbreaking work of full-time farming," writes historical essayist Arno Karlen.[17] Some 9,000 to 8,000 years ago at Tell Abu Hureyra in Syria, women and children worked at grinding grain by pushing and pulling heavy stones, kneeling before them "beyond the limit of pain," according to Theya Molleson of the Natural History Museum of London.[18]

Nutrition declined as farmers relied on a few easy-to-grow, high-calorie crops rather than on the nutrient-dense diversity of tables set by nature. Excavated jaws of farmers tell of cavities and root abscesses. Childhood anemia became common at unprecedentedly young weaning ages, as one or two kinds of cereal mash replaced mother's milk in children's diets. In the Americas, a study of seven health indicators among 12,500 excavated skeletons found that a marked deterioration of health began around the time various peoples took up farming and living in dense urban settlements.[19] Dried-up ancient feces that have been found and probed in the American Southwest show that parasites such as tapeworms were all but absent among hunters and gathers there. They were nearly ubiquitous among early farmers.

"No matter how you look at it," Smithsonian Institute forensics expert Douglas Ubelaker told the *Washington Post*, "infant mortality, tooth decay, anemia, infectious disease—it all went downhill with agriculture and sedentism."[20]

Leaving Eden

You might even call the transition from hunting and gathering to intensive agriculture a fall from grace. In fact, some scholars have. Colin Tudge and archaeologist Juris Zarins see the Bible story of Adam and Eve's expulsion from Eden as a parable that recalled, thousands of years after the fact, this irreversible shift and the massive cultural changes it provoked. The First Couple left their garden paradise to a new life of farming in which men had to earn their living "in the sweat of thy face" and to "rule over" women.[21] In other words, the invigorating simplicity of the hunting and gathering life gave way to the risks and discomforts of agriculture and the tiresome complexities of larger groups.

With a little geographical sleuthing—and a healthy dose of imagination—it's not hard to locate the Garden of Eden on a modern map of Iraq and its environs. The creation story that opens Judaism and Christianity's scriptures relates that "a river went out of Eden . . . into four heads."[22] Once we understand this to mean that the river flowed *into* Eden from four tributaries, we can try to decipher the names and courses of those tributaries and pinpoint their meeting place.

The book of Genesis names the Fertile Crescent's famed Euphrates and the Hiddekel, commonly understood to be the Tigris. In Biblical times the two mighty rivers ran more or less next to each other from the highlands of Turkey all the way to the Persian Gulf. Zarins, of Missouri State University, uses some of the additional details Genesis offers to identify the Pison as the Wadi Riniah and its continuation, Wadi Batin. Today this dry "fossil" riverbed (*wadi* in Arabic) leads out of eastern Saudi Arabia and runs along the border that divides Iraq and Kuwait. Zarins believes the biblical Gihon is the similar-sounding Karun of the present, which flows south out of the highlands of Iran. Seven thousand years ago the four streams converged above what is now the head of the Persian Gulf, forming a mighty river that flowed through a low, fertile plain.

Today that plain lies beneath the waters of the gulf. If Zarins's argument is correct, this plain was the Garden of Eden. Until about 7,000 years ago— close to the time some Christians maintain that God created the universe— this seabed of the Persian Gulf had been above sea level for tens of thousands of years. Melting ice inundated it as the last glaciers and ice sheets of the Pleistocene retreated and the world's oceans slowly rose to today's shorelines. Zarins backs his claim with linguistic evidence: In the language of Sumer, the later Mesopotamian civilization generally considered the world's first, the word *eden* means "fertile plain," while the word *adam* appears to mean "settlement on the plain." Both words came to Sumerian from an even older ancestral culture.[23]

Eden was a verdant land, a well-watered paradise for the hunters, gatherers, and occasional farmers who populated it—"real, glorious and remembered," in the words of Tudge. Like many scholars, Tudge contends that early forms of farming began almost as hobbies among hunter-gatherers well before 10,000 years ago, the date generally associated with the opening of the agricultural revolution. In this temperate land, during the waning days of the last ice age, Tudge notes, "there was no shortage of water. There would have been shellfish galore, and great flocks of water birds, with gazelles and fallow deer and fruiting trees. This would have been the place where the people congregated [and they] would have lived as if in Paradise. They could have cultivated here and there, as they chose: groves of favored fruiting trees, a little horticulture, perhaps a little manipulation of the shallows to encourage the fish and shellfish."[24]

So it was, that is, until the final flooding of Eden, perhaps in a matter of a few decades as seas rose rapidly in response to the natural global warming that ended the last ice age. The surging waters concentrated Eden's thriving population along the higher riverbanks and eventually forced them to migrate into nearby highlands that are now the coastal areas of Iraq, Kuwait, and Saudi Arabia. There the hunter-gatherers, with their occasional commitment to light gardening, Tudge writes, "had to crowd into a much smaller space and were obliged to farm [full-time] to support the augmented population."[25]

Their migration would have brought them into an uncomfortable confrontation with other populations, even more densely settled and also swelling in size. These were full-time farmers, working their drier and less-wild land much more intensively than the gardeners of Eden had done. Some farmers cultivated wheat and barley, possibly at this point already breaking the soil with the world's earliest plows. Others raised sheep and goats. The story of the slaying of Adam and Eve's son Abel, a herder, by his brother Cain, a cultivator, may recall the conflicts that beset these early cultivators and herders when forced to share land as populations grew.

Rubbing shoulders can lead to trading blows, and the changing nature of conflict as human density increased must have been a driving force in the evolution of both war and social institutions. When group size was still fairly small, warfare provided a way for victors to punish and disperse the defeated. Some outrage may have sparked the violence, perhaps, but the underlying point was to put distance between groups so they wouldn't come into conflict over the land's resources. "This is our territory," warriors were saying as they spilled blood. "You guys stay away." Not long after the beginnings of intensive agriculture, by some accounts, the motivation for and the intensity of fighting changed dramatically. Groups had land, bins bursting with stored grain, and large families to protect and defend.

"Aggregative war began only after steadily increasing human numbers created acute shortages of arable land," anthropologist Robert Carneiro has written. "War now took a decisive turn. Not only did it become more frequent and more intense, it came to have different objectives. Instead of fighting to avenge murder or wife stealing or witchcraft, as before, villages now fought, first, to obtain land to be able to feed an increasing population, and next, to incorporate enemy villages themselves, exacting labor and tribute from their inhabitants."[26]

Similarly, less lethal conflicts within groups also changed in nature. As we saw in the last chapter, humanity evolved to cope with larger groups first through language, and then, as communities became ever larger and more complex, through institutions and formalized social roles. Let's assume that Robin Dunbar is right that the early stirrings of language facilitated a tripling of basic group size to 150 or so individuals. In a group of this size, everyone knows each other and can remember their interactions over time. If you list the names of your family members, relatives, friends, close neighbors, and work colleagues, without much effort beyond concentration you can probably identify 150 people you know pretty well. Doubling that number would probably be much more than twice as hard.

Disputes in fairly small groups are generally mediated by kin or friends of both parties, another point suggested by the quip about perpetrator Dwayne in the last chapter. But, as Carneiro and Jared Diamond have pointed out, as the size of a group grows by small increments, the number of possible one-on-one quarrels grows by a function that is almost exponential.[27] Dunbar used the same function to analyze the relationship between group size, social complexity, and brain structure in apes and monkeys. He concluded that the larger the social group, the more complicated the relationships among individuals and the larger the brain size relative to body size, presumably to handle all the data processing needed for successful social relations.

One of my sisters-in-law, a mathematics teacher, once said that what she liked most about her subject is that it's "all about relationships." Here's an illustration of the truth of that statement. If you're walking with a friend, only one quarreling duo is possible. (It could be a happy conversation, but let's talk about quarrels.) You and two friends make for three possible quarreling duos—you with each of your two friends and them with each other. You and five friends make for fifteen possible quarrels. You and 149 friends and relatives have 11,750 possible combinations of two-person disputes. If, in a few generations, the group doubles in size, the possible number of quarrels almost quadruples, to 44,850.

Who knows what the threshold of feasible quarrels is among people who know each other? But it's easy to see that as more third children survived in prehistory and group size increased, the need for new arrangements and new approaches to leadership for mediating quarrels became pressing. With many more than 150 people in your group, you're unlikely to know the name or the kin of the person who aggravates you. You'll need a strong leader to issue, and enforce, a fair verdict on the dispute. Such powerful leaders were something entirely new in primate social relations. In hunter-gatherer societies leadership tends to be collective, with consensus among elders—often elders of both sexes—sufficient to mediate disputes and make group decisions. Primates have pecking orders, but not leaders of dozens of individuals.

The problem isn't just quarrels. Reciprocity of all kinds is harder to keep track of when group size grows. With a small enough group, you can be confident that you'll run into the person you've done a favor for, and he or she is likely to keep the collaboration going by offering you a favor in return. But as group size increases, the people asking you for favors may be strangers. You need some immediate return from them, because you can't be sure they'll ever make good on an IOU. The old adage "fool me once, shame on you; fool me twice, shame on me" is well established in troops of apes and monkeys, who can be unforgiving of individuals that betray trust. Early adaptations to larger groups included the development of kin groups such as clans that were larger than families, smaller than tribes. But eventually organization by kinship became impossible. No one could know or vouch for everyone else. In such social environments of distrust, people invented barter, money, courts, and lawyers.

This movement toward more elaborate social structures and food-production methods has been an ongoing march throughout history—not surprising, given the overall direction of demographic growth. "Over the past 13,000 years," Jared Diamond notes, "the predominant trend in human society has been the replacement of smaller, less complex units by larger, more complex ones."[28] Not many of us would wish this development had never occurred. Technological and social innovations took us further from our animal past and led us toward where we are today. For good or ill, it's a long way from the Garden of Eden.

Nature's Howl

One challenge for growing and increasingly structured societies is how to manage human relations while sustaining livelihoods for large groups. As we've seen, the population growth that accompanies most successful cultures eventually undermines the environmental base on which such a culture thrives. Through environmental degradation and the multiplication of arguments and conflicts, population growth beyond certain points also complicates and stresses governance and the other social bonds by which cultures function. Sometimes political and social structures can cope; sometimes they can't.

Among the earliest societies that failed to cope was that of the Sumerians of southern Mesopotamia, the "first civilization" mentioned in the Eden story above, in the once-fertile Fertile Crescent. Centuries of rising population and increasingly intensive irrigation raised water tables on the Sumerian croplands, bringing salt to the surface of saturated soils. Evaporation left this salt in the soil, forcing a shift from wheat to a more salt-tolerant grain, barley. Eventually the layers of salt so reduced crop yields that by 1800 BC the population was plummeting. Sumer sank into oblivion, its once-glorious cities and farm fields a backwater in the empires of Babylonians and others who based their farming farther north. In later millennia, these peoples repeated the Sumerians' error and salinized their own fields.

Ronald Wright calls such situations "progress traps."[29] Successful innovation facilitates population growth and encourages new kinds of livelihood and governance. These are built for large-scale functionality when conditions are normal, but they lack flexibility for responding to the environmental degradation that eventually results from continued population growth. Societies float on their innovations down a stream of demographic expansion toward conditions that make it ever harder for further innovation to succeed. Population size and cumulative damage to the environment make it impossible merely to back out of the predicament.

That oft-heard toehold of environmental optimism—"we got ourselves into this situation, so we can get ourselves out of it"—sounds comforting, even logical. But it naïvely fails to account for this dynamic. Societies might be able to invent ways to lighten their footprint on the environment. The history of agriculture, in fact, is in part a story of wresting more food from the earth while allowing more people to live on less land. Once tipping points are passed and critical natural thresholds exceeded, however, few populous societies can manage the stately retreat of human numbers needed to return to balance with finite natural resources. The only route to population decline for most has been the kind of catastrophic jumps in death rates that spell collapse to archaeologists.

Most of the societies Diamond studied collapsed within decades of reaching their peak population. "The reason is simple," he writes. "Maximum population . . . means maximum environmental impact."[30] Farmers couldn't go home again to the hunting-and-gathering Eden they had left. There were too many of them.

Many early societies may have been aware of the impacts of population growth, even without understanding all the dynamics. Today, groups that live closest to nature tend to be the most aware of their impact. A few years ago, then–Population Action International videographer Daniele Anastasion and I interviewed several elders of the village of Antsakarivo in the hills of east-central Madagascar. Sitting in a row on a sunlit bench with their sloping farm fields behind them, the men explained to us that the name of their village means "thousands cross over."

"Because of their multitude," one man in his late sixties said, describing the founders of the village. "They were a large number of people." So large and growing so rapidly, he said, that the thick surrounding forests retreated faster than anyone had thought possible, before the advancing machetes and torches of the slash-and-burn farmers.

"Before 1960 there was still plenty of forest, and nature was still abundant," said a man named Jean Botoamby. "Fruits you could eat were everywhere, and living things in the water. But when the forest disappeared, starting around 1980, 1990, everything in nature that can serve as food disappeared. The number of kids has increased, but the food available in nature has decreased. We've entered headlong into a period of shortage and hardship."[31]

People have always been aware of their own numbers, at least those they live among day to day. Not that anyone routinely counts family members or friends, unless asking for a table at a restaurant. But we know the different feel, the different chemistry of groups that have a dozen, or 120, or 1,200 of our fellow beings. So did our remote ancestors, even those that walked on four feet. Animals are acutely conscious of group size. A school of fish, a flying V of migrating geese, even the larvae of German cockroaches will break into two groups when their numbers reach certain thresholds. Prides of lions tend to remain stable in size despite changes in their food supply, then suddenly break into two at certain points, based not only on food available but on the way group size affects their social relations.[32]

It should not surprise us, then, to learn that musings about human population go back to some of the earliest writings and are scattered across cultures and eras up to the present. The earliest known examples of symbolic writing are lists tabulating trade goods—"four sheep, two jars of oil, seven small bundles of acacia wood"—from the city of Uruk in Mesopotamia, dating from around 3000 BC.[33] The counting of farmers or soldiers or a king's subjects was no great leap for writers. The Atrahasis Epic quoted in this chapter's epigraph was a Babylonian antecedent of Genesis's flood story, already ancient when written in cuneiform script on three clay tablets sometime before 1600 BC. No older reference to human population is known. Although only a few tens of millions of people lived on earth at the time, the Atrahasis story depicts *overpopulation*, a surfeit of people, as so painful that the land itself howls.

The image was to reappear regularly, if not always so evocatively, over the next four millennia. The epic finishes "with the observation that barrenness, stillbirth and natural disasters were all part of the cosmic order to balance humankind's numbers with the land's bounty," comments writer Richard Harrow Feen.[34] And it describes what must be the earliest recorded population policy: conscious of the dominant female influence on the growth of population, kings assigned certain classes of women to jobs in temples that cloistered them for life.[35] Population control thus began, if we can believe the Atrahasis, with male rulers forcing some women to abandon sex and motherhood.

There couldn't have been enough temples by the waters of Babylon, however, to make much of a demographic difference. Even in this rare early instance of trying to adjust population *downward*, men didn't quite get it. They lacked a grasp of the conditions that could allow human numbers to be sustained over time. That grasp largely eludes us still. Among the likely results of this ignorance have been many of history's most spectacular demographic implosions, one more of which we'll visit in chapter 8.

Yet some cultures and civilizations found ways to last for thousands of years. And here we are today, riding an all-time peak of human population in ways that seem pretty successful, albeit increasingly risky. That there are demographic roots to social and environmental collapse may not surprise us. It may be just as interesting to probe why so many groups have thrived over time and what their long survival may have to do with successful innovation—and with women's lives and reproductive intentions.

FIVE

A Sense of Timing

To everything there is a season, . . . a time to be born, . . . a time to embrace, and a time to refrain from embracing.

    —Ecclesiastes 3:1–2, 5

Conceiving is nice; pregnancy is irksome.

    —Mesopotamian proverb

Until well after sunset my two West African colleagues and I weren't sure anyone would talk to us. We had invited all the reproductive-age women in the village of Djole, in south-central Mali, to an evening meeting. The community was participating in a development project supported by Oklahoma City–based World Neighbors, for which my colleagues worked. The topic that night was one any sensible focus-group leader would have judged too sensitive to be attempt in this setting: managing the timing of pregnancy and the size of families.

The word had gone out earlier in the day. The only man there would be myself, the foreigner whom the women had seen earlier in the village scribbling notes during a series of meetings to prioritize community needs. What chance, I wondered as I sat waiting, did a white American male have of drawing pious Muslim women out of their earthen-walled homes to talk about family planning?

Then, when the daylight had vanished so completely that I gripped my small flashlight in my teeth to illuminate my notebook, the sounds of rustling fabric, settling bodies, and soft voices slowly filled the covered space we had selected for the meeting. Over the next hour I scribbled, squint-eyed but feverishly, as a current of human energy surged through the darkness. The two dozen or so women wanted their opinions known—and acted on.

Where were the pills and other contraceptives, they demanded, that they had learned about two years earlier when a delegation from a Malian family planning organization had visited the village? Using one of these methods, the visitors had confirmed, a woman could have sex without fear of pregnancy. Then, when she wanted a child, she could stop using the contraceptives and conceive.

"We're tired of having one in front and one behind," one woman told us. It was a folk reference to carrying one child on the back while pregnant with a second. Others agreed, and the talk went on into the night. To my discomfort, I began to realize they thought I had the answer to their questions—and maybe some contraceptives.

Family planning is anything but a foreign concept to women in even the remotest reaches of the poorest developing countries. In industrialized countries most of us take for granted the relatively easy access to a range of contraceptive options. It's annoying that my local urban drug store has encased its condoms behind a locked plastic pane—they're being stolen, apparently—but if I need some, they're there. We can easily forget that any sexually active woman might want the option of safely and easily preventing pregnancy, at every point along her nearly four decades of reproductive potential. She need not be planning far ahead. She might not be working out her desired family size. She might just want to postpone motherhood or to get a break after her last pregnancy. (She might also want to reduce her exposure to a fatal infection, but I'll be sticking mainly to reproduction here.) Next door to Mali in Niger, women call contraceptives "rest medicine."[1] Enough use of rest medicine adds up to later childbearing, smaller completed families, and slower population growth.

Not that women and their partners are thinking about population when they practice contraception. Few if any have just read the latest report on global warming and decided that a smaller family would mean lower greenhouse gas emissions. Rather, they're making a calculus about their lives, livelihoods, and relationships at any given moment. They're aiming to maximize the satisfaction and pleasures of sex while minimizing its risks. Although intensely personal, collectively these childbearing decisions shape the dynamics and structures of human populations—assuming the intentions are realized.

As the author of Ecclesiastes recognized, some times are ripe for parenting and others are not. Women tend to be in the best position to know which is which. If nothing else, they may endeavor to "refrain from embracing" (though the men they're with may have other ideas). But if effective contraception is available and its use is allowed (and the men are supportive), it tends to be used. And there have always been at least a few options available to those most anxious to avoid pregnancy at any specific time.

The concept of reproductive *timing* is broader and more useful here than the concept of family-size *limitation*. Functionally, the two objectives are similar. "Timers" generally end up with smaller families than would otherwise be the case. And each decision that "limiters" make is really about the appropriateness of childbearing at *a moment in time*. The key question a prospective mother faces at each moment of her reproductive life is, when is the right time?

Reproductive timing may refer mostly to preventing an unwanted conception at a given moment, but it also includes the encouragement of conception and healthy pregnancy when a birth is wanted. It can include fostering and adoption, if willing and qualified parents are available. It can include the always-divisive concept of abortion. And it can include strategies more universally disturbing than abortion but that today gain much less attention: infanticide and two less directly murderous ways of escaping parental investment, child neglect and abandonment.

Females have long evolved and developed ways to improve their chances of delivering healthy offspring at term. Biologists at the University of Chicago found that the scent of a breastfeeding woman can enhance the libido of nearby reproductive-age women, suggesting a kind of olfactory signal that *someone has successfully given birth; the time must be right for me to try.*[2] The history of natural fertility enhancers may be as old as that of fertility repressors, though there seem to be many fewer of them.

Either way, timing is the key. Even if women start out, like Henrietta in Accra, with a family-size ideal, their goal is rarely to achieve it as fast as possible and then stop having kids. Recall that Henrietta herself hoped to wait until she was established in a good job, was married, and had reached the age of twenty-four. Rather, women more often seek to raise their chances of having and raising a child when the time is right and—if their culture and compatriots allow them this choice—to reduce the chances of conceiving at other times. Given the length of time sexually active women must live with pregnancy as a possibility, reproductive timing is most often a matter of using contraception rather than trying to enhance fecundity. Sometimes contraception fails, and other options for avoiding reproduction may come into play.

How long has this been going on, the intentional management of one's own childbearing? There are no fossilized pessaries from the Paleolithic, no cave paintings of condoms. But there is good reason to believe that at least the urge—and possibly some capacity—to have your sex and enjoy it, too, without fear of pregnancy, goes very far back in human history. It's even possible that contraceptive and other fertility-regulating practices influenced changes in human population long before modern contraception became widespread.

Ancient Options

Sex, as we've seen, is only sometimes specifically about making babies and is much more often about the sex. For most of those heterosexual couples having sex without contraception, however, pregnancy happens. On average, 85 percent of women in such couples will become pregnant during any given year.[3] Any single act of unprotected heterosexual intercourse may be followed in nine months by a notice of payment due, in the form of a nearly two-decade commitment to raising a new human being to adulthood. It's logical that not long after women figured out that pregnancy resulted from sexual intercourse, they began asking, Does it have to be this way? Couldn't I enjoy the sex, but wait until later—and maybe with some other guy—to have the baby?

Conventional wisdom tells us that until the invention of modern contraception over the last few centuries, the answer was pretty much no, you can't. In the view of most demographers, intentional pregnancy prevention played no significant role in depressing population growth until the invention of modern contraception. Instead, human population hobbled along at consistently low levels throughout prehistory because the natural world was a Malthusian hell for parents and their children. Women were pregnant or breastfeeding much of their adult lives, wasting most of this effort because all but two of their many children routinely died before adulthood from infection, accidents, predators, or starvation.

But what if childhood weren't always so deadly and the timing of reproduction not so far beyond a woman and her partner's control? There are so many places, after all, where cold feet can step off the parenthood path, from before sex to after birth.

Couples can decide mutually to just say no to sex, for example, as Ecclesiastes suggests they do when it's the "season" for abstinence. Or women can refuse eager suitors and partners—sometimes. In the 1970 Swedish film *The Emigrants*, a character played by Liv Ullmann tells her aroused husband that another child would doom their homesteading effort in the bleak winter landscape of nineteenth-century Minnesota. The husband, played by Max von Sydow, forlornly turns away from her in their bed and sulks. Elsewhere and at other times, another husband might respond to such a refusal with violence. Whichever is the more common reaction will make a difference to reproductive timing, family size, and even population growth—not to mention to the wife.

Abstinence is unlikely, though, to be the long-term contraceptive some religious leaders and politicians dream about. As most human beings learn early in life, the sexual urge is insistent and sometimes all-consuming, especially when strong mutual attraction is in the mix. But nonprocreative sex is an option. Couples who can't abstain can enjoy alternatives to vaginal intercourse, such as mutual masturbation. In eighteenth-century France this common practice was called "the pleasures of the little goose," a culinary metaphor for second best.[4] More adventurous nonprocreative sex acts were well enough accepted in ancient times to be depicted in art. In the bedroom of the Roman emperor Tiberius, a painting depicted the goddess Juno performing fellatio on Jupiter.[5] A few centuries later and half a world away in Peru, ceramic figurines from the Moche culture also depict oral sex—and a husband enjoying anal sex with his wife while she cuddles a sleeping child, who apparently did not need a younger sibling.[6]

Such diversity in sexual connections may have encouraged the proliferation of sexually transmitted infections. This could be one reason that societies proscribed nonprocreative sex. A more likely reason, however, is simply that it was nonprocreative. Societies sometimes have an interest, as we'll see later, in making sure that sex results in babies. Over time, as well, sexually active heterosexuals may simply miss the sexual and emotional sat-isfactions of conventional vaginal intercourse, as Monica Lewinsky report-edly did during her oral-only affair with President Bill Clinton. So the challenge of separating intercourse from reproduction remains.

Perhaps the best-known natural contraceptive method is *withdrawal*, the interruption of sexual intercourse just before male climax to avoid the risk of conception. The technique may be as old as the insight that male orgasm in vaginal intercourse is, literally, the seminal event in initiating conception. Withdrawal gained scriptural fame in the Old Testament story of Onan, who "spilled his seed on the ground" rather than inseminate his brother's widow.[7] An Arab writer commented in the ninth century that contraceptive withdrawal was the major distinction between men and ani-mals, the latter of which knew no better than to abandon themselves to the moment.[8] And the method was probably what Governor Bradford of the Plimoth Plantation had in mind when he wrote of one colonial couple, in what must be the earliest documentation of contraception in North America, "for though he satisfied his lust on her, he endeavored to hinder conception."[9]

Consider, however, who is withdrawing what from whom. The tech-nique can be effective when couples are communicating well and men are disciplined and highly motivated to prevent conception. But this is pre-cisely the method's weak point: a woman has to rely on her partner to act on the mantra *no baby* at precisely the moment when the future is the last thing on a man's mind. "Sorry, honey," he remarks postcoitally to his soon-to-be-pregnant partner. "I couldn't help myself." More accurately, like many men before him, he couldn't help *her*. This, in fact, is the con-ceit of a French pornographic novel published in 1741. In it, a boy fails to make good on his promise to a young partner, who allows him to try withdrawal despite her protests that it's not a practical technique.[10] Withdrawal survives today in Turkey and in much of Europe as a tradi-tional method of contraception, at least when nothing else is handy. In much of Europe it may have been among the most popular methods of contraception for centuries prior to the introduction of the oral contraceptive pill in the 1960s.

A piece of wisdom that must long have been shared among women is that the simple and instinctive act of breastfeeding can be a powerful natural contraceptive. Nursing is all the more supportive for reproductive success because of its compelling main function in nurturing the child most recently born. The suckling raises levels of the hormone prolactin, which effectively represses a nursing mother's ovulation—if the feeding is frequent and regular, day and night, whenever the infant demands.

Leanness on the mother's part may be important as well. Breastfeeding in combination with low fat levels stemming from regular exercise, some scholars believe, may explain much of the sustained low populations of hunter-gathering humans before the invention of agriculture. Anthropologists have documented this among hunter-gatherers who held on to this ancient lifestyle in relatively recent times. The !Kung San of southern Africa have been known to maintain birth intervals of four years or more, apparently through breastfeeding, with the intervals longer when natural resources are scarce and shorter when times are good. Families tended to be small by traditional African standards, with fewer than five children on average, which facilitated the !Kung San's nomadic hunter-gatherer lifestyle.

"Their genes hardly seem to be screaming out for replication; and economic considerations, as virtually always, lie to the fore," wrote paleoanthropologist Ian Tattersal of !Kung San contraceptive breastfeeding. "For hunters and gatherers, then, it's fertility, not its lack, that is the enemy. Individual [!Kung San] women show no sign, conscious or unconscious, of wishing to maximize their output of progeny. And that, folks, is the ancestral environment."[11] An ancestral environment, Tattersal might have added, in which human populations grew relatively slowly—at times perhaps not at all—for centuries on end.

As modernity increasingly hemmed in the !Kung San in the late twentieth century, they encountered pastoralists and farmers and began shifting
their livelihoods to these ways of life. In this process, breastfeeding gave way
to feeding children mashes of grains or tubers. By most accounts, birth intervals shrank and family size and population growth rates increased. It's hazardous to extrapolate the experience of modernizing hunter-gatherers into
the deep human past, but, as Tattersal suggests, comparable behavioral shifts
may help explain why human numbers expanded at unprecedented rates
among the earliest agricultural populations. A major boost in fertility may
have compensated for higher childhood death rates caused by less varied
diets and the new infectious diseases that arrived with settlement.

One problem with breastfeeding as a contraceptive, of course, is that
it's useless for delaying first births and not so great for making your most
recent birth your last. Moreover, it's not always easy for women to breastfeed as intensely as needed to securely prevent ovulation. !Kung San
infants feed three to four times an hour, for just two minutes each time,
with the longest average gap between feedings less than one hour.[12] Try
that with a nine-to-five job downtown, or with almost any livelihood
other than that of a forager. An absence of menstruation is a helpful indicator that things are going well, but the first postpartum ovulation occurs
before the first postpartum period, so there's no real margin of error
before method failure means another pregnancy. And pregnancy may be
harder to discern early on because, after all, menstruation has been absent
since the last child's birth. Breastfeeding and the other traditional methods I've discussed certainly prevented pregnancy in some cases. But they
hardly provided the dependable 99 percent effectiveness we associate with
modern birth control.

The Birth of Birth Control

What women and sympathetic male partners really needed, in prehistory as today, was exactly what the Malian women I interviewed were

demanding: a safe and convenient method they could use to have unin-
terrupted vaginal intercourse without fear of pregnancy and without
undermining their ability to conceive when they wanted to. Could such
contraception have existed in the deep past? Possibly, but only if we don't
expect too much of it.

For tens of thousands of years women spent much of their time collecting and learning about the plants and small animals their environment
offered for food. Early rock art in southern Africa suggests that some artists
altered their consciousness by ingesting local hallucinogenic plants when
they covered outcrops and cave walls with dreamlike imagery. Some of this
knowledge of the effects of natural substances, accumulated over millennia, could have been applied to identifying substances that healed illness or
wounds and relieved pain. Might the accumulation of such wisdom have
led eventually to the use of nature to help women time their reproduction?
Might local environments have offered substances to enhance the chances
of conception and pregnancy, when that's what women were hoping for in
having sex, and to repress the reproductive process when it was sex but not
a child they wanted?

Biological and documentary evidence suggests that nature indeed may
offer plant and animal substances that have at least some effect on human
fertility. Consider the possibility that some plants and animals have evolved
a capacity to reduce the fertility of their predators. That would be a shrewd
survival adaptation. In recent decades experiments have indicated that some
plants produce substances that may reduce animal fertility. These aren't the
kinds of experiments one can easily duplicate with human test subjects, but
some of the animal results correspond intriguingly with accounts of natural contraceptives and abortifacients documented from ancient Egypt to
modern Colombia.

John Riddle, a historian of pharmacology based at North Carolina State
University, has tabulated dozens of herbs and other natural substances that
are mentioned as regulators of fertility in historic texts *and* that contain

pharmacologic agents that may depress mammalian fertility. Many of them contain estrogenic sterols similar to those in today's hormonal contraceptives. Some are still used in traditional medicines around the world. One of these is the common roadside wildflower Queen Anne's lace, which women in both the Appalachian mountains of Watauga County, North Carolina, and rural areas of the state of Rajasthan in India have used in relatively recent times for contraception.[13]

Some scientists dismiss the idea that natural herbs could act block ovulation or conception. It took decades, after all, to develop the complex formulations of modern oral contraception. Would natural equivalents literally be hanging from trees or popping out of the ground? And any substances effective enough to abort a pregnancy would almost certainly be dangerously toxic and potentially fatal to the woman herself. A middle option of natural fertility regulators, however—something that has elements of both contraception and abortion—crops up often in the historical and ethnographic literature and is easier, forgiving the pun, to conceive of.

These are the *emmenagogues.* That's a gem of a word you'll never encounter in a spelling bee or a college-entrance vocabulary test. Emmenagogues induce menstruation, regardless of when—or whether—it was previously scheduled. Intentionally bringing on a period might be useful just to reassure women with late or irregular menses that their bodies are behaving as they should. Of course, menstruation also flushes away any products of a recent conception and implantation in the uterine wall, if these are present. Emmenagogues thus can bring on what amounts to a very early abortion, but in such a way that the woman herself—let alone her partner, her family, or the local authorities—need never know she had been in the earliest stage of pregnancy. It's easy to see how popular emmenagogues might have been to sexually active women who wished to avoid the birth of an unwelcome child. And, indeed, the most reliably documented fertility-regulating plants tend to act as emmenagogues rather than as contraceptives or as abortifacients for later and more obvious pregnancies.

Riddle lists emmenagogues and a few contraceptives he found in a contemporary mail-order catalog of herbal nutritional supplements, each of which he has also seen documented in antiquity or in contemporary oral accounts: aloe, angelica, catnip, coltsfoot, feverfew, hyssop, juniper berries, mint, myrrh, pennyroyal, pleurisy root, sage, spikenard, tansy, and wormwood.[14]

A field guide to eastern North American medicinal plants that I happened to find on my own study bookshelf lists the following species used by Native Americans or European colonists as emmenagogues (the term is even listed in its index), or in some cases as contraceptives: false Solomon's seal, Canadian sanicle, various snakeroots, mayweed, trout lily, golden ragwort, sweet goldenrod, common milkweed, American dittany, common speedwell, pasqueflower, American pennyroyal, rough blazing star, various mugworts, spicebush, mistletoe, American bittersweet, and Dutchman's-pipe. A few other herbs are identified as possible abortifacients and highly toxic.[15] Don't try any of these at home, by the way. Unlike modern contraceptives, there is no scientifically demonstrated effectiveness or safety for any of them. Even if some are effective, at what dosages? Two women died in the United States in recent decades after taking large amounts of pennyroyal oil in efforts to self-induce abortion.

Whatever the dose, many of these plants were imbibed whole or in solutions, like some folk version of the birth control pill. But there's a more likely bodily route to effective contraception or menstrual inducement: pessaries, something a woman places in her vagina just in front of the cervix before having sex. The objective is to keep the man's spermatozoa from entering the uterus and fertilizing any egg making its way down one of the fallopian tubes. Pessaries made of substances from acacia oil to crocodile dung are described in Egyptian papyri that record efforts at contraception at least as old as the Atrahasis Epic of Mesopotamia.[16] Based on logic alone, pessaries have a better claim to contraceptive effectiveness than anything taken orally. They provide a physical obstacle to sperm and also can alter the local chemical environment around the cervix in ways that may kill or at least fend off the male seed.

Some classical Mediterranean pessaries contained "misy," believed to be a copper compound comparable to the copper used in modern intrauterine devices to kill or immobilize sperm. Others featured acidic substances such as lemon juice, still used by sex workers in Nigeria in the hopes it will prevent both conception and HIV infection, though there is no scientific evidence it does either.[17]

Intriguingly, the female condom appears both in ancient times and in at least one indigenous culture, though the male version has no obvious counterpart in either sphere. A Greek legend holds that women who cohabited with King Minos of Crete inserted membranes made from goats' bladders into their vaginas to protect themselves from the "serpents and scorpions" his semen contained.[18] For two thousand years or more these animals served as archetypes for infection in Europe. Apparently, the objective here was prophylaxis. But in other cases the condoms were for contraception. Women among the Djukas people, descendents of African slaves who had escaped deep into the forests of what is now Surinam, clipped off one end of five-inch seed pods of what may have been a variety of okra and used these, in the words of contraceptive historian Norman Himes, as "a kind of vegetable condom held in place by the vagina."[19]

One other point about ancient use of contraception is worth making: if women or couples wanted to be as certain as possible about avoiding pregnancy while enjoying sex, combining two reasonably effective methods was just as wise then as it is today. A contemporary couple properly using both hormonal contraception and condoms have less than a one-tenth of 1 percent probability of beginning a pregnancy in any given year. The equivalent in prehistory might have been to combine consistent withdrawal with a reasonably effective pessary. As human populations began to gather in city-states and communication methods improved, any midwives who made this insight and spread the word might have become very well appreciated. They might also have nudged downward the curve of the local population's growth.

Most demographers and physicians tend to doubt that such potions and pessaries from wild plants made much of an impact on individual reproduction or past demographic trends, but I don't find their arguments convincing.[20] Certainly anyone wishing safe and effective pregnancy prevention today would choose modern contraceptives over folk fertility regulators. But, as British medical demographer John Cleland and several colleagues point out, "even the least effective method is better than using nothing."[21] Even if typical effectiveness was a fraction of that of modern contraception, the cumulative demographic impact of widespread use over time might nonetheless have been significant despite the many disappointed individual users.

The folk wisdom of generations of women, Riddle argues, would have eliminated plants and substances that were broadly ineffectual in preventing pregnancy and childbirth. "The hailed placebo effect does not apply to birth control measures," he wrote in 1992. "Full-term pregnancy simply cannot be psychosomatic."[22] The diversity of natural contraceptives and emmenagogues convinced Riddle that until sometime in the late Middle Ages, women were managing their own childbearing as they saw fit and having children, for all practical purposes, when and only when they wanted to.

At the very least, the stories of plant-based contraception encountered in this and later chapters demonstrate women's strong interest over thousands of years in avoiding unwanted childbearing. Billions of women must have given birth at times when they had no desire to begin a new round of mothering. Even if a woman welcomed one birth, she might not the next. As with the women I met in Mali, a social interest in having a large family often masks and conflicts with a private interest in having a healthy and prosperous one.

But Riddle, like some of the anthropologists who held that premodern peoples kept their populations in balance with their environments, goes too far in contending that ancient women really *controlled* their own reproduction. Women rarely have full control of childbearing today, even in developed countries with a range of safe and effective modern contraceptive options. In the United States, despite a health system some claim is the most advanced in the world, nearly half of all pregnancies are unintended. Among some low-income U.S. populations the proportion is higher than that and appears to be rising.[23] Sex is too powerful an urge and the availability of reliable contraception—ancient or modern—is too variable for humanity ever to have achieved the Planned Parenthood ideal of "every child a wanted child." Not yet, at least.

Last Resorts

The reality of contraceptive failure is the reason that preventing conception and pregnancy has never been the only option for avoiding unwanted reproduction and parenting. Mentions of abortion in literature go back to the Hippocratic oath of classical Greece and possibly longer in ancient China. Efforts to end a pregnancy prematurely were either ineffectual (physicians advised women to jump vigorously) or dangerous, involving toxic herbs or long probing needles inserted into cervix and uterus. It's clear enough, however, that women often sought and attempted abortion in ancient times.

Once an unwelcome birth occurs, the window for avoiding a full investment in parenting begins to close, but is not yet entirely shut. More direct and often violent approaches to family limitation loom as last resorts: child neglect, abandonment, and infanticide. Human infanticide differs from the practice among other primates in that it is much more frequently a female than a male strategy for reproductive success. Where individual female strategy ends and male-dominant cultural pressure begins, however, isn't always easy to see. But in almost all cultures in which infanticide occurs, ancient and modern, it is most likely mothers or occasionally their birth attendants who dispatch the infant. Modern people may interpret infanticide "as lunatic savagery," Canadian psychologists Martin Daly and Margo Wilson wrote in 1984, "but the ethnographic record makes clear that infanticide is nowhere taken lightly."[24] !Kung San women seek solitude for a few days with their newborn. Men are neither consulted nor anywhere nearby when the event takes place. The infant might as easily have taken ill or been lost to a wild animal. No questions, apparently, are asked when the mother returns to the group alone.

In preagricultural cultures, infanticide may be ritualized in ways that make the decision a matter of tradition rather than a mother's reproductive strategy. Among some South American indigenous groups, twins are killed, as are orphans and any child born with a disability or some other distinguishing physical characteristic. In premodern Madagascar, infants born on a Thursday or a Monday might routinely die. Even in Christian Europe, perhaps even in the memory of some now living, mothers sometimes explained suspicious deaths of healthy young infants by claiming they inadvertently "covered" or "overlay" the babies while sleeping. The slumber would have to have been remarkably profound, and these were probably euphemisms for intentional suffocation of the infant. Throughout the late Middle Ages and beyond, the Catholic Church tried to eliminate the alibi of overlying by prohibiting parents from sleeping with their babies. The ban had the additional impact, intended or not, of reducing the contraceptive effect of breastfeeding.[25]

Mothers anxious to avoid raising a newborn don't always need to resort to violence. Those of ancient Sparta "exposed" their infants on remote heights, somewhat comforted by the thought that a passing shepherd might find and adopt the child. The women of other Greek city-states placed their infants near temples, just as later Christian women left nondescript bundles at the doors of churches.

Much as infanticide shocks us today, it is still an occasional outcome of unwanted pregnancy in every society. We may regard the mothers of babies found in dumpsters or toilets as mentally ill, but the line isn't easy to draw between pathology and calculations about the life chances of mother and child. Such calculations have always prompted some mothers to abandon their newborns. In the year 2000, a Bolivian health reform group reported that women in some communities in that country took the lives of 16 percent of babies born. The group explained the practice as an extreme reaction to poverty based on cultural beliefs that infanticide was the only practical form of family planning available.[26]

Among the reasons for the persistence of infanticide is the strong bias against girls from which perhaps no culture is entirely free. Unlike contraception or abortion, parents can select children for survival based on the tiny sex organs they discover at the moment of birth. Indeed, anthropologists have good evidence that infanticide played an important role in early population limitation: in many ancient societies, boys significantly outnumbered girls. We saw in chapter 1 that it's normal for about 105 boys to be born for every 100 girls, but much higher birthrates for boys indicate a deadly bias against girls. As anthropologists Marvin Harris and Eric Ross point out, this might be adaptive for groups interested in managing their population size, especially those in competition for resources with other groups. The fewer girls, the fewer future births; the more boys, the more future warriors.[27]

There's not much scholarly consensus on how common infanticide was in prehistory, of boys or girls—your view may depend on whether you view prehistory as a golden or a dark age—and not much direct evidence to settle the argument.[28] Yet cases of modern infanticide in India and China make clear that some women act in accordance with strong gender preference in their cultures regardless of how repulsive others find this behavior. A grim photograph that sometimes crops up in the public health literature shows how son preference operates even when girls are not dispatched at birth. A sad-looking South Asian mother holds a pudgy, smiling boy toddler on her lap next to his spectral, hollow-eyed sister. The girl, the caption informs us, died from neglect not long after the photo was taken. Favoring boys over girls has not entirely disappeared in the more "civilized" West either. In an airport terminal outside of Washington, D.C., I overheard a flight attendant ask an airline pilot whether he had any daughters. "Girls are like undersized fish," the pilot responded, without answering the question. "We throw them back in."

In any case, the documentation of infanticide from ancient texts to yesterday's newspapers suggests that it plays a disconcertingly consistent role, however small, in reproductive timing and in past population trends. Still, one need not romanticize the maternal instincts of prehistoric females to see that infanticide must have been a last resort along a continuum of strategies for avoiding a mistimed investment in parenthood. Even if a wrenching attachment to a newborn child were not a risk, why would anyone willingly suffer the depletions of pregnancy and the risks of childbirth if one or both of these could be avoided altogether? That question must have occurred to more than one woman—and led more than once to contraceptive experimentation.

Women's Lives

In agricultural and urban societies infanticide often has been an extreme response to an inability to prevent pregnancy and birth much earlier in the process. Barriers to contraception and abortion, in turn, have often stemmed from strong cultural traditions on every continent that tended to boost family size and thus the growth of population. For beyond the question of whether effective birth control methods are accessible, there is another important limitation on women's ability to time their reproduction: they may not be allowed to. Why this has so often been true in so many places, and how restrictions may have changed over time, are closely connected to some difficult and contentious questions: how men and women relate to each other and how their differing interests in sex, reproduction, population, and nature play out in cultural evolution and everyday life.

Human cultures have always exhibited a wide range of gender power balances—assuming you're not expecting to find most females dominating most males. Female dominance has been documented in no human culture of any significant size or duration. Still, evidence suggests that at least some prehistoric societies were characterized by relatively high status for women. Archaeologists see this status in women's burials and in the analysis of their remains. Anthropologists document the roles of women as shamans, judges, and members of leadership councils in hunter-gatherer groups in Africa and the Americas.

Along the Yellow River in northern China, the Yangshao people of about 6,500 years ago buried some women, and almost no men, "in elaborate fashion, with higher-quality grave goods [and] ritually significant postures," according to Chinese historian Kenneth Hammond of New Mexico University. "This suggests that at this time the societies that were emerging had a leadership provided by women."[29]

Just as intriguing as the possibility of women's leadership may be hints of day-to-day gender equality provided by 9,000-year-old Çatalhöyük, a large town of a few thousand people that thrived in south-central Turkey shortly after the dawn of settled agriculture. Hunting and horticulture, intriguingly, both contributed to the compact town's food supply. Analyzing patterns of skeletal wear, Theya Molleson concluded that both sexes engaged in similar tasks. Patterns of soot accumulation within the rib cage suggested that women and men spent identical amounts of time indoors. That's a remarkable contrast to the much later observation of the Greek historian Xenophon in the fourth century BC that "the gods created the woman for the indoors function, the man for all others," a view that has survived in some cultures to the present day.[30]

While women enjoyed high status in some cultures in some time peri-ods, equality was the exception rather than the rule. True, anthropologists have identified dozens, even hundreds, of cultures that were *matrilineal* (in which descent is tracked and accorded value through maternal lines) or *matrilocal* (in which husbands live with the families of their wives, rather than the more common reverse arrangement). Don't confuse these with genuine female status and autonomy, however. Such social arrangements relate more to specific economic and livelihood arrangements, especially the need to ascertain paternity in premodern cultures.[31] Even in matrilin-eal and matrilocal cultures, some male domination is common. Does this mean that a tendency toward such gender relations is "natural" and all but inevitable in human societies? Men are, on average, bigger and stronger than women, for example, and thus are able and likely to physically over-power them. Moreover, in the majority of primate species, males dominate females. Maybe when it comes to gender attitudes, men are basically just chimpanzees wearing pants.

Such theories quickly break down when you survey the many past and contemporary cultures around the world. If you try to track gender relations across time, it becomes apparent that no specific pattern of gender relations is encoded in our DNA. To the extent that archaeologists, anthropologists, and historians can discern trends, male subjugation of women seems to have increased markedly as human numbers expanded and societies necessarily grew more complex. Why this should be remains one of humanity's great mysteries, but I would argue that it is linked to the changing ways our ances-tors earned their livings.

Earth Mothers, Male Gods

Women's status has traditionally ebbed and flowed with their contribution to the group's livelihood or food production. As we've seen, females in hunter-gathering societies enjoyed relatively high status since the food they gathered often made the difference between a decent meal and starvation when large game was scarce. That status may have been enhanced during the revolutionary transition to agricultural lifestyles. Ancient art suggests that during this period women were frequently associated with the bounty of nature and the mysteries of fertility, birth, and creation itself—an association that survives today in concepts like Mother Earth.

Meanwhile, men may have lost some status as animal extinctions and scarcity of game gradually marginalized the importance of hunting. "Men, whose bows had lost much of their usefulness," historian William McNeill comments in one of few references to women in his epic work *The Rise of the West*, "may have been persuaded to take on part of the work of the fields— fencing to keep out animals [and] may in some communities have taken spade or hoe reluctantly in hand to work the fields side by side with their womenfolk." We see a few of these men, limbs and backs just as ravaged as those of women, kneeling at the grindstones of Tell Abu Hureyra or working indoors at Çatalhöyük. Families sometimes must have worked as single production units, the old sexual divisions of hunting and gathering erased by necessity. "Correspondingly," McNeill adds, writing of the Near East, "the spread of agriculture was connected everywhere with the rise of females priestesses and deities to prominence."[32]

Men soon reasserted their authority over food production and, correspondingly, over women's lives. The slightly later domestication of animals probably contributed to the shift from female to male power that occurred in Europe, Asia, and perhaps Africa. (The peoples of the Americas before European contact domesticated only a few animals, and those they did were small.) There's no reason to believe that the average woman is unable to corral, break, or drive livestock or horses. But over time men may simply have outcompeted them for the assignment through their usual advantage in upper-body strength.

Nomadic pastoralism, the lifestyle of Abraham and Lot in Genesis, gradually separated from crop cultivation and became a way of life for millions of people living where altitudes were too high or climates too dry to support crops. Lacking any role for women in improving livelihoods, pastoralism tended to marginalize women's productive capacity. Women were confined mostly to the interiors of tents and wagons,where they gave birth to babies and cared for children. Pastoralism generated some of the most rapid population growth the world had seen up to that time. Those who still grew grain developed a less intensive animal husbandry, learning how to fertilize tired soil and warm the walls of their houses with the manure of their livestock. Sometimes the animals lived indoors, serving as natural furnaces inside farm homes—transferring not only heat but pathogens that adapted to the plentiful new human hosts.[33]

Sometime well before 3000 BC, as growing agricultural populations depleted the most easily tilled woodland soil and pushed farmers toward the tougher and weedier grassland soil, necessity mothered the invention of the earliest traction plows. These offered yet another route to male advancement. Scraping out a furrow through hard soil behind the rear end of an ox, like breaking oxen itself, was strenuous upper-body work. The shift in farming practices may have been pivotal to gender relations, the growth of population, and history itself, because it was plow agriculture that spread from the Fertile Crescent to Europe, North Africa, Asia and eventually to the Americas and Oceania. "Hunting and tending animals had always been primarily a man's job," McNeill writes. "And when animals came into the field, men came with them. Women lost their earlier dominion over the grain fields; and as followers of the plow, men became once again the principal providers of food. Therewith they were able to reinforce or restore masculine primacy in family and society."[34]

The violent conflicts that erupted as plow farmers fanned out across new lands may have further promoted male dominance. Warfare is an almost uniformly male domain. Not being childbearers, individual men were more expendable to their groups and were thus more valuable as fighters. And their muscular edge would have been decisive in positioning them along perimeters, given the occasional need for hand-to-hand combat in hostile border encounters. Years ago some writers speculated that men consciously took on—perhaps even invented—warfare at least in part as a specialty in which they could excel, to balance women's capacities for childbearing and the production of plant food.[35] The idea hasn't held up well. Who would risk being impaled, disfigured, or killed out of gender envy? Still, the intensification of violence that accompanied increasingly sophisticated food production perversely gained men status, even as it sometimes took their lives.

By the time of the earliest written records, patrilineal families and male dominance were universal among plowing peoples in the Middle East. "The rise of male deities and priests—established features of Sumerian and Egyptian religion—may also be connected with the new masculine role in agriculture," McNeill notes.[36]

Taming Women

Each of these developments—all traceable to population growth—opened up new possibilities for males to develop specialties naturally favored by their body types. Under these circumstances, natural tensions over reproductive timing would have arisen between men and women and between rulers and the ruled. Women's interest in conserving their own childbearing energies to assure that their children survived to adulthood would have collided with male rulers' evolving interest in population growth and youthful population age structures—to assure a consistent supply of followers, workers, and soldiers. As farming changed from slash-and-burn methods to high-maintenance, fertilizer-hungry ones, and as cattle and other livestock grew in number and importance, human experience and awareness shifted from a world of nature in which all people once had lived. In that world, knowledge of plant and animal behavior-often the province of women, at least as much as of men-offered sustenance and power. In the new human-dominated world of farm fields, caches of stored grain, villages and towns and eventually cities, knowledge counted for less than physical strength. With the bounty of the world now quantifiable, storable, and controllable by those who could defend food surpluses, new ideas of property, wealth, and inheritance emerged. All these shifts tended to favor males with their upper-body strength and brought them to the fore as authorities and leaders. Women dropped back, and their value as childbearers came to overshadow the roles they had had in societies more oriented toward natural livelihoods.

Not through any particular malevolence but simply by practical necessity in this new post-natural world, men looked with suspicion and concern at whatever contraceptive and other reproductive timing methods women may have used. And with time and more cultural evolution in populous societies, women often came to depend almost completely on the influence and power of the males in their lives—fathers, brothers, husbands, even in-laws. Women and their reproductive powers came to be seen as a special kind of property, intensified by female competition for the best male providers and by such male interests as certainty about paternity.

By 3100 BC in lake villages in the foothills of the Alps, decorations and other artistic depictions could not have been more different from the naked and voluptuous females of the past. Now the ornaments were pendants of male genitals and symbolic bows, arrows, axes, and daggers. Women's elaborate dress and ornamentation found in burials indicate marital status. Some "decoration" physically confined its wearers. In the Swabian Alb in southwestern Germany, archaeologists found female skeletons buried with pairs of leg rings joined by short chains at midcalf. British archaeological student Amanda Giles interpreted these "as female ornaments of sexual restriction," comparable to the foot binding practiced in imperial China.[37]

Pastoral societies were, and generally still are, almost universally sex-segregated and patriarchal. Women process food and other animal resources and attend to household and childraising tasks. Although they perform an estimated 55 percent of work in such societies, based on surveys of 156 well-documented societies summarized by anthropologist Peggy Reeves Sanday, women contribute little to actual food production. Men in such societies tend to have little involvement in childraising but do direct the reproduction of livestock and horses. Men's growing expertise and familiarity with this animal task may have easily extended to the women in their lives.

"In their capacity as childbearers, women are often equated with the animals men control," Sanday writes. "Men carve a separate domain for themselves by taking public responsibility for female and animal fertility."[38] Even etymology testifies to this as a male domain. One word for *wife* among the ancient Greeks was *damar*, meaning "tamed." The word *vagina* is derived from the Latin word for "sheath."[39] Had linguistic power relations been reversed, the penis might have been named after the Latin for "stuffing." The idea that men are the appropriate decision makers on reproduction, in any event, eventually linked with male enthusiasm for population growth that even today often recoils at the prospect of low birthrates and demographic stability. While men in hunter-gatherer groups, living close to nature, sometimes tolerated or even endorsed infanticide to achieve population stability, the male elites of larger, more organized societies—who stood to gain power through increases in soldiers, workers, and the numbers of the ruled—tended toward optimism that natural limits posed no significant barriers to indefinite human expansion. The attitude survives today among such elites, who add consumers, taxpayers, and voters to the list of those characterized by a key attribute: it's always good to have more.

Even in organized and patriarchal states, a few women may have achieved the high status of queens or queen mothers, though such exalted positions tended to be rarities. In some of the settled societies on the cusp of the classical Mediterranean age, however, there is evidence of relatively high status for women in general. In Minoan Crete, acrobatic women are depicted somersaulting over charging bulls in ritual partnership with men. In Etruscan Italy, women drove chariots, owned real estate, and ran shops.[40] These societies tended to be based on diverse livelihoods, including trade in a world of growing human numbers and waterborne mobility in the Mediterranean world. Yet this relative gender equality may have cost these societies the population growth they eventually needed to defend themselves from more demographically dynamic pastoralist invaders. Both Minoan Crete and Etruscan Italy fell after centuries of relative stability to militaristic and male-dominated outsiders. The societies that replaced them had altogether different ideas about women, and the populations of these societies grew for some time to come.

SIX

Axial Age

In a multitude of people is a king's honor, but in the lack of
people is the downfall of a prince.
   —Proverbs 14:28

V isiting the hazardously sloping farm fields of southwestern Uganda, I
met Emannuel Kasigwa—elder of the village of Rubuguri, husband of
two, and father of eleven.

"We used to go by the Bible," Emannuel told me with a slight smile
when I asked about his family in a meeting with a group of the village
elders. All were male. "People were going by the idea of filling the world.
Mothers would be breastfeeding and expecting at the same time. Now
that's rare."

Why rare? I asked. We were sitting in a sparsely furnished wooden shelter used for community meetings. The equatorial sun was brilliant on the
green fields outside. All the men chimed in. The rains fall differently than
they once did, the men explained, and food is less abundant and nutritious
than before. Parents no longer want lots of children. The development
group CARE had been working in Rubuguri to provide family planning

and other health services, and between the hard times and the available contraception, family size was going down.

"It's almost too late," one of the men said. It would have been better to have learned about family planning much earlier, he added, when times were better and people fewer. Several other men nodded in agreement.

For at least 2,500 years, cultures from the Mediterranean Sea east to China have been "going by the Bible"—or equivalent forms of scriptural authority—in the ways they approach sexuality and reproduction. For no aspect of cultural tradition has been as influential on sex and parenting as organized religion. And the world's great religions and the civilizations to which they gave shape reached a formative apex in an era historians call the Axial Age. The age extended from around 800 to 200 BC. The term *axial* derives from the historical sense that humanity—Eurasian humanity, at least— literally shifted on its axis at this time. Societies from the Mediterranean to eastern China rotated as if on the same gear shaft into spiritual and secular belief systems that characterized Europe and Asia at least until the Age of Enlightenment and the births of modern science and democracy.

The Axial Age was a time in which new tools of hard iron made it easier than ever before to level forests and to plow soil. The resulting food surpluses stimulated the fastest urban growth the world had ever seen. Religion and secular institutions raced to keep pace. At the peak of the period around 500 BC, Socrates held forth on ethical living in Athens, Confucius puzzled over the erosion of state authority in China's late Chou dynasty, Lao-tzu developed the philosophy of Taoism, and several of the later prophets of the Hebrews refined a religion dedicated to the one god Yahweh. In the same era, the Buddha preached detachment from the world in northern India and Zoroaster launched a scriptural religion in Persia.

What Lies Beyond

The Axial civilizations were distinguished from those that preceded them more than anything else by the concept of *transcendence*, a view of "what lies beyond." The idea was that there is something more important than experiencing pleasures and building up treasures in this life. S. D. Eisenstadt, among the chief historians of this era, calls the beginnings of the Axial Age a "sharp disjunction between the mundane and the transmundane." This wasn't just a discussion among a few visionaries and prophets; entire civilizations were organized around the Axial ideas. The central importance of the "beyond" was institutionalized in monarchies, in which kings were no longer gods and the personal embodiment of the cosmic order, but rather secular rulers accountable to a less immediately accessible higher order.[1]

Why did these profound changes in philosophy, government, and social custom occur in so many places during this period? Historians find no single unifying force to explain it. Some societies were undergoing rapid changes around this time from migration or marauders, but others experienced neither. Only a handful of scholars have noted that demographic and environmental change wove a common thread in each Axial civilization. The underlying catalyst once again could well have been population growth, with its related themes of environmental disruption and changing gender relations. The fact of dwindling natural resources is mentioned or alluded to by some Axial Age writers; in other cases, such depletion is apparent in the nature of the institutional changes themselves.

The king-gods of pre-Axial times were distributors of plenty. That's what made them believable as gods among people. Such generous rulers existed in some indigenous societies well into recent centuries—in New Guinea and the South Pacific islands, for example, or on the northwest coast of North America. Anthropologists call such tribal chiefs Big Men, and the key to their status and power is maintaining the personal loyalty of their subjects through frequent distribution of food, animals, and other forms of wealth.

As populations grew in fertile agricultural regions, however, abundance led to scarcity, as it so often does when enough third children survive. Gifting festivals became less frequent and eventually faded from the scene. But Big Men cannot be small, and king-gods can't fail in their generosity. What kind of god fails to offer bounty to his people? Since abundance could not be produced, the nature of kingship itself had to change. Rulers now merely petitioned or mediated with remote deities, rather than providing goods directly. The deities might not deign to grant the rulers' wishes.

Other aspects of religion also adjusted to account for the new hardships of earthly life and offered tantalizing improvements in the "beyond." The afterlife became a release from human suffering, and food and festivities became less central to religious experience. To receive spiritual bounty, all you had to do was die, or at least spend long hours meditating while consuming as little food and water as possible.

Reflecting the relatively rapid population growth that continued until shortly after the Axial apex, the literature of Greece and India speaks compellingly of the destruction of forests, the expansion of farmland to every available niche, the fast-paced and disorienting life of the cities, and the need to relieve population pressure by establishing colonies or picking fights with neighbors. In classical Greece, Athens exemplified the colonial strategy, Sparta the bellicose one.[2]

There's clear documentation from some Axial societies of resources growing scarce because of population growth, often in combination with climate change. (We saw this interaction operating in chapters 3 and 4 in the much earlier extinction of Pleistocene animals and the dawn of agriculture.) India in particular experienced rapid changes in both its population and environment just before the Axial Age began, when the line blurred between human and natural effects on the land. The shifts in climate documented in India as populations grew in the early Axial Age may have been partially human-induced, given the known effects of large-scale deforestation on local temperatures and patterns of rainfall.

"Some time around 1000 B.C.E. or slightly later a change occurred in the Vedic society," writes historian Hermann Kulke, referring to the ancient

Hindu culture of the time. "The late books of the Rigveda [among the world's first scriptural texts] contain several elegies with a hitherto unknown lamentation over the complaints of the daily life. Slowly the pristine worldview and its norms were questioned. The reasons of this new restlessness are not clear but usually it is attributed to population growth and a scarcity of food and land which might have increased dramatically through a climatic change during these centuries."[3]

Religious historian Karen Armstrong notes that the ancient practice of animal sacrifice was fading in India even before the Buddha rejected it in his teaching. Anthropologist Marvin Harris suggests a plausible reason why: animal protein was simply becoming too scarce to give away to gods. Harris sees the Axial Age religious shift toward the inner life and the afterlife as a response to worsening natural-resource scarcity and the increasing inability of rulers to act as providers of last resort. In the new era of shortages, kingdoms of plenty all too conveniently were, in the words of Jesus, "not of this world."[4]

In Buddhist scripture, an Indian king personifies this reversal: depressed by the state of his kingdom—the conversion of nature into farmland, the rapid urbanization, the lust for wealth only a few could gain, and his own impotence in the face of all this—he takes a carriage ride through one of the last remaining primeval forests in the plain of the Ganges River. The monarch finds peace among the ancient trees, their buttressed roots as big as a man, and is inspired to follow the Buddha's teachings.[5]

Farther east in Asia, the population of dynastic China was also growing rapidly at the opening of the Axial Age. Despite the vastness of its territory and the productivity of its agricultural land, ancient China endured periods of political strain that may have been linked to its demographic growth. The Chou dynasty, for example, offers a classic case of abundance leading not only to scarcity but to social disorder. Initially successful rulers, the Chou emperors vastly expanded and enriched the territory of their empire. They oversaw dramatic increases in population over several centuries that eventually made

the vast country governable only through devolution to imperial representatives in distant provinces. Far from the capital city, these satraps began to
claim for themselves the title of emperor, a development the central rulers
tried unsuccessfully to stop.

As the political order crumbled around 500 BC, Confucius and Lao-tzu
both pondered what China had lost and arrived at different explanations for
the social and natural harmony the empire had previously experienced. For
Confucius, the secret was respect for family, authority, and law. For Lao-tzu,
it was the inner balance that the natural, simple life provides. Both of these
conditions—though neither philosopher made the connection—are more
common in societies in which population is relatively stable, where there's
a balance of young and old citizens, and where natural resources are sufficient.[6] Without these demographic and environmental conditions, neither
order nor nature was easily regained.

Lovers, Wives, and Mothers

The second great Axial Age theme, linked to that of environmental disruption, is a significant shift in attitudes about gender. These were especially evident in the evolution of people's sense of how they fit into the
cosmos. With the development of full-scale agriculture, religious historian
Mircea Eliade writes, "religious experience becomes . . . more intimately
connected with life. The great mother-goddesses and . . . the spirits of fertility are markedly more dynamic and accessible to men than was the
Creator God. Yet . . . in cases of extreme distress, when everything had
been tried in vain, and especially in cases of disaster proceeding from the
sky—drought, storm, epidemic—men turn to the supreme being again
and entreat him."[7]

As human populations grew, resource scarcity and environmental
degradation brought more than a few sky disasters and pushed groups into
continuing confrontations with nature's fury and that of their neighbors.
Though gods and goddesses coexisted for some time—often paired up like

Zeus and Hera as married couples, and each with legions of worshippers of their own gender—the males tended to take on more power and authority over time. With the advent of the monotheistic religions—first Judaism, and then, growing out of it, Christianity and later Islam—goddesses disappeared altogether, and belief in them became proof of heathenness. Among the polytheistic religions that endured in the Greek and Roman worlds, some strong goddesses survived, like relics of a distantly remembered more egalitarian past. By the time the Roman Empire was at its height, however, even these goddesses had been largely abandoned. Most of the remaining goddesses in the Greco-Roman pantheon adopted the roles of lovers, wives, and mothers. So did the mortal women around them, for a long time to come.

Every one of the Axial societies institutionalized the subjugation of women. Women were confined and veiled in harems in Persia and Mesopotamia, secluded in their homes in classical Athens, and treated as male property by the Hebrews. Buddha stands out in having reluctantly agreed to admit women to his order, but even he mandated that the most senior nuns defer to the least senior monks.[8]

Such female subjugation helped guarantee that maximum childbearing would grow the local population. Unlike the pre-Axial Babylonians, Axial rulers seem not to have connected the scarcity from which their societies suffered to the population growth that eventually made scarcity all but inevitable. Rather the reverse: with enough farmers, the rulers were convinced, they could command nature to yield food and water no matter how harsh and unfriendly the landscape. With enough soldiers, they could force neighboring groups to pay tribute. With enough workers, they could erect awe-inspiring monuments to themselves. Multitude and increase were essential to the culture. This is evident throughout the Old Testament, as the epigraphs from Proverbs for this chapter and from Genesis in chapter 2 make clear. One of the books of the Pentateuch is even called (in languages other than Hebrew) Numbers, after two censuses of the Israelites it describes. Unlike the

Babylonian gods, the Israelites' Yahweh endorsed population growth and even liked to track it. "Count my people" was at times a divine command, almost as explicitly as "increase and multiply." Yahweh's interest, however, seemed to be in knowing his chosen people's military strength. There were two censuses in Numbers, and both tallied only males twenty and older. God promised Abraham progeny as countless as the stars, making him the paragon of patriarchs ever since.[9]

Few laws in such scriptural texts mentioned sex, contraception, or abortion. They didn't need to. Women and children were male property. And the seclusion of women in most of these societies limited access to the female networks that in the past had disseminated ancient wisdom on these issues.

Checking Growth

Ancient population growth and resulting natural resource scarcity encouraged the subjugation of women and discouraged birth control. Shouldn't this interaction have fueled unlimited expansion?

In fact, growth may have slowed, leveled off, or even gone negative in most Axial societies in the fifth century BC or not long after. Demographic estimates are based on circumstantial evidence and guesswork, but the dominant view is that human population either remained fairly constant for the next two millennia or declined around the birth of Christ before rising in the Middle Ages.

Among the possible reasons are the "positive checks" that Thomas Robert Malthus elaborated on much later. Among the most "positive"—that is, deadly—was pestilence. The first known epidemic of plague in Europe struck Athens in 430 BC, after surrounding villagers poured into the city for protection from the attacking Spartans during the Peloponnesian War. The sickness may have been typhoid fever, typhus, smallpox, or bubonic plague, but the symptoms historian Thucydides described don't match any modern disorder. It was clearly, however, a crowd disease.

The epidemic killed a third of Athens's inhabitants and handed victory to the Spartans.[10]

Cities were warrens of human waste and infectious disease until relatively recent times. In classical Greece and Rome, any conveniences offered by the increasingly concentrated urban centers were probably more than offset by the ease of infection promoted by crowded living conditions. Even in the advanced (for its time) civilization of the Roman Empire, a quarter to a third of babies died before their first birthdays.[11]

Another reason that Axial Age populations eventually began to level off may be that women maintained some control over their own reproduction even during the height of their subjugation, regaining more personal control as the age began to wane. As early as 400 BC, Hippocrates mentioned abortion (proscribing the use of a pessary to effect one in his famous oath), and later Greek medical texts listed contraceptives and emmenagogues as well as abortifacients. Some of these substances were accessible because of their value as spices, perfumes or incense-such as the frankincense and myrrh that the Wise Man brought as gifts in the Christian nativity story. Most women could not read, but they could have passed knowledge about pregnancy prevention among themselves, sometimes applying methods that were hidden in plain sight from the ruling males around them.

In Greek mythology, Hades kidnapped Persephone, daughter of the harvest goddess Demeter, and spirited her away to the land of the dead. Demeter successfully appealed to Zeus for her release, but Persephone spoiled this by eating the seed of a pomegranate. As a result, she was required to go back to Hades for four wintry months each year, to Demeter's dismay, spending the more fertile spring and summer months above ground with her mother. The pomegranate has never been accorded significance in conventional mythological interpretation, but classical Greek medical writers reported the use of pomegranate rinds and peels for birth control. John Riddle documents the discovery in 1933 that the plant produces female mammalian sex hormones capable of discouraging ovulation. Demeter thus resembles a modern mother who finds a cycle of pills in her daughter's dresser drawer and reluctantly acknowledges that her daughter will not be staying long in her girlhood home.[12]

The Juice of Cyrene

Could women have applied contraceptive knowledge even from their posts in the lowly domiciles of classical Greece and Rome? Marital fertility among the wealthy Roman citizenry fell so low by the decades just before the Christian era that Emperor Augustus Caesar promulgated legislation to forbid adultery and punish childlessness among the upper classes. The laws don't seem to have had much impact.

Perhaps women's status improved slightly. Or perhaps their desire to regulate their fertility simply was strong enough even in times of abysmal status to encourage secret efforts to contracept or abort. Such secrecy remains important in some places today. The fastest growing method of contraception in sub-Saharan Africa, for example, is Depo-Provera, an injection of a synthetic version of the hormone progesterone administered every three months. A likely reason for its popularity is that clinics can provide the injections during regular health checkups, and husbands unsympathetic to pregnancy prevention are none the wiser. Among more than a quarter of the married couples recently surveyed in Malawi on the family planning methods they used, the wives reported using Depo-Provera while their husbands reported that their wives used no contraception at all.[13]

We do know a bit about one method of birth control that was used in classical Greece and Rome—and indeed became so popular that it entered the literature of the time and was depicted on a coin. This was silphium—or, in Greek, *silphion*. A kind of giant fennel, silphium was the best documented fertility regulator of the premodern world, and the story of its rise and fall touches on many of this book's main themes. Growing wild on sea-facing slopes near the Greek colonial city of Cyrene, in present-day Libya, silphium was pressed for a sap used to make "Cyrenaic juice." Its main use, so far as historians can tell, was to prevent or end pregnancy.[14]

Originally harvested by Cyrenean women for their own use, silphium over time gained such popularity in the expanding Greek colonies that entrepreneurs co-opted the plant as a trade good and made it the mainstay of Cyrene's export economy in the miniglobalized Mediterranean world. Catullus, a first-century BC Roman poet, mentioned the plant in a poem about the satisfaction of sexual desire.[15]

On a four-drachma coin of the fifth or sixth century BC, at the height of the Axial Age, a seated woman touches a silphium plant with one hand and holds the open palm of her other hand over her reproductive organs. Farmers tried to cultivate the herb in other parts of the Mediterranean, but it refused to be tamed. As wild specimens became more scare, their value rose, until a rare silphium plant found in the wild came to be worth its weight in silver.

All this suggests that the herb worked as advertised. We can't be certain, though, because the rage for it and the traders who exploited it eventually drove silphium into extinction. The plant's trajectory is testament not only to the loss of species, but to the tendencies of open markets to inflate the value of natural rarities and to the drive of women—in the past, just as today—to prevent unwanted pregnancy.

Second Opinions

Whatever was happening in women's lives, the topic of population began to gain attention of its own as the Axial Age began to fade. Views on population growth were hardly any more uniform than they are today. Like the author of Proverbs, the kings of classical Persia primed the pump of women's fertility. They richly rewarded the fathers of many sons, the Greek historian Herodotus reported, "for they hold that number is strength."[16]

Not everyone agreed. Even Yahweh, much as he enjoyed counting his soldiers, was at times capable of his own Malthusian streak. On a few occasions
he seems to have regretted creating such a hyperfertile species. Noah's Flood,
the toppling of the Tower of Babel, and the annihilation of Sodom and
Gomorrah all bespeak a certain divine distaste for people who were under-
pious, oversexed, and overcrowded. The residents of Sodom and Gomorrah
suffered far more for their sins than Adam and Eve had—they were burned
alive. But, as in Eden, a woman is portrayed as the sinning spouse of an essentially God-fearing man. Leaving the flames of the city that once was her
home, Lot's wife—Genesis never dignifies her with a name—looks back
longingly on all she is losing. For that crime, God turns her into a pillar of
salt.[17] In a preview of the ecological concept of carrying capacity, the herds-
men of Abraham fought with those of Lot because "the land was not able to
bear them . . . for their substance was great, so that they could not dwell
together." Centuries later, Malthus cited these verses as scriptural support for
his own conviction that agricultural limits always eventually check population growth.[18]

In Greece, Plato and Aristotle also leaned toward a pessimistic view of mul-
titudes and promoted the ideal of small populations that neither expanded nor
shrank. They wrote in the fourth century BC, after decades of rapid population growth had filled the available farmland of Attica and spurred the various
Greek city-states to conquer their neighbors or send out colonists across the
Mediterranean. Plato expressed the hope that governments could maintain a
stable population through the regulation of marriage. He suggested 5,040 to
be the precise, optimum number of free male heads of household. Remarkably,
this number of households implied a total of not many more than 40,000 people at a time when Athens had roughly ten times that number. In earlier ages,
Plato noted, the Greek forests had been thicker and its soils more fertile and
better able to store moisture and prevent flooding.[19]

Aristotle saw population in similar terms, arguing that large populations
were harder to govern than small ones. Given the emergence of an Athenian

democracy based on citizen assemblies, the conclusion may not be surprising. But Aristotle was less confident than Plato that regulation of marriage would keep population from growing. Abortion and infanticide were among the remedies Aristotle proposed for population growth that threatened the rule of law. He appears to have been the first writer to promote the practice of contraception for the limitation of population. In a biological treatise, Aristotle described the use of cedar oil, olive oil, frankincense, and—again, don't try this at home—"ointment of lead" as vaginal suppositories to prevent pregnancy.[20]

Beyond the Mediterranean, Zoroastrians in Persia discussed the tensions that large populations could produce, and around 300 BC an Indian sage named Kautilya wrote of the dangers of unbalanced populations, suggesting an optimum of five hundred farming families on about two square miles of land. In China, the third-century BC legal scholar Han Fei Tzu noted how quickly the male descendants of one man could proliferate if he had five sons and each of them had five sons, and so on. In the less populated past, he added, men made light of the essentials of life, but the "men of today quarrel and snatch."[21]

The diversity of views on population growth in the Axial Age parallels the ambivalence human beings have felt about their numbers ever after. It also illustrates the difficulty of judging the costs and benefits of ongoing demographic growth. Even though Axial Age civilizations were chronically stressed by their rising numbers, they remained wedded to a value system in which women had little choice but to produce as many children as chance and the constant attention of their husbands dictated. Yet these societies were also hotbeds of technological, institutional, and cultural innovation. While some (Persia, Greece, Israel, and Rome) eventually declined or were conquered, others (China, and to a large extent India) simply evolved and continue growing to this day. Then, as now, demographic and non-demographic factors interacted in ways specific to each place and culture.

Societies that were the first to look to a transcendent cosmos for relief from worldly scarcity and stress nonetheless left descendents, and their legacy lives on 2,500 years later. This may offer us hope in considering the role of population growth, women's lives, and the interaction of both with nature in our own era. But we should be cautious in comparing the Axial cultures to our own. Whatever the dynamics of the Axial Age, it was a much less populous and technologically powerful era. Axial peoples were leveling the local forests and degrading the soil. We do that, too, but we are also heating up the planet, depleting the oceans, and threatening an extinction event on the scale of the great ones of the earth's geologic past.

Djenaba

The last expression of the Axial Age, by most historians' reckoning, took place more than 1,100 years after the age's peak, like a time-traveling colonial outpost of fifth-century BC civilizations. This was the birth in Arabia of Islam in the words and thinking of the prophet Muhammad. Like the earlier societies, those organizing themselves around Islamic principles tended to focus on the transcendent rather than the earthly life. And they expanded on the ancient theme of female subordination to males.[22] Inspired by the prophet, Muslim societies grew demographically to become among the world's most populous, urban, and widespread. In the early tenth century AD, Baghdad and Cordoba were the largest cities in the world, with populations that each may have approached 1 million people.[23]

To illustrate the hazards of easy generalizations about these matters, it's worth noting that these societies were also among the world's most scientific, cultured, and tolerant. During the centuries after the fall of the Roman Empire, Arab writers kept alive and built upon the wisdom of their Greek philosophical and scientific predecessors, while European writers remained mostly ignorant of them. Ironically enough, many Arab physicians wrote as well on contraception and other means of regulating fertility. Whether the Islamic world will again achieve a comparable cultural and scientific ascendancy is anyone's guess. Some countries with Muslim majorities today— Iran, Indonesia, and Tunisia, for example—are characterized by fertility rates that are at replacement or not far above. The encouragement of high fertility and restrictions on female freedom nonetheless dominates most of the Islamic world.

In a village in Mali, a predominately Sunni nation, I met Djenaba. She was sixteen or seventeen—she didn't know which—and the mother of two. The new baby, a girl, tugged at her breast as we spoke. Djenaba said she was happy to have just one year between births, if that was Allah's will. And when I asked her how many children she wanted to have in all, she replied quietly, eyes down, "As many as I can." A more nuanced answer surfaced as I pressed on with the interview, asking her about the health of her children, the circumstances of their births, and how she had met their father. Her parents had arranged the marriage, she said, but the wedding hadn't actually taken place until after the birth of her son when she was fourteen or fifteen. Suddenly her composure and her voice both shifted, and she confessed that she wished she could have waited to become a mother. Around the world, 80 million times a year, other women learn, as she had, that they are pregnant and wish, as she had, that they were not. Djenaba had heard of the contraceptive pill, and she understood its appeal.

"You take it, and you don't get pregnant," said this cultural descendent of the Axial Age. "You stop taking it, and you have children." She wished she could wait now, at least three years, before becoming pregnant. She wondered where she could find some of these pills, because she did not want many more children, and none any time soon.

"It's too hard," she said. "We don't have any wealth."

SEVEN

Punishing Eve

I was an unmarried girl—I'd just turned 27—
  When they sent me to the sisters for the way men looked at me.
Branded as a Jezebel, I knew I was not bound for Heaven.
  I'd be cast in shame into the Magdalene Laundries.
    —Joni Mitchell, "The Magdalene Laundries"

In sixth century Ireland, according to an ancient account, an abbess and saint named Brigid took pity on a nun under her supervision who, "through youthful exuberance of pleasure [had] swelled with child." Brigid magically made the fetus disappear "without coming to birth, and without pain," so that the lucky sister could remain in the abbess's convent.[1]

Fourteen centuries later, Brigid's religious successors on the island ran a network of institutions designed to isolate prostitutes, unwed mothers, and other female sexual transgressors from society. Abortion was not an option. Sent away by their own families, the "penitents" remained in these homes for the rest of their lives after being forced to give up children they had never meant to conceive. They spent their days washing and drying clothes to help the nuns earn income from commercial laundries. These so-called Magdalene asylums, named for Mary Magdalene of the Gospels, were little-noted institutions of Irish life from the mid-nineteenth century until at least the 1970s.[2]

During most of the 1,400 years that separated Brigid from the Magdalene Laundries, the Christian Church dominated European public and private life in ways that we can scarcely imagine today. Even by Brigid's day, the Church had established itself as a formidable authority on procreation and sexual mores—though its reach was at first less assured in distant outposts of the faith such as Ireland. In the Middle Ages and early modern period, Christianity forged an amalgam of religious and political power of historically unprecedented scope and influence. Earlier and more securely than any of its counterparts, it was Catholic Christianity in western Europe that achieved this level of authority, but its Eastern Orthodox counterpart and its later Protestant offshoots held comparable aspirations. The Church used its power for social control, seeking to impose order and morality on increasingly populous and complex societies. Stringent codes of sexuality were ascribed to the scriptures, though no consistent message about women and their reproductive entitlements is inherent in the text.

Like the Axial Age societies from which it had sprung, the Church allowed no input from women in developing its views on these matters. But Catholicism went further, requiring that the bishops and others shaping shaping religious orthodoxy abstain from sex. Some clerics remained sexually active, either clandestinely or openly, despite their vows of celibacy. No doubt many others lived up to the ideal, which meant their views on sexual and reproductive matters either had no basis in personal experience or were colored by memories of sexual lives they had put behind them. Some of the Church fathers had been sexual libertines before conversion or admission to the clergy—then wrote afterward about women and sex with such venom we can only wonder what in their sexual experience might have so filled them with loathing. Considering the hints we have about communication between the sexes in antiquity, it wouldn't be surprising if unsatisfying sex lives were more the rule than the exception. And that simple reality may have influenced the course of doctrine and policy on sex and reproduction as societies grew in size and complexity.

Neither sex can fully penetrate the sexual and reproductive experience of the other. Until recently few women wrote about their own experience, and the literature of sex and reproduction has often been as wrongheaded as it was self-assured. Aristotle and the classical Greek physicians Diocles and Empedocles believed that all women menstruated at the same time of the month (Aristotle specified "at the decrease of the moon"), an error that easily could have been set straight by a quick survey of some of these men's female neighbors.[3] The ancient Greeks considered sexual intercourse an act of primal male domination, but the later Christian fathers offered a more subtle insight (and worried about its implications)—that in sex men lose control and assume unusual vulnerability. Doubts may plague them not only about whether they father their own children, but about whether they satisfy their partners. "Is that all?" a woman can always ask after sex, and at some point a man must suffer the humiliation of conceding that, yes, it is.

It's thus not surprising that most patriarchal cultures try to control not just female reproduction but sex itself. This hardly makes men naturally insensitive or power-crazed. Male attitudes about sex and reproduction may have grown almost organically from the physical and reproductive differences between the sexes as male roles became dominant in farming and settled life. Early Christianity gave such attitudes their fullest expression yet.

The most influential Church father of all was Augustine, a fourth-century orator who lived in the decades just after the Emperor Constantine reversed three centuries of persecution of Christians and embraced the young church as a spiritual partner to his own imperial authority. As a young man, Augustine lived and fathered a son with a woman he never married. He was engaged to be married to another woman when he decided instead to renounce the pleasures of the world to help shape the thinking of the Church. Augustine's conviction that even newborn babies were guilty of "original sin," as the children of Adam and the product of carnal relations, was soon adopted as the official position of Roman Catholicism. In the view of historian of religion Elaine Pagels, the Church adopted this radical view of human and divine nature—which made all human beings dependent on religious authority to avoid eternal damnation—because it suited so well the ambitions of social control mutually held by the new alliance of Church and Empire. In the fourth and fifth centuries, Pages writes, "Christianity . . . was the religion of emperors obligated to govern a vast and diffuse population . . . Augustine's theory of human depravity—and, correspondingly, the political means to control it—replaced the previous ideology of human freedom."

Certainly such a position had no clear connection with the life or words of Jesus. In the Hebrew scriptures, God warns Eve that she will be ruled by her husband and bear many children, always in pain. In the Christian holy writings, by contrast, Mary Magdalene and two other women, Joanna and Susanna, have enough of their own money to help fund the ministry of Jesus and his twelve disciples. Jesus' relative tolerance of sex is evident in his intervention to save the life of an adulteress, whom he dismisses with the simple recommendation that she "go, and sin no more."[4] Yet as Christianity developed in Europe and the authorities of the Catholic Church joined forces with secular kings and later captains of mercantilism, the church hardened in its conviction that sex was as a loathsome physical drive, unfit for those made in the image of God and existing for one purpose only: procreation.

Spontaneous Uprisings

By the third century, when the early church had settled on most of its scripture, the canonized books of both Old and New Testaments were feeding a growing industry of exegesis and advice for the faithful. Opinions on how to treat women and how to approach sex and procreation quickly took shape for debate and dialogue. In the early church some women were able to serve as abbesses, as Brigid did, at least in remote outposts such as Ireland. But few if any wrote down their thoughts or otherwise influenced the overwhelmingly male Church hierarchy. Those wrestling with these issues were almost entirely men, and these men were committed, publicly at least, to celibacy.

Perhaps partly in reaction to the licentiousness of the Romans and Greeks, Christian views on sex and the place of women early on became restrictive and definitions of proper behavior narrowed. Clement, a first-century pope who may have known the apostle Paul, ordered the limitation of sex not only to marriage, but to just those acts within the sacramental union that were capable of producing offspring. Not only did Clement proscribe nonvaginal intercourse as perverse; he forbade any intercourse with a menstruating, pregnant, barren, or menopausal wife. "Even that union which is legitimate is still dangerous, except in so far as it is engaged in procreation of children," Clement warned.[5] The distinction guided doctrine on sex for well over one thousand years. Later church fathers stirred such admonitions into a thickening stew of misogyny, based (intellectually, at least; the emotional origins are much more difficult to sort out) on the rebellion of Eve against the rule of God and his earthly surrogate, Adam. In this set piece, Eve represented the irrational body and Adam the rational mind. Through their domination by males, all women were punished for the first sin of Eve, the temptress.

Augustine was especially concerned by a universal physical reenactment of this original rebellion. He acknowledged that he never met a couple who only had sex when they wanted to have a child.[6] The male erection, Augustine argued, was "a spontaneous uprising" (credit historian of religion Elaine Pagels for the pun) of a man's "lower servant"—his body—demonstrating a mindless will of its own, despite rational man's intention to resist a woman's temptation. "You are the devil's gateway," Tertullian wrote of women. "You are she who persuaded him whom the devil did not dare attack . . . Do you not know that everyone of you is an Eve? The sentence of God on your sex lives on in this age; the guilt, of necessity, lives on, too."[7]

It's not clear how influential these views of sexuality and procreation were in the average couple's experience of sex and family. But historical records reveal couples' use of contraception as well as clergymen's efforts to persuade them to stop. One of the most intriguing findings comes from an elegant linking of disparate but contemporaneous documents by English demographic historian Peter Biller. Researching the late ninth-century Kingdom of Lotharingia in the Ardennes, in what is now Belgium and Luxembourg, Biller compares censuses of the estate of Prüm Abbey with manuals that instructed the abbey's priests on questioning parishioners during confession. A manual written at Prüm in the 890s is the earliest one known to spell out withdrawal as a contraceptive method (often known by its Latin name *coitus interruptus*) and to warn the abbey's priests to root it out. During the same decade, land records show the population density on the abbey's estate amounted to three or four times that of surrounding areas. Not until the eighteenth century did the area again record such high rural population densities. Biller quotes the French historian Georges Duby, who called the crowded estate lands of Prüm Abbey "overpopulated islands, where biological increase stimulated by agrarian prosperity pushed men to the verge of scarcity." Abundance was leading to scarcity—just as it had for early modern humans described in chapter 4, for whom successful animal predation boosted population, which pushed people to forage progressively farther down the food chain. And married couples, it seems, were coming to the attention of the local church authorities because they were seeking to reduce their childbearing in response.

"The chronological and geographical coincidences are so remarkable that they look almost too neat," Biller writes. The pastoral concern that parishioners were practicing contraception "was an alert response to patterns of sin among the flock: one sin [contraception] was being committed more than it had been, in an area suffering from we call overpopulation . . . There may well have been behind this response . . . the *awareness* and *thought* of 'many people', 'they are poor', and 'they are avoiding conceiving.'"[8]

European Slow Change

Could individual efforts to prevent pregnancy have depressed population growth in the "Dark" and Middle Ages? Possibly. By most demographic calculations, the world's population at the end of the first millennium AD numbered no more than 250 million to 300 million, the same level of population that began the millennium. Whether high death rates or low birthrates were more responsible for this relative demographic stasis is probably impossible to ascertain. But attempts to prevent pregnancy, at least in Europe, are clearly documented.

Biller cites dozens of mentions of contraception and abortion during this period, including what may be the earliest account in Europe of a named individual—a married woman—using birth control: Clémence, wife of an eleventh-century nobleman named Robert II of Flanders. According to a monk identified as Hermann in the abbey of St. Martin of Tournai, Clémence had three sons in quick succession and, in order not to further complicate the question of future inheritance, "acted with a womanly skill not to give birth any more." Some medieval marriage contracts in western Europe, Biller finds, included language obligating the partners either to use withdrawal, "potions of sterility" (oral contraceptives or emmenagogues), or "impediments" (pessaries) to avoid producing offspring. One account suggests that some couples making such covenants limited sex to those times of the month they believed least conducive to conceiving. "Here," Biller says of this fourteenth-century account, "is one of the best examples of [bringing] into the text the couple themselves, engaging in pacts, too poor to have more children, and using coitus inter-ruptus, infertile times, and potions."[9]

Beyond questions about the efficacy of contraceptive "potions," is it possible that the rhythm method actually worked for medieval couples? Some writings of classical Greek and Roman times do hint at early experimentation with the concept, by which couples refrain from sex at the time of the month when women are least likely to conceive. Unfortunately for these experimenters, most premodern cultures seem to have gotten women's cycles of fecundity precisely backward, believing that conception was most likely at the waning of menstruation and least likely midway between periods. From Hippocrates and the second-century Greek physician Soranos to some indigenous cultures of more recent times, this error has persisted. Perhaps the misunderstanding is even more ancient than the Greeks. The old joke must have been especially apt in such cultures: What do you call people who practice the rhythm method? *Parents.* It could be that the couples of medieval Europe improved on the ancient understanding of women's cycles of reproduction. Or, like so many parents before and since, they simply came to love and care for the children who arrived despite failed efforts at contraception.

Large families, in any event, were not routine in Europe during the Middle Ages, though they certainly existed, especially among the wealthy. Medieval historians Frances and Joseph Gies report about three children per household in the village of Elton in the English Midlands around 1300. But the end of the thirteenth century was a time of relatively rapid growth in England and elsewhere in Europe, and this size family may have been closer to a high point than an overall average for the preceding centuries.[10] Certainly, there doesn't appear to be much evidence during the Middle Ages that the efforts of church authorities to discourage contraception and non-procreative sex resulted in either infrequent sex or high fertility. (Even in the case of the Prüm priests, we have no reason to assume their admonitions against contraception effectively discouraged the practice.) Nor did the sexual proscriptions prevent untold numbers of supposedly celibate ecclesiastics (including popes) from being led by the spontaneous uprisings of their lower servants.

Because of one such wayward priest's behavior, an ecclesiastical court record from the year 1319 preserves what must be the oldest known account by a woman of her own experience with sex and contraception. According to the document, now housed in the Vatican, Béatrice de Planisolles was a young widow in the village of Montaillou, in the Pyrenees of southwestern France, who had an affair with a wolfish priest named Pierre Clergue. The affair took place around 1300. Two decades later Béatrice faced trial during the Inquisition as a heretic and answered questions about the illicit relationship. She testified that the priest had proposed sex the day she first visited his church. "What shall I do if I am made pregnant by you?" she asked pragmatically, to which he replied that he "possessed a certain herb" that prevented conception. Clergue carried this herb—John Riddle believes it was *Ferula asafedia*, of the same genus as silphium—to their subsequent trysts. Béatrice described it as about an inch in diameter and attached to a long string.

"When he wished to ravish me," she told her inquisitors, "he put [the string] around my neck," to avoid misplacing the herb while the two slept. "He would place [the herb] in the opening of my abdomen, the string passing between my breasts. In this way he could unite with me, and in no other way." The clerical priest who scribbled down this remarkable account may be forgiven if he fumbled some of its details in his excitement—he mentioned the detail about the breasts three times—but the use of a pessary is obvious.[11]

A philanderer such as Pierre Clergue probably picked up his expertise on birth control from one or more women along his trail of seduction. Such informational networks, however, would have been useless to those, presumably including Clémence of Flanders, who followed the socially sanctioned route of waiting for sex until marriage. What most married women needed were mothers, aunts, grandmothers, or other sympathetic women who could pass on ancient wisdom about the prevention of unwanted pregnancy. In Europe, much of the gynecological writings of the classical Greek and later Arab physicians had long been forgotten. The obvious candidate for the medieval keeper of this knowledge is the midwife, who until fairly recently in history was the near-universal deliverer of human babies.

"And it is more than likely, is it not, that no one can tell so well as a midwife whether women are pregnant or not?" Socrates asked his student Theaetetus in Plato's dialogue of that name. Socrates spoke from experience; his mother was a midwife. "Moreover, with the drugs and incantations they administer, midwives can either bring on the pains of travail or allay them at their will, make a difficult labor easy, and at an early stage cause a miscarriage if they so decide."[12] It's not as surprising as it might appear that women who bring life into the world would also specialize in the prevention of pregnancy or birth. Among the first questions many women ask their attendants after giving birth is how to prevent or postpone the next one. (Men, none the worse for wear after a birth, often have a contrasting hope. "What's the very first thing a baby does in being born?" an Irish acquaintance of mine once asked, having learned the riddle from an uncle. Breathe? Cry? No. "He makes room for the next one.") A woman also may need her midwife for much more than advice. As a mid-fifteenth-century English manuscript noted, "When the woman is feeble and the child may not come out, then it is better that the child be slain than that the mother of the child also die."[13]

Such knowledge eventually may have proved deadly to midwives and to the wisdom they had carried across the generations. A perfect storm of three historical currents seems to have converged on Europe beginning in the late fourteenth century, shaping societal attitudes toward midwifery, reproductive health care, and women for centuries to come.

The Season of the Witch

The first of these historical currents was a cataclysm that began drawing down the continent's population early in the fourteenth century. In the previous century, the demographic stasis that had characterized most of the Middle Ages gave way to growth. Human numbers began to rise as a temperate climate and improved agricultural technology—better plows and pumps, wetlands drained to make cropland, new roads to carry farm goods to market, and much more—boosted food production and wealth. In many places the limits of arable land were reached—and then exceeded. In the early to middle 1300s even boys knew the boundaries of their village land, which for the first time ever ran up against the land of the surrounding hamlets. (Every seven years the town of Llantrisant, Wales, still re-enacts a tradition, dating from 1346 and called "beating the bounds," in which much of the town's population walks its seven-mile perimeter. At each boundary marker, the procession stops while male elders men pick up young boys and gently bounce their rumps on the stones, so none will forget where the edge of the town lies.) "Then the downswing of the Malthusian cycle common to pre-modern rural societies set in," writes historian Norman Cantor.[14] The climate began cooling, limiting formerly generous harvests. A rolling series of famines struck northern Europe, culling some of its population. But this was just the beginning.

In 1348 a pestilence arrived in England from the Continent, apparently flea-borne in the fur of rats. In city and village whole families succumbed to dark swellings in the armpits and groin and developed the fetid breath of lung decay before suffocating on their own blood. Four years later, the Black Death—presumably bubonic plague, but possibly mixed as well with cattle-borne anthrax—had swept through most of Europe, killing roughly 25 million out of a peak population of about 75 million. Most countries, including England, would not recover their early fourteenth-century population levels for another three or four centuries.[15]

Aftershocks of plague and famine occasionally struck Europe over the next few centuries. Yet mortality rates don't seem high enough in this period to fully explain the sluggishness of population growth during the post–Black Death recovery. Late marriages and increases in the proportion of people never marrying would have reduced birthrates and thus helped depress population growth. But given the documented evidence that many women and couples were comfortable using contraception despite the teachings of the church, it's likely that many were trying and perhaps sometimes succeeding in preventing unwanted births during these insecure decades.

Couples might have had good reason to attempt later births and smaller families to take advantage of emerging opportunities. These arose from the second historical current during the Middle Ages, which closely followed the first. By reducing the supply of labor, the famine- and plague-driven depopulation of northern Europe eventually raised the status and pay of workers. Women especially benefited, taking on such economically important positions as brewers and shopkeepers. Wealthier ones enjoyed "dowers" of income from the estates of dead husbands, while male heirs litigated the inheritance. Women's wages grew even faster than men's. In Bristol, one study found, the average woman's wage amounted to about two-thirds the average man's before the plague, and three-fourths afterward.[16]

The higher value of labor in the second half of the fourteenth century rattled the evolving wage-labor system, a new approach to manual work that had been undermining feudalism as early as the mini–population boom of the thirteenth century. That century's abundance of working-age peasants meant landowners could cast off feudal obligations to their serfs and rely instead on hired workers to whom they had no responsibility beyond low wages. When the population crashes of the fourteenth century made workers scarce and drove wages up, landowners could only regret the fading of feudalism. Responding to the laboring class's new power over wages, craftsmen's guilds exercised unprecedented influence over job entry and compensation. Guilds remained influential until the return to population increase and the accompanying mass industrialization of the late eighteenth century.

In 1381, England's laborers—their militancy stoked not only by their greater wage value but by clerics shouting the revolutionary new phrase "the equality of man"—rose up in the Peasants' Revolt.[17] The forces of King Richard II and His Majesty himself, all of fourteen years old, quickly put down the uprising, and the world saw no similar rebellion until the nineteenth century. But these social changes brought a dawning awareness among the newly moneyed classes and the Catholic Church, landowner of a third of the best farmland in England, that stable populations were a problem. "They are mistaken who worry about scarcity owing to a multitude of children and citizens," wrote French lawyer and political writer Jean Bodin in 1576, "when no cities are richer and more famous . . . than those that abound the most with citizens."[18]

The third historical current, related to the other two, was the growing conviction of the church that it was time to enforce its prohibitions on the common practices of contraception, abortion, and the "overlying" or other killing of unwanted infants. In the late 1300s, Geoffrey Chaucer expressed in popular English the emerging intent to criminalize birth control through the words of a parson who is clearly speaking for the author. "If a woman by negligence overlies her child in sleeping," asserts the parson in *The Canterbury Tales*, or if she drinks "venomous herbs through which she may not conceive, . . . or else puts certain materials in her secret places to slay the child . . . it is homicide."[19] This harsh judgment seems at odds with Chaucer's bawdy depictions elsewhere in the *Tales* of extramarital "swyving" (Middle English for "copulating," surviving today in the word *swivel*)—none of which, for some reason, ever seems to result in pregnancy. The author's personal behavior may have been similarly inconsistent. Court records show that in 1380 Chaucer paid the sum of ten pounds, equal to more than half his yearly income as a London customs official, to settle an accusation of rape.[20]

A century and a half later, the founding men of the Reformation differed with Rome on countless liturgical matters. Martin Luther posted ninety-five of them on a German church door in 1517. But not one of these doctrinal differences related to sexuality, reproduction, or the place of women in society. Indeed, the prevailing Protestant misogyny and sexual phobia may have spurred on the Catholic authorities. How, after all, could they be softer on these issues than their new religious adversaries?

In the wider world, all three of these currents—the consequences of the Black Death, the elevated status of workers, and increasingly stringent church prohibitions on interfering with pregnancy—may have converged to bring on a mass hysteria that has long baffled historians: namely, the identification, trial, and execution of tens of thousands of supposed witches that preoccupied much of Europe from the fifteenth through the early eighteenth centuries. A briefer transatlantic manifestation in colonial New England is well known to Americans, but the European expression of witch phobia was much longer lasting and deadlier. Most of those executed for witchcraft were older women, an age group from which were drawn not only midwives but also herbalists and other health specialists. Younger women were far too busy being wives and mothers to gain these types of expertise.

The precise proportion of executed "witches" who practiced midwifery or who might have advised younger women on birth control is the subject of controversy that data are insufficient to resolve. Women's professions were recorded spottily at best. German legal scholar Manfred Hammes believed that virtually all of Cologne's midwives lost their lives during a particularly intense period of witch prosecution in the late 1620s, with every third woman executed at this time a midwife. Historian Carol Karlsen, by contrast, found only 22 out of 267 women accused of witchcraft in New England specifically identified as midwives. Karlsen argued, however, that the real proportion was probably much higher, since many women assisted births without pay. In July 2006, Virginia governor Timothy Kaine posthumously pardoned Grace Sherwood, a lifelong midwife and herbalist, who in 1706 became the only person convicted of witchcraft in Virginia by being "ducked" in a river. (A woman who sank and drowned was not a witch, by traditional belief. Mrs. Sherwood floated, despite having her thumbs tied to her feet.) What is clear, at least, is that many midwives were accused, prosecuted, found guilty and executed as witches.[21]

Why might older women involved in birth and healing be vulnerable to charges of witchcraft? The debates on the causes of the witch hunts show no sign of resolution. Probably multiple causes interacted, but such an explanation always begs the question of which among them was decisive. In 1973, Barbara Ehrenreich and Dierdre English suggested that the execution of older women was one way for the emerging science and practice of medicine—university-based and uniformly male—to eliminate the last of its female competitors in the lucrative business of delivering babies and addressing women's health concerns.[22]

In recent decades, three scholars—German historians Gunnar Heinsohn and Otto Steiger, joined by John Riddle—have advanced a comparable thesis too provocative and germane not to mention here. The hysterical fear of witches, these scholars believe, was strategically stoked by religious and secular leaders to drive contraception and abortion into the shadows once and for all and to guarantee the unfettered increase of Christian European populations.[23]

Misogyny and the distrust of sex had built up over the centuries and played a leading role in inciting mass fear of witches. In 1484, Pope Innocent VIII published *Summis Desiderantes*, which reported the proliferation of witches in several parts of Germany and noted their power to "hinder men from begetting and women from conceiving." Pope Innocent was frank about his overarching objectives in calling attention to this, which were not only evangelistic but demographic. "Desiring with the most heartfelt anxiety," began the papal bull, "that the Catholic faith should especially in this our day increase and flourish everywhere . . ."[24] The pope did his own part to help the faith flourish, fathering at least seven illegitimate children. To help eliminate obstacles to the growth of Catholicism, Innocent deputized two Dominican inquisitors, Heinrich Krämer and Jakob Sprenger. Witches were at the top of the list of enemies.

A few years later, the two inquisitors published the infamous *Malleus Maleficarum* (The hammer of the witches), which over the next 150 years became the primer for hunting down and killing witches. Protestant as well as Catholic accusers and prosecutors relied on it—helped by the proliferation of the new technology of printing across Europe, and little hindered by the fact the Catholic Church soon repudiated the book. By the early 1600s it had been reprinted more than two dozen times. The *Malleus* specifically addressed the problem of "witch midwives," arguing that they had special power over sex because it was the source of the world's first sin, and that midwives routinely prevented conception, killed fetuses in the womb, and kidnapped living children to deliver to devils. "No one does more harm to the Catholic Faith than midwives," Krämer and Sprenger wrote.[25]

In 2004, Heinsohn, Steiger, and Riddle had an opportunity to refine and defend their view that Renaissance-era elites had whipped up popular fear of witches to wipe out contraception. In that year Harvard University statistician Emily Oster proposed that the European witchcraft trials were a response to crop failures and food shortages brought on by a climatic cold snap called the Little Ice Age. Oster noted a surprisingly consistent correlation between the frequency of witchcraft trials and European population growth rates in the years from 1520 to 1770. The more rapid the demographic growth, she found, the fewer the trials. She argued that when the climate was favorable to food production, and hence to population growth, fewer witches became scapegoats for local hunger and high death rates.[26] Heinsohn, Steiger, and Riddle accepted the correlation but turned Oster's logic on its head. Population trends, not climatic ones, drove the witch trials, they argued. It was when population was relatively stagnant that accusers and prosecutors, frenzied by the fear of demographic stasis, were most apt to stigmatize birth control by identifying and executing witches. As populations grew, the need to root out these practices was less urgent.[27]

Ultimately, we don't need to prove that midwives were the principle targets of witch trials, or that the Catholic Church and its Protestant spinoffs competed in stoking witchcraft hysteria solely to drive up the populations of their flocks. Whatever was behind the witchcraft frenzy, the social upheaval it sowed cast a chill for centuries on contraception, the use of emmenagogues, and abortion. In such a social environment, what young woman would have put herself at risk—along with a respected older neighbor or relative—by inquiring about such things? And if desperation led to infanticide, women in much of Europe could expect the most brutal penalties to make them examples to wavering expectant mothers. In May 1715, on a rise in southwestern Austria named Gallows Hill for its executions, an unmarried woman convicted of killing her infant had her right hand cut off as the first act of her slow punishment, which ended with her death on a wheel of torture.[28]

No doubt other factors contributed to the fog of forgetfulness that appears to have descended on ancient birth-control folk wisdom. The rise of sexually transmitted diseases may have discouraged older women from passing on pregnancy-prevention remedies that offered no protection from infection and death. Urbanization meant that apothecaries supplied such remedies in boxes and bottles, probably with little or no counseling about mixing and doses. Once upon a time these remedies had come straight from the forest or meadow, along with the careful advice of a village wise woman. After evolving and enduring for countless generations, traditional woman-centered birth control disappeared from most of Europe. Eventually, men assumed nearly complete control of reproductive health care and childbirth, as they did of medicine generally. Few males had any sympathetic counseling to offer young women about sex and birth control, even if they were seducers.

Around the time of the execution on Gallows Hill in Austria, the idea that a married European woman might seek help in preventing pregnancy or birth had become anathema in respectable society. In 1727 Daniel Defoe, author of *Robinson Crusoe*, published a tract called *Conjugal Lewdness; or, Matrimonial Whoredom*. In it he depicted a feckless young bride futilely seeking advice on contraception from a shocked cousin. By his title alone, Defoe made clear that "the diabolical practice of attempting to prevent childbearing by physical preparations" effectively turned wives into prostitutes.[29]

By the early eighteenth century, the witch trials were fading from both European and North American life. The physical preparations to which Defoe referred were forgotten or at least nowhere to be found. The demise of birth control may have contributed, along with steady improvements in infant and child survival, to demographic impacts that were direct, cumulative, and substantial. In the five centuries that followed the Black Death, the population of Europe more than tripled. Human numbers on the continent would have multiplied even more, but Europe's newly populous nation-states and their expanding business enterprises were cascading into the rest of the world. By the eighteenth and nineteenth centuries, populations of Europeans were ballooning in the faraway Americas, Australia, New Zealand, southern Africa, and pockets of Asia. It would be some time before women once again would seek help to prevent childbearing while remaining sexually active. Even when they did, the intermingled fears of sex, contraception, women's autonomy, and population stasis would endure, throwing up barriers to the use of birth control all over the world, right up to the present day.

EIGHT

Age of Enlightenment

Thomas Robert Malthus, the second son of eight kids, grew up with a stutter.
   Uh oh, uh oh.
With the Revolution came a lot of high hopes. Malthus took a good look.
   Uh oh, uh oh.
   —Artichoke, "Thomas Robert Malthus"

O n Easter Sunday, 1722, Dutch explorer Jacob Roggeveen beached his ship on a sixty-four-square-mile island off the coast of Chile. There he encountered a small group of warring and cannibalistic tribes. Aside from each other, there was little left to eat on the once lush island. They were descendants of Polynesian chief Hotu Matu'a and his six sons, who folk tradition suggests had settled the island centuries earlier. In the intervening years, the number of islanders grew beyond what the modest-sized island could support. By the time Roggeveen arrived, the inhabitants had stripped bare the once-verdant forests of giant palm trees. They could no longer build boats, or fish the oceans, or use the wood and wildlife resources they had exploited for centuries.

The potent brew of population growth, environmental deterioration, and social collapse has made Easter Island a popular metaphor for what could happen on our own "Earth Island" if we fail to learn the lessons of the past. Absent from the green fable's retelling, however, is that natural contraception was familiar to the women of Easter Island, at least to those who survived into the early twentieth century. European sailors who slept with some of them around this time reported their using a wad of seaweed as a pessary.[1] What does this suggest about population and the environment on the ill-fated island? The women living in the waning days of Easter Island's social cohesion may have tried to limit their childbearing, given the precarious condition of their environment and community. But managing fertility is hardly a controlled process today, let alone in a collapsing eighteenth-century island society. On Easter Island the use of seaweed pessaries and other natural contraception might have slowed population growth and delayed the eventual environmental reckoning. But without reliable birth control, the collapse nonetheless eventually occurred.

"The Earth Is Inexhaustible"

As Easter Island was reaching a breaking point, Roggeveen's brethren in Europe were weighing the consequences of their own population dynamics. With the flourishing of science and philosophy that characterized seventeenth- and eighteenth-century Europe, the period often called the Age of Enlightenment, human numbers came to the fore of public discourse. The debate over the benefits and hazards of growth began to build in the years leading up to the dawn of this age, with intense views on both sides.

In the sixteenth century, Niccolò Machiavelli imagined a hellish world in which "every province of the world so teams with inhabitants that they can neither subsist where they are nor remove elsewhere, every region being equally crowded and over-peopled." Moreover, he reasoned, "when human craft and wickedness have reached their highest pitch, it must needs come about that the world will purge itself in one or another of these three ways (floods, plagues, or famine)." During the same period in Britain, with urban poverty and unemployment rising and a growing stream of people willing to risk their lives in the New World, Sir Walter Raleigh warned of "the danger of pestilence, often visiting them which live in throngs."[2]

In the seventeenth century, a jurist named Sir Matthew Hale, who late in life became lord chief justice of England, observed that populations often "will continually increase in a kind of Geometrical Progression," an early term for exponential growth. Hale also noticed that many animals had greater reproductive power than people and yet failed to overrun the earth. He supposed there were opposing "Motions of Generation and Corruption" that counterbalanced each other to keep animal numbers constant.[3]

In this period of dawning science, however, generalizations about such matters increasingly required observations that were quantitative as well as qualitative. Anyone could offer impressions about the way human numbers worked; to back these up required actually working with numbers. The seventeenth century saw the birth of statistical demography in the career of John Graunt, a London haberdasher who from time to time accepted minor government positions and who took up what was then called "political arithmetic" as a hobby. Graunt combed records of baptisms in London and a few nearby rural communities to calculate sex ratios at birth. Comparisons with burial records enabled him to estimate ratios between births and deaths, thus developing a quantification of natural increase. His work led eventually to the development of life tables, which show the number of people in different age groups and indicate what proportions in each group survive to specific ages. The life insurance industry, just starting out on its road to global profitability, took an understandable interest. But the concepts also served as the foundation for demography, a social science that uniquely combined the study of human lives and relationships (eventually even sex acts) with the precision of statistics.

Graunt himself approved of large and growing populations, "hands being . . . the father of wealth." But like many demographers since, his passion leaned far more to tabulation than to the pros and cons of population increase. He remains an iconic figure to many demographers today, who believe that the polemical work of Thomas Robert Malthus unjustifiably overshadows the earlier thinker's more pragmatic mathematical contributions to the specialty.[4]

The turn of the seventeenth to eighteenth century and the formative decades that followed saw a continued flowering of arguments on both sides of the population question. It is characteristic of the European intellectual mood of the time that optimists on population growth dominated the conversation. "The earth is inexhaustible," wrote one, a teacher of the French royal family with the pen name Fénelon, "and increases its fertility in proportion to the number of inhabitants who cultivate it." That assertion may have been the earliest expression of an idea that guides cornucopian conviction up to the present. But pessimists did not yield the field entirely. Among them was Benjamin Franklin, who argued that the number of any people was limited by "the means provided for their subsistence."[5] Not that such limits were an issue for his own countrymen, scattered thinly across eastern North America when he wrote this in 1751. But in more densely peopled Europe, population growth had shifted into a higher gear after centuries of slow increase or none at all. Mere subsistence was becoming a challenge for many farm families, sharpened by the ongoing enclosure of common land and the concentration of ownership in the hands of the wealthy and powerful. Europe's cities, fed both by their own natural increase and streams of rural emigration, had begun to grow more rapidly than ever before.

Seven years after Franklin's comment, a Danish parish rector named Otto Diederich Lütken published an "enquiry into the proposition that the number of people is the happiness of the realm"—and concluded that it was not. "Since the circumference of the globe is given and does not expand with the increased number of its inhabitants, and as travel to other planets thought to be inhabitable has not yet been invented," Lütken wrote, "it follows that the proposition 'that the world's inhabitants will be happier, the greater the number' cannot be maintained . . . The wise Creator . . . did not intend . . . multiplication should continue without limit."[6] But Lütken wrote in Danish. Any fame he gained for this reasoning seems not to have reached beyond Denmark. In fact, while the population debate was rich and varied, few who wrote or spoke about population dynamics during this period have garnered anything like the notoriety of Thomas Robert Malthus.

Population Malthus

Perhaps it was the dozens of pages of baptisms in the register of Surrey's Okewood parish church, vastly outnumbering the pages of burials, that first led the curate there to ask himself what would happen if the imbalance continued.[7] His name was Thomas Robert Malthus, and the answers he came up with over a decades-long preoccupation with the question turned his last name into an adjective, often pejorative, like those associated with Niccolò Machiavelli and Karl Marx. Reduced to its essence, what Malthus argued was that no plant, animal, or human population can grow indefinitely in the finite physical space of a planet. At some point, something has to give. To give his critics their due, he did express the concept rather darkly, famously writing, "The power of population is so superior to the power of the earth to produce subsistence for man, that premature death must in some shape or other visit the human race."[8]

The seemingly doleful figure of Malthus looms over the population debate even today. Why do we remember him and not the many others who expressed their views on human numbers? "In the history of science . . . timing is all," University of British Columbia philosopher Margaret Schabas writes of Malthus.[9] That much he had going for him. The final decade of the eighteenth century was a time of explosive expansion in science, and nowhere more so than in Great Britain. Scotsman James Hutton was founding the new discipline of geology with his mammoth *Theory of the Earth*, published in 1795. Three years later, the eccentric polymath

Henry Cavendish completed a year's worth of measurements of the mass of the earth, arriving at a figure—6 billion trillion metric tons—that's only 1 percent higher than the figure estimated by scientists in the twenty-first century.[10]

It was also a time of social upheaval, ripe for consideration of numbers describing human rather than planetary mass. London and other European capitals were filling rapidly with migrants displaced from rural land, where big families and small opportunities were the rule. The Industrial Revolution was only beginning to gather steam, so to speak, and there were not nearly enough jobs for these rural migrants. England's Poor Laws had offered jobs and even direct payments to those with no means since the Elizabethan era. The gentry may have seen this early version of government welfare as generous, but the poor they nonetheless had always with them—and in greater numbers than ever. In France, revolutionaries had toppled the royalty and an entire social structure with it, and yet their success did not appear to be turning France into the egalitarian society many educated Europeans had expectantly awaited. Frustration with the persistence of poverty, despite the success of scientific, industrial, and political revolutions, was running at a high pitch in Great Britain. The willingness among educated and leisured readers to believe that large families caused persistent poverty was probably equally high.

So Malthus had a ready audience, though neither he nor his readers knew for certain whether the English population was actually growing. Other countries had counted their citizens—Iceland in 1703, Sweden in 1749, Spain in 1787, and the newly independent United States of America in 1790. But England, despite its overwhelming scientific dominance and its development of demography, somehow failed to manage a serious count of its own people until 1801.

In fact, some English observers suspected the nation's population was in decline. The fear was hardly unfounded; the seeming ubiquity of infant and child death was obvious to any Londoner. But by the late 1700s, as Malthus could see in his rural parish, the perception was out of date. England's population probably had been roughly stable at slightly more than 5 million from the middle of the seventeenth century to the middle of the eighteenth. But then the population had resumed growing, reaching 8 million people by 1798. Overall care of infants seems to have improved at this time, and child survival benefited from such developments in hygiene as English chemist James Keir's invention of an inexpensive but effective soap.[11] With contraception proscribed as never before in the aftermath of the witchcraft hysteria, there may have been a rise in family size as well. When the first census was completed, at any rate, the accumulated data demonstrated that population was growing steadily in the sceptered isle.

As England's population passed the 8 million mark, Malthus pulled together the disparate reasoning on demography that had accumulated over the centuries and developed a powerful, intuitively understandable principle. In 1798, he anonymously published *An Essay on the Principle of Population*, but he was immediately "outed" as its author when the hastily written polemic became a bestseller. In it he argued that human population grows "geometrically." The larger the base population, the larger each year's increase, with no extra "effort" required. Food production, by contrast, grows by the much slower "arithmetic" function. Each incremental increase requires the same extra effort, no matter how much food was produced to start with. Inevitably, boosting production reached points of diminishing returns as more land was farmed and as once-rich soils gradually were exhausted through long use. The result, Malthus argued, was that population always tended to outrun food production, until the "misery" of famine, war, or disease—the apocalyptic horsemen—brought matters back to equilibrium.

For Malthus, poverty was simply a natural and inevitable consequence of population growth. It couldn't be prevented no matter how society was organized, because populations tended to grow beyond their means of subsistence. It wasn't capitalism or any other organization of society (as Karl Marx and Friedrich Engels came to argue), but simply the growth of population that consistently drove the less fortunate and less skilled into poverty. Malthus initially saw no way out of this dilemma, though later he argued that late marriage could help slow the growth of population, and, hence, of poverty. But it was his conviction of the inevitability of poverty as populations grow that has most animated his critics since his short essay was first published.

In the next five years, Malthus transformed that essay into a much longer scholarly work that can be considered fully a second essay. He then revised that second book a half dozen more times, reworking his one fresh idea continually. (This wasn't unusual for the era. A few decades later, Charles Darwin produced nearly a dozen editions of his masterpiece *On the Origin of Species*, leaving scholars ever after uncertain which to quote as the authoritative Darwinian statement.) Unfortunately for Malthus's reputation, none of the later editions achieved anything like the fame and readership of the first. The evolution of the author's views beyond the bleak pessimism of the initial essay is today little known.[12]

So was Malthus a misanthrope? What can we say of the man whose name became synonymous with demographic fatalism? His life began in 1766 and ended in 1834, perfectly bracketing the turn of the nineteenth century. Thomas Robert Malthus went by his middle name, not by Thomas as so often assumed by those who mention him today. He appears to have been a studious child, distinguishing himself in Latin, Greek, French, and mathematics at Jesus College of Cambridge University. His writings give evidence of a strong but independent-minded belief in God, and at twenty-seven he was ordained a minister in the Church of England.[13]

Through most of the second half of his life, he was a professor of political economy at a university designed to prepare young men for service in British-ruled India. While friends and family called him Bob, admirers dubbed him Population Malthus, which his students affectionately shortened to Pop. Until a surgical procedure late in life, he had a slight harelip that marred his speech, discomfiting many who heard him speak.

Malthus was the son of a country landowner, a fact that critics Marx and Engels were quick to point out in their early writings. But even a cursory reading of the various editions of *Principle of Population* undermines Marx's charge that Malthus was "a professional sycophant of the landed aristocracy," bent on building the capitalist case for the inevitability of poverty.[14] Robert Malthus came from and remained within an intellectual community that grappled with the problem of poverty, and he was a man infatuated by what he believed was his own discovery about the way the world worked.

He called "the present great inequality of property . . . an evil." He questioned Britain's death penalty. He proposed universal education to empower the poor and suggested that women's intellects were equal to those of men. And he proposed that laborers would improve their lot if they could somehow "agree among themselves never to work more than six or seven hours in a day."[15] Some of his descriptions of England's poor certainly strike modern readers as insensitive, perhaps offensive. But at no point does he suggest that the poor deserve their lot or that poverty is socially acceptable because it is demographically inevitable. The logic seems not to have occurred to him, as it does to so many of his critics, that poverty must be neither or both. "His work as a whole," writes anthropologist James Wood, "is consistently motivated by a desire, perhaps paternalistic but nonetheless real, to ameliorate the plight of the poor."[16]

The Malthusian Legacy

Malthus hoped his writings would somehow contribute to a reconciliation of the differential growth rates of population and food production, and that this would ameliorate poverty. Yet the infamous *Essay* inspired theories, critiques, and policies beyond what he could have imagined—some of them less than admirable. Some industrialists embraced his ideas to justify low wages for laborers. A few governments applied his reasoning to build networks of punitive workhouses for the poor. Social Darwinists and assorted eugenicists interested in "high-quality" populations found in Malthus's writing a rationale for exerting control, including reproductive control, over the poor and powerless.

But Malthus influenced later thinkers in more benign ways as well. Reading his first essay in the 1830s provided Eureka moments to both Charles Darwin and Alfred Russel Wallace, who independently of one another developed the idea of natural selection as a force in biological evolution. (It's an intriguing historical footnote that demography and evolutionary biology, like two individuals whose genetic makeup researchers can compare, thus derive to some extent from a common lineage.) Malthus's treatment of wage labor and diminishing returns in production inspired later economics writers from David Ricardo to John Maynard Keynes.

For the purposes of my inquiry, however, Malthus's important contribution remains his articulation of the differential growing power of population and food production. Historians examining European famines and plagues of the late Middle Ages and early modern times often invoke the adjective *Malthusian* to describe the dynamics of growing populations outrunning the productive capacity of their arable land. University of California–Davis economist Gregory Clark has argued provocatively that only at about the time Malthus wrote did England's economy escape from the Malthusian trap of each agricultural innovation being negated by subsequent population growth.[17] This period of frequent hunger and disease was, in fact, the historical experience out of which Malthus's ideas evolved. Unfortunately for his reputation, however, he thought it obvious that food production had only modest prospects for further growth. As luck would have it, he wrote precisely at the dawn of a two-hundred-year era in which farm acreage and crop yields each more than doubled, and food production expanded faster than the number of food consumers.

The concept of finite natural resources made Engels, writing a decade after Malthus's death, apoplectic. "This vile and infamous doctrine," he called the central Malthusian principle, "this repulsive blasphemy against man and nature." Why, Engels asked, should the earth's power to feed growing populations face any limits at all? "The productive power at the disposal of mankind is unmeasurable," he wrote. "The productivity of the land can be infinitely increased by the application of capital, labor and science."[18]

We could call this the Fénelonian view, after the eighteenth-century French author quoted earlier on the earth's inexhaustibility. Ironically, in recent decades its foremost adherents have been not Marxists, but conservative neoclassical economics writers such as the late Julian Simon. A professor of marketing at the University of Maryland who died in 1998, the two-hundredth anniversary of the publication of Malthus's first essay, Simon influenced the Reagan administration's thinking on population by arguing that natural resources really are effectively infinite. The increase of human population continually produces more minds, Simon proposed. That means more innovations for substituting scarce resources with more abundant ones, or for recycling used resources, or for using what's left with ever greater efficiency.

"The more [natural resources] we use, the better off we become," Simon wrote, his idealism barely tempered by the parentheses to come, "and there's no practical limit to improving our lot forever (or for at least seven billion years)." I knew Simon slightly, and I regret that I never probed him about what could happen to spoil a streak of prosperity lasting billions of years. Perhaps, Oxford University demographer David Coleman suggested to me, Simon lacked confidence that we could survive the exhaustion of the sun.[19]

Regardless of Simon's limitless optimism, the world food situation has become in recent years less reassuring, less comfortably a refutation to Malthus's predictions. He could never have foreseen that the production of biofuels for internal-combustion vehicles would begin to compete with the production of food on some of the world's best cropland, pushing up food prices from Mexico to India in 2007. With global reserves of staple grains reaching their lowest levels in years, the number of malnourished approached 850 million, many more people than ever suffered consistently from a lack of food while Malthus lived.[20] Indeed, the phenomenon of entire nations almost perpetually in need of foreign supplies of food emerged only after world population passed 3 billion people in the 1960s. As hazardous as prediction is, it's getting hard to be confident that farmers and fishers will easily feed the 9.2 billion people projected to be alive in 2050. Will we keep innovating successfully, expanding our prosperity with our numbers? Your guess is as good as mine. But I would bet most of us would agree with Robert Malthus in disputing the notion that "trees may be made to grow indefinitely high, or potatoes indefinitely large."[21]

The Cordial Drop

Of course, there is a way to slow population growth before famine sets in, but Malthus and his contemporaries were loathe to consider it. The idea that women's own decisions about their childbearing might be the best guarantor of demographic stability showed up only in the last century or so. This was true despite the fact that the Enlightenment ushered in new attitudes about women and sexuality, at least among the wealthier and educated classes of Europe. It would be overstatement to say that women's standing improved everywhere or even generally. But the rights of man kept arising in public discussions, and the question of whether there were any for women could not long be avoided. A handful of individual women established names for themselves in realms that for centuries had been exclusively male. In 1699, German naturalist Maria Sibylla Merian sailed to Dutch Guiana (Surinam) and documented the use by enslaved Indians of a plant she named *flos pavonis* ("peacock flower") to avoid giving birth. In later decades male biologists acknowledged Merian's scientific work, but ignored its connection to abortion; one dismissed *flos pavonis* as "a pretty hedge." [22]

Some male scientists in Age of Enlightenment did inquire about sex and reproduction. Sex may still have been sinful, but it was also acknowledged as part of the natural order. As early as the seventeenth century, the Dutch developer of microscopes, Antoni van Leeuwenhoek, examined his own semen, magnified 275 times, and reported its appearance. (He did apologize to his readers for the unsavoriness of the investigation.) Erasmus Darwin, a physician and the grandfather of Charles Darwin, wrote a two-hundred-page poem extolling the diversity of sexual reproduction in the plant kingdom. Titled *The Loves of the Plants*, it was one of the bestsellers of 1789. Darwin called sex itself "the cordial drop in the otherwise vapid cup of life." And the pioneer taxonomist Carolus Linnaeus lavished sexual imagery on flora and fauna as he carried out his self-appointed task of naming nature like some latter-day scientific Adam. Bivalves reminded him of female genitalia, the parts of which—vulva, labia, hymen—contributed names to body parts of a species of clam. He dubbed an entire genus of plants *Clitoria*. He called the reproductive strategy of flowers, with male stamens casting their spermlike pollen on the wind to settle randomly on female stigmas, "promiscuous intercourse." Most famously, he named mammals for the mammary glands with which females nourish their young.[23]

Linnaeus's fixation with breasts went beyond taxonomy. In an era in which most middle- and upper-class parents on the continent of Europe packed their infants off to wet nurses (the practice was less common in Britain), Linnaeus was a rare activist for maternal breastfeeding. Like many writers in eighteenth-century Europe, he believed that the Continent's population was falling because so many infants died in the indifferent care of breastfeeders for hire. If mothers would only nurse their own children, he reasoned, more children would survive and Europe's population would again begin to grow. Linnaeus's wife did her part, giving birth to seven children, five of whom survived.[24]

As it happens, the practice of wet nursing may actually have contributed to higher birthrates than otherwise would have occurred. True, many infants did die in the care of wet nurses. For parents, in fact, the institution often amounted to a reproductive timing strategy, somewhere just short of abandonment and infanticide. But wet nurses were scarcely incompetent as a class, and more infants survived than perished. And since maternal breastfeeding acts as a natural contraceptive, in its absence many mothers must have quickly become pregnant yet again. Only one eighteenth-century writer appears to have grasped the link between breastfeeding and population growth, as we'll see, and she was neither naturalist nor demographer, but a writer and mother.

Clearly, scientists were not the only ones reconsidering traditional attitudes about sexuality and reproduction. The nature of marriage shifted around this time, with unions likely to be based less on parents' economic strategies and more on mutual affection. At the same time, many people of wealth and education tolerated extramarital liaisons and the offspring that resulted from them. Published pornography began to appear.[25]

The year 1798 saw the death of Giacomo Girolamo Casanova, another writer whose last name, like Malthus's, has evolved into a word of its own in many languages. The prolific lover's autobiography celebrated the pleasures of sexual intercourse free from the fear of infection or pregnancy. His well-advertised secret was the use of small sheaths made out of lamb's gut, which he tested by filling with air. Although his were manufactured in the French port city of Marseilles, he called them "English riding coats." Today we know them as condoms, though the origin of that word remains a mystery.[26] Casanova was an exceptional male for his time, needing reliable contraception for an aristocratic sexual hobby he could only sustain if few of his lovers troubled him with pregnancies and children. The real and ubiquitous need, however, was for safe and effective contraception that worked for women.

Moral Restraint

Despite the loosening of some mores, eighteenth-century Europe was a long way from social acceptance of birth control. Rather, churches and governments continued to counsel abstinence as the only acceptable way to prevent pregnancy. Malthus himself couldn't bear even to mention contraception. In his original 1798 essay, he argued that the only check on population growth aside from death was what he called vice ("vicious customs . . . with regard to women").[27] He squeamishly failed to detail these customs, but they seem to have included infanticide, abortion, and contraception, the last of which the Church of England would not approve for use by married couples until 140 years later. Vice also clearly included nonprocreative sex, such as male ejaculation outside "the appropriate vessel," which Christian authorities had long condemned.

In his more scholarly second edition, Malthus amended his theory to recognize the one benign check on population growth that he could imagine and endorse: "moral restraint," which amounted to delaying both sexual activity and marriage until children could be provided for. (The second essay also expanded on steps governments could take to ameliorate the impacts of population growth.) The late population writer Jack Parsons provocatively suggested that the views Malthus espoused in this second essay resemble those of today's Vatican. The focus of both Malthus and the Holy See is on "responsible parenthood," a prohibition on contraception, and condemnation of the idea that government should play any role in limiting family size. Malthus even suggested that governments should subsidize the parents of large families if their "prolifickness" arose despite the moral restraint of late marriage.[28]

That restraint was indeed a "check" on European population in the eighteenth and nineteenth centuries, and in some places a moderately effective one. Late marriages slow population growth in two ways, first by stretching out the succession of generations over longer time periods, and second by allowing women fewer years in which to bear children. By themselves, late marriages don't bring fertility close to replacement levels, however, so populations keep growing. And late marriages are only effective to the extent that premarital sex and pregnancy are the exceptions rather than the rule, which was pretty much the case in most places during these centuries. But not for all people.

If late marriage can slow population growth, might prohibiting marriage altogether among certain subpopulations stop and even reverse their growth? So thought some in Germany who read Malthus in translation early in the nineteenth century. Actually, while Malthus thought governments might usefully discourage "improvident" marriages, he opposed their prohibition. The subtlety of that distinction seems not to have survived translation into German. By the middle of the nineteenth century, some German states were forbidding men under thirty or with low incomes to marry, with the predictable result that as marriage declined the number of babies born out of wedlock rose. In 1851 in a number of parishes in Mecklenberg, one writer reported, no babies were born to married parents.[29]

Evidence of contraceptive need was hidden in plain sight, not only in Europe but halfway across the globe in Japan, where an unusual reproductive and demographic story was unfolding just as Malthus was developing his ideas on population. In the late eighteenth century, the Tokugawa shogunate was two centuries into its militarized rule of feudal Japan. Among peasants, struggling to survive in a population of 30 million people with food expensive and in short supply, family size dropped to two children or even fewer. Population leveled off and then actually declined after centuries of growth. How did couples achieve fertility so low that demographic growth actually reversed course? As it happens, it's not certain they did. They may have achieved such small families mostly through widespread, culturally accepted infanticide. Estimates of the proportion of infants killed run as high as 25 percent. Ironically, boys were more likely than girls to be dispatched after a first birth, at least if a woman was young enough to expect two or three later chances of giving birth to a son. A first-born daughter could help her mother raise younger brothers, but a first-born son would be useless for that task. Infanticide was so routine that custom discouraged congratulating a couple who had just given birth. Only after it was clear they would raise the child did the customary congratulations and gifts flow.[30]

Leaving aside our own horror that parents could behave this way, infanticide is an absurdly wasteful and hazardous expenditure of maternal resources. It requires women to invest the energy and risk of pregnancy and childbirth to no purpose. In the absence of modern health care, any pregnancy and childbirth present a significant risk of killing or permanently disabling a woman. Those of late Tokugawa Japan were in an obvious state of what demographers call unmet need for safe and effective contraception.

Moreover, women and couples' efforts to keep family size small put them at odds, as so often, with powerful governmental interests in maintaining the growth of population. Throughout the two and a half centuries of Tokugawa rule, the central Japanese government encouraged and even rewarded couples for having large families. The tension between governmental and parental reproductive intentions found graphic illustration in a propaganda scroll produced in 1788. The government of the northeastern municipality of Sendai sought to boost the area's long-stagnant population by eliminating the killing of infants. As the document unrolls, a just-delivered woman is shown throttling her newborn while a midwife shakes out a birthing mat and the infant's father nonchalantly brews tea. With further unrolling of the scroll, we see the murderous mother tumbling headlong into hell, where demons force her to witness the infanticide in a magic mirror. Later she is lowered upside down into a boiling caldron, while other women who shirked motherhood wade forlornly in a lake of blood, and the spirits of dispatched babies gambol on the barren landscape. This propaganda campaign appears to have been demographically effective. Average fertility rates recorded in one community in Sendai, which had hovered around two children per woman for the previous fifty years, immediately began rising and doubled over the next sixty. This trend was typical of Japan in this period.[31]

A further illustration of the need for contraception was unfolding around the same time in Sweden, not far from where Malthus was pondering population and food production. Comparing data on fertility and grain prices in southern Sweden from 1766 to 1864, economic historians Tommy Bengtsson and Martin Dribe find that the two trends moved consistently and inversely, higher prices for staple foods correlating neatly with lower birthrates. Disappointing harvests routinely were followed within months by significant declines in births; baby boomlets followed hard on the heels of harvests that brought bulging grain bins.

"In an agriculturally based economy, one of the most pressing concerns was how to deal with short-term economic stress owing to fluctuations in food prices," Bengtsson and Dribe write. "Our results strongly suggest that when faced with this kind of stress, preindustrial families actively controlled the timing of childbirth." The authors speculate that abstinence and withdrawal, along with an unspecified "range of other traditional contraceptive techniques combined with low coital frequency was quite effective in limiting the number of births." Intriguingly, they find that existing family size had little bearing on this reproductive decision making. Rather, the decision seemed related to whether a given harvest rendered the following year an auspicious time to have a new child.[32]

The fact that contraception was intended and used in response to harvests and food prices suggests a feedback effect that would have interested Malthus, had he known what was unfolding a thousand miles from his parish while he wrote his first essay. Under the right circumstances, the Swedish experience suggests, declining birthrates may lead to sustainable populations purely through the intentions of women and their partners.

A Vindication and an Alternative

Just six years prior to 1798, Malthus's London publisher brought out a work destined to make its own history: *A Vindication of the Rights of Women*, by the pioneer feminist Mary Wollstonecraft. The book proposed a check on population that was neither misery, vice, nor moral restraint, but something altogether different: regular breastfeeding, a mother's gift of her own body to nurture her child. "For nature has so wisely ordered things," Wollstonecraft wrote, "that did women suckle their children, they would preserve their own health, and there would be such an interval between the birth of each child, that we should seldom see a houseful of babes."[33]

It seems unlikely that Malthus ever read Wollstonecraft, though the two writers did have a connection. Five years after she wrote *Vindication* Wollstonecraft was rescued from an unsuccessful suicide attempt by the writer William Godwin, whom she married. Godwin, an optimist on the perfectibility of man, so influenced Malthus that the subtitle to the first *Principle on Population* includes the words, *With Remarks on the Speculations of Mr. Godwin*.

Eleven days after giving birth to her and Godwin's child, Wollstonecraft died from puerperal, or "childbed," fever, a once-common postnatal infection of the reproductive tract. The baby girl beat the odds of motherlessness to survive to her own adulthood. At age twenty-two, under the name Mary Shelley, she wrote the book *Frankenstein*. In what makes a sad footnote, Godwin recorded in a memoir of Wollstonecraft that during the short time she lived after giving birth, the doctor would not allow her to breastfeed her newborn baby "and procured puppies to draw off the milk."[34]

Centuries earlier, both Aristotle and the twelfth-century Spanish Islamic physician Averroës had observed that nursing women rarely seemed to become pregnant.[35] Wollstonecraft was likely the first woman, however, to publish a secret that must have been shared orally among her sex for thousands of years. The idea that frequent nursing could prevent large families never occurred to Malthus, though he fathered three children. Wollstonecraft whispered what others came to clamor: that women could and should direct their own childbearing. Eventually that clamor would change everything about human population and even influence the course of nature itself.

NINE

Zen and the Art of Population Maintenance

Every human society is faced not with one population problem but with two: how to beget and rear enough children and how not to beget and rear too many. The definition of "enough" and "too many" varies enormously.

—Margaret Mead

Somewhere on this globe, every 10 seconds, there is a woman giving birth to a child. She must be found and stopped.

—Sam Levenson, American humorist

The day I met "Condom Sister" Henrietta in Accra, I also made the acquaintance of Florence Aku, a nurse at a small reproductive health clinic attached to the youth center where Henrietta worked. As Ms. Aku instructed me on the contraceptives the clinic offered, my eyes occasionally strayed to a life-sized figure on her desk, skillfully sculpted from a dark tropical wood and rising out of a square base. It was an erect penis. This one had nothing to do with male domination, as it might have in ancient

Greece, where columns adorned with bearded heads and erect phalluses were common. It was merely a prop for demonstrating the proper application of condoms.

You get an odd mix of feelings in such clinics. Surrounded by white-coated specialists, the faint chemical odor of latex, models of intimate human anatomy, and shelves of packaged contraceptives, you start out thinking you'd rather be anywhere else in the world. Stick around, however, and you soon find yourself intrigued, curious, oddly upbeat. Women and men speak openly about sex, but no one is hitting on anyone. The pervasive message is that staying healthy and making life plans are good—and not hard to do. Here's help. It's a one-stop shop specializing in sex, reproduction, and health. Want to have sex without having a child? Stop here. Want to have sex and have a healthy baby? Here. Want to be tested for and counseled on HIV or another sexually transmitted infection? For breast or testicular cancer? Here. You can plan your family, making sure it doesn't arrive until you're ready and gets no bigger than you want it to be. And you can enjoy sex without risking your future—or your life—in the bargain.

Visitors often surprise themselves by reacting warmly to reproductive health clinics, despite the lineups of genital devices. Colleagues of mine at Population Action International have taken members of Congress to see how family planning services actually work in developing countries, and these visits sometimes change the politicians' lives—and their voting records. That's vital, because the survival of many of these little shops on main street in Accra and thousands of places like it depends, sadly enough, on contentious legislative battles in capitals like Washington, D.C.

In sharp contrast to the herbs and practices women used to prevent pregnancy in the past, modern contraception requires quality control, global distribution networks, and careful and empathetic counseling from trained personnel. None of this is expensive the way open-heart surgery or occupying a hostile country is expensive. But the cost of safe and effective contraception is nonetheless more than many people in developing countries can afford. And this raises a critical point. World population isn't likely to stabilize at 9 billion or 10 billion people sometime in this century or the next, as UN and other demographers are said to "expect," unless one of two things occurs: higher death rates, or governments of the world making sure clinics and contraception are available to reproductive-age women. These women number 1.7 billion today, and that number is projected to grow by 400 million, much higher than today's entire U.S. population, by 2035. Governments aren't taking on this challenge in any serious way right now, and—thanks in large part to the global silence on population—they aren't under much pressure to improve their act.

None of the staff at the clinic in Accra said anything at all about population, yet their work is one outcome of the long history of concern about human numbers that I've traced in earlier chapters. Family planning service providers facilitate the later pregnancies and smaller families that bring down birthrates and slow the growth of population. Their job, however, is not to preach population control or family limitation—despite Sam Levenson's laugh line that opens this chapter—but rather to help women bear children in good health, when women want to do so. Women have their own reasons for postponing or preventing pregnancy. When those intentions are realized, the delays and reductions in births ripple out into the larger world in positive demographic outcomes. It resembles a Zen Buddhist approach to dealing with unsustainable population growth. Zen masters counsel their adherents to achieve enlightenment not by striving for it, but by creating the mental and spiritual conditions through which it will occur naturally and spontaneously. Reproductive health workers rarely if ever mention population to their clients—few clinic workers take an interest in human numbers, unless in their private thoughts—but the safe and healthy reproductive habits these workers promote do create conditions out of which population stability tends to arise.

It's not hard to see why population size is not a pressing day-to-day concern among clinic staffs. Working with people, it can be difficult to keep a focus on slowing population growth, if you had one to begin with. Faces are so unique, personalities so distinct, babies so appealing, and human beings so essentially interesting that any visceral feeling that there are just *too many people* often fades as the work proceeds. And with population size itself so sensitive and controversial, a common strategy for traveling through this minefield is to simply ignore the issue altogether and lift your load.

This scarcely means that the rest of us need to ignore human numbers. Population is too vital a human issue to be swept under rugs for long. It will always out, often unpleasantly. *Overpopulation. Uncontrolled. Breeding. Teeming. She must be found and stopped.* Such phrases hardly launch a good conversation, and they miss the nuances of what's actually happening. Some writers refer to populations in many developing countries as "out of control," while those of most industrialized countries have been "successfully limited," or words to this effect. The reality is that *all populations are out of control.* None are limited. Not even in Communist China can the government actually micromanage the reproductive decisions, let alone the reproductive *outcomes*, of millions of women and men. Migration streams, too, have mostly mocked governmental efforts at control. What governments can do is establish the policies, set up the programs, and create the conditions under which population trends are likely to bend in good directions.

The best way to "control" population is to give up control, in fact to give control *away* to those who can best decide for themselves when to bear a child. Enlightenment will arrive only after one has given up the search, and positive population outcomes only after the forcing stops. It's worth considering where this Zen-like approach to population came from, where it has detoured, and where it's headed.[1]

"A Dirty, Filthy Book"

From at least the Axial Age until the late eighteenth century, most organized efforts to influence the size of populations aimed at boosting it. Women have been extolled, pressured, or coerced into having children early and often, whether or not they would have timed their own childbearing that way if left to their own devices (contraceptive or otherwise). But let's consider for a moment the strategies that have gained the greater attention since Malthus wrote, the kind designed to slow demographic growth by reducing family size and birthrates.

Malthus didn't have a distinct plan for addressing the forces behind his "principle of population." Maybe it would help if people exercised "moral restraint," meaning marrying later in life. That worked, a bit, but population growth rates in England and elsewhere nonetheless kept rising at a pretty rapid clip despite Malthus's warnings. Given the importance of family size to population change, Mary Wollstonecraft may have been the first since Aristotle to write about contraception in a demographic context with her recommendation that breastfeeding could prevent a "houseful of babes." One year before Malthus's essay appeared, the idealistic Utilitarian philosopher Jeremy Bentham suggested that if enough women used the contraceptive sponge, a type of pessary, England's poverty rate might fall. But Bentham saw this as a private matter, a mere suggestion to couples, and left it at that.

The first true promoter of actually *acting* on population issues appears to have been Francis Place, a self-educated son of the English working class. Married at age nineteen to a woman two years his junior, Place fathered fifteen children and lived in poverty. In late middle age he became the world's first birth control theorist and propagandist. In an 1822 book on Malthus's population principle, Place proposed substituting contraception for late marriage to moderate birthrates. Not content to let the book plead his case, the author wandered the streets of London and northern English industrial cities the following year, posting anonymous handbills addressed "to the married of both sexes." The handbills argued that large families risked the health of mothers and children, caused economic anxiety and suffering, and led to low wages because large cohorts of workers flooded labor markets. If couples would just use the sponge, Place suggested, they could solve these problems.[2]

By joining Malthus in identifying population growth as a driver of poverty, Place proposed a function for population policy and for family planning that would both help and haunt the two concepts ever after. On the one hand, the alleviation of poverty has been one of the great endeavors of humanity since the French Revolution. If bringing population growth to an end could demonstrably help that cause, the future of the effort might be secure. If the goal was to eliminate not poverty but the poor themselves, on the other hand, only a handful of well-off misanthropes were likely to sign up for the cause.

Place did stress one value that underlies mainstream population policies up to the present: control of births not by government or other outsiders, but by women and couples themselves, "so that none," in Place's words, "need to have more [children] than they wish to have."[3] Yet some later theorists doubted that women could be trusted to actually *want* the small families needed to slow or end population growth. "It is an empirical fact," biologist Garrett Hardin argued in 1980, "that in every country in the world the number of children wanted by the average family is greater than the number needed to produce population equilibrium in that nation."[4] Less than two decades later, physician Malcolm Potts demonstrated that this was anything but an empirical fact; even as early as the 1960s, countries that provided relatively unconstrained access to family planning and safe abortion services saw fertility rates heading toward or going below replacement levels of two (and a fraction) children per woman.[5]

Perhaps the eighteenth- and nineteenth-century writers on contraception and population had some inkling that this would be true; admonishments of the need to convince women and couples to have fewer children are hard to find. Annie Besant, a procontraception activist in the late nineteenth century and later a leader in the spiritual movement Theosophy, did write in her book *The Law of Population* that women in rapidly growing populations such as Britain's had a "duty" to have small families. But she believed women would perceive this duty for themselves. She wrote, as she noted in her dedication, "in the hope that [the book] may point out a path from poverty, and may make easier the life of British mothers."[6] The tension between empowering all sexually active people to make their own reproductive decisions and the perceived need to guide these decisions toward less childbearing (or, in some cases, more) has pervaded population policy since its origins.

In stressing the childbearing intentions of couples themselves, however, Place established a standard for judging population-related policies and programs: their conformance with individual rights and choices. The word "voluntary" hardly does the concept justice. Do policies help women and their partners have children when and only when that is their intention, or do they hinder this reproductive autonomy? Had the early pioneers of birth control focused more on this distinction, which shines more brightly in our day than in theirs, they might have avoided some damaging detours and dangerous liaisons that have marred the struggle for universal access to family planning ever since.

Just as Place promoted the sponge, most nineteenth-century writers on birth control stressed their own preferred contraceptive methods. Ten years after Place wrote in Britain, the Massachusetts physician Charles Knowlton claimed a right of discovery for douching in an 1832 work, *Fruits of Philosophy*. (Medical historian Norman Himes, writing in the 1930s, reported that he looked but found no earlier mention of the method.)[7] British physician George Drysdale appears to have been the first to chronicle a variety of birth control techniques. He also expressed the insight, which women may have long noted on their own, that using two methods at the same time can dramatically reduce the chances of pregnancy. Similarly, well-stocked reproductive health clinics today offer clients a variety of choices: condoms for those with multiple partners or otherwise risking sexual infection, for example, and intrauterine devices (IUDs) or hormonal methods for those in monogamous relationships with uninfected partners.

Not surprisingly, civic groups and civil authorities challenged many of the nineteenth-century writers as purveyors of indecency. The tracts and books were, after all, discussing sexual intercourse. In the late 1870s, Besant and iconoclastic attorney Charles Bradlaugh published Knowlton's *Fruits of Philosophy* for the British market and were quickly charged with spreading obscenity. Their trial turned into a publicity bonanza for birth control. Prosecutor Hardinge Gifford called *Fruits* "a dirty, filthy book" and added that "no decently educated British husband would allow even his wife to have it. The object of it is to enable a person to have sexual intercourse, and not to have that which in the order of Providence is the natural result of that sexual intercourse."[8] Besant and Bradlaugh were convicted and sentenced to six months in jail, but the verdict was reversed on appeal. That judgment effectively ended contraception's legal status as obscene in the United Kingdom. Sales of books on contraception soared into the hundreds of thousands throughout Europe and North America. The Besant-Bradlaugh trial helped launch a slowing of demographic growth within England and Wales that continued for decades. Births peaked around the time of the trial at about 35 per 1,000 people per year and then slid down a steady slope to 17 per 1,000 per year by the 1930s.

Not only in England but in several European countries and as far away as Brazil and Cuba, organizations calling themselves Malthusian and Neo-Malthusian Leagues sprang up in the early 1880s to promote wider use of contraception. The naming convention is hard to explain, given Malthus's abhorrence of this "vice," but the new Malthusians seem to have finessed this point. In Germany, physician Wilhelm Mensinga developed a hollow half hemisphere of rubber with a watch spring threaded around its rim to hold it over the cervix. This advanced pessary, soon known as the diaphragm, was easier to use and more effective than anything then available. Recommended by health practitioners and controlled by women users, the diaphragm was in some ways "the Pill" of its era, as birth control clinics began to proliferate early in the twentieth century. Some women, however, found diaphragms difficult to insert and uncomfortable, and they required soap, running water, and the fitting expertise of a medical professional. Withdrawal and condoms remained more popular methods for some time.

In the Netherlands, the country's first woman physician, Aletta Jacobs, established centers for instructing midwives in how to teach contraceptive methods to women in their homes. The need for such instruction is an ironic indicator of the folk wisdom that midwives must have lost since the Middle Ages—including, perhaps, the memory of their predecessors' persecution in the witch trials. Nonetheless, with Dr. Jacobs's medical supervision as a defining feature, these centers mark the origin of reproductive health education and provision as practiced today.[9]

Obscenity in America

Across the Atlantic, the winds of change blew in the opposite direction. In a uniquely American development, a Protestant moral arbiter named Anthony Comstock crusaded for laws to criminalize as obscene the advertising and sale of contraceptives. A receptive U.S. Congress in 1873 rushed through passage of what came to be known as the Comstock Act to accomplish these objectives. For the District of Columbia and federal territories, the act banned even the possession of contraceptives. A woman inserting a diaphragm before having sex with her husband in her Georgetown or Anacostia bedroom was technically violating the law. "In penalizing the possession of contraceptives Congress went further than any pope or canonist," notes contraceptive historian John Noonan.[10] Comstock himself was deputized as a special agent of the Post Office Department, authorized to inspect suspicious mailings and to make arrests. State laws along the same lines as the federal one soon followed and, in some northeastern states where the Catholic Church wielded political influence, legislatures prohibited physicians from prescribing or even advising on contraception. Connecticut made any use of contraception a misdemeanor, criminalizing pregnancy prevention until the U.S. Supreme Court found the law unconstitutional—in 1965.

Abortion was the target of even more-severe state laws. Once again, midwives found themselves tarred by their association with the practice. "The practice of abortion has become a very great evil," lamented a leading Chicago obstetrician in 1896, "largely as a result of a lack of midwife control." The city government tried to remedy that lack, prohibiting birth attendants from possessing "any drug or instrument . . . which may be used to procure an abortion."[11]

Burly and bald with bushy whiskers that drew a large *W* across his face, Anthony Comstock was virtually a caricature of the male moralist, righteously determined that women should bear all the children whom God and their husbands sent their way. His nemesis, emerging a few decades after enactment of his laws, was physically much smaller but driven just as powerfully by precisely the opposite idea: that women should determine for themselves if and when to have children, based not on abstinence but on birth control.

Her name was Margaret Sanger, and earlier and more energetically than any other single individual she honed and promoted the idea that women freely choosing when to become pregnant would improve not only their own lives, but humanity itself. That conviction led her to the conclusion that the spread of birth control would slow or end world population growth—and also that it could improve the genetic quality of the human species. In this complex and ambiguous legacy, she represents to some extent the equally complex and ambiguous history of modern population policy itself.[12]

She was born Margaret Louise Higgins in 1879, the sixth child to a devout and tubercular Irish American mother who endured seven miscarriages as well as eleven successful pregnancies. Fiercely independent from her earliest years, Margaret concluded early in life that large families and near-annual childbearing were a source of misery for women and their families. Her Irish-born father, a raconteur and radical, struggled to lift his family into the middle class through his work as a stonemason. During her girlhood in Corning, New York, Margaret carefully observed the town's wealthier women strolling on fine afternoons. In contrast to her own overworked and sickly mother, these women cheerily devoted their attention to each of their two or three children. How do they do that? she wondered. And could their less frequent childbearing contribute (along with their wealth) to their happiness and well-being?

Marrying architect William Sanger at age twenty-two, Margaret bore three children over the next eight years. Along with her husband, whom she later divorced, she became a socialist and moved to New York City four years before the outbreak of World War I. Some historians see these pre-war years —during which communist journalist John Reed, whom Warren Beatty portrayed in the film *Reds*, made his mark—as the golden age of American radicalism.

Trained as a nurse, Sanger worked with immigrant women on the Lower East Side and witnessed the impacts of unplanned childbearing and unsafe abortion. These women had none of the access to private physicians and surreptitious medical advice on postponing pregnancy that the well-to-do women of Corning took for granted. When one mother injured herself aborting her own pregnancy, she asked a visiting doctor how to avoid another one. According to the story Sanger recounted, the physician replied, "Tell Jake to sleep on the roof." Several months later, Sanger and the same doctor watched this woman die after a botched second abortion.[13]

Thus began Sanger's lifelong commitment to make *birth control*—two words she was the first to link together, in her monthly newspaper *The Woman Rebel*—available to any woman who wanted to use it. By 1916, after visiting clinics in the Netherlands, the descendants of Aletta Jacobs's training centers, Sanger had set up the first birth control clinic in the United States in the Brownsville neighborhood of Brooklyn. Though she spent a month in a jail cell the next year, her prosecution for promoting birth control yielded a legal victory in the state and a political one nationally. The court case led to an exemption under the New York state Comstock laws by which physicians could provide contraception for medical reasons. That exemption led to the spread of legal birth control clinics under the supervision of doctors, first in New York and then elsewhere.

Sanger founded the American Birth Control League in 1921 and opened the doctor-operated Birth Control Clinical Research Bureau under league auspices. In 1939 the bureau and league merged, and three years later the new organization was renamed the Planned Parenthood Federation of America, a name maintained to this day by the nation's predominant nongovernmental reproductive health care provider. Returning from semiretirement after World War II, Sanger helped to found the International Committee on Planned Parenthood in 1948, which became the International Planned Parenthood Federation four years later. Again, the new name stuck. Sanger was president of the federation from its renaming in late 1952 until resigning in 1959 at the age of eighty.

An advocate more than an ideologue, Sanger worked after World War I to expand support for birth control to as broad a public as possible. Women may have been using contraception for thousands of years, but public promotion of birth control as a woman's need and right arose in the early twentieth century largely out of feminist and leftist thought. Feminism and left-leaning ideologies generally moved to the margins of public attention in the economic boom times that followed World War I. Sanger also had grown impatient with her radical male colleagues' lack of commitment to the birth control cause, despite their enthusiastic embrace of free sex. After World War I, she courted the altogether different movement that sought to restrain the growth of world population, then approaching all of 2 billion people. The population movement was small but influential with key elites whom Sanger believed could help the cause of birth control. Trips to England and Germany in 1920 and to China and Japan two years later elevated her to international standing as a leading population activist. In both Asian countries she organized groups that promoted contraception for years after her visit.

Sanger's contributions to this field were all the more impressive given her lack of expertise in either population or policy. In the two decades or so after World War I, demography was not yet a well-established scientific discipline, and the topic of conception control still carried the whiff of smuttiness among the era's mostly upper-class scholars. From her own backers Sanger raised private funding and, through that, gained scientific support for a first-ever conference on world population. The meeting, held in 1927 in Geneva, Switzerland, was designed in large part to bring the issue to the attention of the League of Nations, the precursor to today's United Nations. Sanger clearly grasped the momentousness of her own role in organizing such an august gathering—and played down her usual mode of operation accordingly. Normally a headstrong advocate, she yielded to the insistence of the delegates—they were mainly statisticians, biologists, and economists, and all male—that there be no discussion of birth control and that Sanger herself stay behind the scenes at the conference.[14]

"The papers were mostly long and highly technical treatises on differential fertility by nation and region, and on patterns of migration, the consumption of natural resources, and mortality," wrote Sanger biographer Ellen Chesler. Sanger later edited these page-turners into a published volume of proceedings. The conference led to the establishment of the International

Union for the Scientific Study of Population, a still-thriving association of demographers that, Chesler wrote, "for years had not one woman among its members."[15]

"Good Stock," Bad Idea

For much of the rest of her long career, Sanger traveled the world promoting her vision: when all women could safely and effectively direct their own childbearing, world population problems would take care of themselves. Unfortunately for her reputation, the world's most famous advocate for birth control had sought another alliance even before she reached out to demographers and advocates of slower population growth. Indeed, her interest in population seems to have grown in tandem with her interest in eugenics, the "science" of human genetic improvement.

Sanger was drawn to the concept during a period that was, in demographic terms, somewhat similar to our own. In the decades between the world wars, the use of contraception had caused birthrates to fall among the wealthy and well-educated in industrialized countries, while large numbers of surviving children and falling death rates in poorer countries were beginning to call attention to the challenges of rising populations in those regions. In other respects, that era and this one are decidedly different, and Sanger's alliance with eugenics is the one that modern public opinion is least likely to forgive.

The English scientist-inventor Francis Galton, building on the ideas about evolution and reproductive fitness developed by his cousin Charles Darwin, coined the word *eugenics* in 1883 from Greek words meaning "well born" or "of good stock." Galton concluded from the principle of natural selection that humanity had earned its perch as the crown of creation through eons in which only the fittest survived. Yet somehow, civilization had reached a point at which any imbecile—the word grates on contemporary ears, but once it was common—could raise children to the age of their own reproduction.

Galton and his immediate followers had no particular interest in birth control. They hoped that by encouraging the right reproductive matches and discouraging the wrong ones they could head off the deterioration of the "race." In those days, the word *race* referred at least as often to the human "race"— as in this case—as to racial groups as we know them today.

The first eugenicists were clueless about the actual genetics of reproduction. Everyone was, until the early twentieth-century discovery of the Mendelian model of paired genes and chromosomes. This improvement in scientific understanding only hardened the conviction of eugenicists that heritable genes drove virtually all important human qualities. Even then, however, eugenics advocates had no clear scientific basis for distinguishing good from bad genes, little appreciation of the interaction of multiple genes, and no realistic policies to propose. The concept of voluntarism featured vaguely in the writings of some eugenicists, but the movement by its nature amounted to advocating that women in favored groups give birth to more children than they might otherwise have intended (*positive* eugenics) and that women in disfavored groups have fewer (*negative* eugenics). Though the mechanisms were rarely if ever spelled out, an elite of some kind clearly would need to determine which group was which.

Before the Nazis co-opted it into their own racist policies, eugenics enjoyed considerable cachet in influential scientific and progressive circles throughout Europe, the United States, and in racially diverse Brazil.[16] Traveling in England in the years around World War I, Sanger met and was impressed by such prominent eugenicists as Havelock Ellis, a psychologist who specialized in human sexuality, and the author H. G. Wells. She had affairs with both men. The popularity of eugenics made it a tempting ally to someone like Sanger, who understood that neither improving women's health nor slowing world population growth were easy sells in the marketplace of public opinion.

In 1916 Sanger also met the British contraception activist Marie Stopes. The two should have been fast friends, for even down to their initials and more importantly in their ideals they quite resembled one another. Each was a birth control pioneer who promoted women's enjoyment of their own sexuality. Just as Sanger helped found Planned Parenthood, Stopes founded a British organization of family planning providers. In 1976 it became Marie Stopes International and now operates around the world. Stopes, too, achieved fame by writing prolifically on birth control and, like Sanger, endured her share of snickering for her interests. During the 1920s London schoolchildren skipped rope to the rhyme, "Jeanie, Jeanie, full of hopes, / Read a book by Marie Stopes, / Now, to judge by her condition, / She must have read the wrong edition."[17] Despite the cause they shared and the resemblances between them, however, the American and British reformers never warmed to one another, and each woman appears to have resented whatever fame the other achieved.

In 1922, Sanger's *The Pivot of Civilization* was published, its characteristically over-the-top title a synonym for birth control as the key to improving humanity. Part of this improvement, Sanger argued, would stem from the likelihood that society's "unfit" would eventually join the "fit" in having small families. Arguing for the promotion of birth control to support negative eugenics (she never endorsed the positive kind), Sanger wrote that "we are paying for and even submitting to the dictates of an ever increasing, unceasingly spawning class of human beings who never should have been born at all."[18] Unlike some of the ugliest quotes on the anti-Sanger Web sites, this one is accurate, albeit out of context and using language that rings more harshly to modern ears than to those of the 1920s. "Every feeble-minded girl or women of the hereditary type, especially of the moron class, should be segregated during the reproductive period," Sanger wrote. As "an emergency measure," she added, "we prefer the policy of immediate sterilization, of making sure parenthood is absolutely prohibited for the feeble-minded."[19]

To comprehend such a thought, it helps to recall that in Sanger's time care was abysmal and social stigma overwhelming for people with disabilities. Parents today might choose not to give birth to children diagnosed prenatally with severe disabilities, but in Sanger's day neither diagnostic tests nor legal abortions were available. More than a few politicians in state governments shared her fear that the "feeble-minded" might increase their numbers by reproducing freely. Several states developed policies and programs for sterilizing young people perceived as likely to pass on genetic defects and disabilities to a new generation.[20]

Despite modern accusations to the contrary, Sanger's writings make clear that she was no racist. She refused to tolerate bigotry in those who worked for her. In May 1966, a few months before Sanger died, Martin Luther King Jr., became the first recipient of Planned Parenthood's Margaret Sanger Award. "There is a striking kinship between our [civil rights] movement and Margaret Sanger's early efforts," King noted in his prepared acceptance speech, delivered by his wife, Coretta Scott King. "Our sure beginning in the struggle for equality by nonviolent direct action may not have been so resolute without the tradition established by Margaret Sanger and people like her."[21]

A rebel in so many ways, Sanger disappoints her admirers today not for racial prejudice but for the conviction that differential genetic endowments threatened progress and justified reproductive coercion. That view was widespread and freely expressed in the 1920s and survives today as a much less common private view. Sanger was overawed by the scientists of her day, and eugenics was seen—inaccurately—as an outgrowth of evolutionary biology. A heroine of reproductive rights, Sanger was nonetheless all too human and all too much a person of her time. Heroes and heroines usually are.

Though she repudiated any connection, the eugenic ideals she and others espoused influenced the Nazis and hence played some role in the forced sterilizations and the genocidal mania that swept Germany. As early as

1933, however, Sanger herself spoke out against Nazism and Fascism and used her connections to help Jews leave Austria and Germany. To Sanger's redeeming credit, we know something else about her influence among the Nazis: they burned her books.[22] Among the targets of the Third Reich's persecutions were midwives. Once again, birth attendants were despised as birth preventers, purveyors of contraceptives, and worse. Midwives risked the death penalty if they performed abortions for Aryan women, who on occasion sought the pleasures of sex without accepting the duties of German motherhood.[23] Chief among Hitler's demographic concerns were the childbearing patterns of *der deutschen Mutter,* who had been failing to replace herself during the years of the Weimar Republic. If she was "fit"—that is, Aryan—the German mother could earn a bronze Honor Cross for four or five children, a silver cross for six or seven, and a gold one for eight or more. "Unfit" mothers, by contrast, were shuffled off on the orders of local medical commissions for state-sanctioned sterilizations or, if already pregnant, abortions.

"In every nation of militaristic tendencies," Sanger had argued in *Woman and the New Race,* published in 1920, "we find the reactionaries demanding a higher and still higher birthrate . . . As soon as the country becomes overpopulated, these reactionaries proclaim loudly its moral right to expand [and] to take by force such room as it needs." In the decades that followed, Hitler proved her words prophetic. "In my state," he declared in a 1934 speech, "the mother is the most important citizen." That a woman might enjoy her body's sexual expression and determine for herself when to bear a child was not an idea *der Führer* could stomach for his Reich of a thousand years.[24]

The horrors of Nazism, exposed most vividly as Allied troops entered the concentration camps of central Europe, brought a swift end to the popularity of eugenics. A few scholars with interest in the field soldiered on, and two scientific journals carried the word in their names until the late

1960s, publishing papers on demography and contraception (and little on eugenics per se), some of which are still cited today. A fading eugenic culture in some southern state governments still left room for dozens of documented cases of coerced sterilizations, most often of African Americans, as late as the early 1970s. These abuses eventually fueled an important counterpoint to Sanger's focus on a women's right to say no to childbearing. Women also needed the right to say *yes* to childbearing, despite discouragement from the larger society. Carried into the reproductive rights advocacy community mostly by minority women, this crucial point brought diversity and balance to what had been a largely white movement. And it refined a message—reproduction *as often*, equally valid to *as rarely*, as a woman chooses—that has infused international advocacy for sexual and reproductive health and rights to this day.

Return to Quantity

To the surprise of demographers and campaigners for birth control, the decades that followed World War II saw the most dramatic increases in population the world had ever known. In industrialized countries, the combination of returning soldiers and the prosperity of postwar reconstruction yielded baby booms no demographer had foreseen. U.S. fertility rates approached four children per woman by the mid-1950s, having bottomed out at little more than two during the Depression. Western European and Canadian women were less fertile than the Americans, but minibooms occurred across the Atlantic and north of the forty-ninth parallel as well. For the many demographers who had argued that prosperity and small families marched in lockstep, the baby buggies of the affluent 1950s were an embarrassing reminder that science is perpetually a work in progress.

The larger influence on global demographic trends, however, was the growth seen outside of North America and Europe. Public health initiatives introduced in the remaining and former European colonies were reducing death rates dramatically—by 30 to 50 percent in some countries. Vaccinations, improved water supply, sanitation, roads and railroads to move crops to markets, food and fertilizer aid, hygiene education, and more than a few applications of the pesticide DDT—each of these steps, large and small, slashed away at the high rates of infant and child death that for centuries had clamped down population growth in Asia, Latin America, and Africa.

Birthrates, too, were rising modestly in some places, making their own small contributions to growth. Improved health and nutrition are the most commonly cited reasons for this, but a loss of traditional contraceptive methods may have played a role as well. As in Europe centuries earlier, juggernauts of economic and social change may have swept aside whatever biologically active herbal contraceptives and emmenogogues had survived the European colonization of the tropical world, leaving behind only a few ineffective charms and amulets for women to rely on.

The surplus of births over deaths, in any event, was large and growing. Within a decade of the World War II's end, populations were growing by more than 3 percent a year in many of Europe's colonies and in newly independent nations. The world's growth rate exceeded 1.8 percent. If humanity had ever multiplied so fast before, it could only have been in the mists of prehistory, when every member of the species *Homo sapiens* would have fit into a football stadium, had one been around.

Scientists, technocrats, bureaucrats, journalists, and more than a few laypersons developed a fretful fascination with this burst of population growth. Where would it lead? When—and how—would it end?[25] In 1949 the new United Nations set up a Population Division, from whose calculator-laden desks emerged thick reports tracking world population and projecting its future. It was obvious to U.S. and European governments that the annual population growth rates of 3 percent in the postcolonial world exceeded the growth rates of most economies. Some experts genuflected to the ghost of

Malthus, noting that many countries were falling steadily behind in the race to feed their own people. Yet few experts at this stage could imagine actually *doing* anything to slow population growth.

Without intending to, industrialized countries themselves had helped bring about this rapid demographic expansion. Public health measures introduced from Europe and North America to keep infants and children alive had the side effect of boosting family size and hence population growth rates in the rest of the world. Less developed countries were struggling to adjust to numbers and densities of people they had never experienced and for which they were scarcely prepared. But reversing this process without giving up the effort to boost child survival was a problem. How could people in wealthy countries promote the use of birth control in poor ones? The topic was always awkward, and often taboo. The influential Roman Catholic Church forcefully opposed "artificial" contraception, which effectively eliminated effective modern methods. Religious leaders in Islamic countries reacted more diversely but often with just as much hostility. So it could not be the West (or, as it came to be called later, "the North") that pushed for the world's first policies aimed to pull down soaring population trajectories. Instead, it was national governments in Asia and North Africa.

In 1948, in the midst of its postwar occupation by U.S. forces, Japan's diet legalized contraceptive sterilization and abortion. News stories depicting the horrors of botched illegal abortions in the wake of Japan's defeat had mobilized public and political support for making both options legally available to Japanese couples. The country's total fertility rate began what must have been the most precipitous fall the world had ever seen, from roughly four to two children per woman in less than a decade. It was almost as if the women of Japan couldn't wait to return to the small families their foremothers had known in the eighteenth century. Within a few years of this postwar reproductive revolution, the recently vanquished nation became a manufacturing and trade powerhouse that drove the phrase "made in Japan" into every corner of the industrialized world. Much later, in the 1990s, economists would recognize that such rapid fertility decline could produce a "demographic dividend" by reducing the proportion of dependent children and allowing more of the wages of working parents and the revenue of governments to flow toward long-term investments rather than short-term consumption.[26]

By 1955, India, Taiwan, Ceylon (now Sri Lanka), and Egypt had taken tentative steps to slow the growth of their populations by establishing programs through which married couples could secure methods to prevent unwanted pregnancy. The strategies followed in the steps of the neo-Malthusians and Margaret Sanger: *Offer all married adults family planning information and contraceptives. Couples will use them. Fertility and population growth rates will fall.* Sanger's prewar visits to Japan and India and the colonial exposure of India and Egypt to British thinking may have played some role. So, no doubt, did the visits of Western experts sponsored by U.S. foundations interested in population. But it would take much more than this to bring the governments of *industrialized* nations into direct action on world population.

Politics

In 1958 President Dwight D. Eisenhower tapped William Draper Jr., a businessman, former general, and veteran of several government assignments, to lead a presidential committee studying U.S. military assistance. Exceeding his orders, Draper pushed the committee to consider foreign aid generally. In a report the following year the committee recommended that the U.S. government "respond to requests for information and technical assistance in connection with population growth" and "increase its assistance to local programs related to maternal and child welfare."[27] The recommendations were euphemistic—a Catholic member of the Draper Committee insisted there be no explicit mention of birth control—but

Eisenhower got the point. "I cannot imagine anything more emphatically a subject that is not a proper political or governmental activity or function or responsibility," he told a press conference when a reporter asked about the commission's recommendation. "The problem of birth control [is] not our business."[28]

The 1960 presidential election was just a year away, and news media pundits considered a young Catholic senator from Massachusetts the likely Democratic standard bearer. "The problem of birth control" looked to Eisenhower like a land mine placed hazardously close to the nation's Catholic voters. But the president's dismissal of a governmental role in birth control was not to prevail. Rapid world population growth had become a palpable worry to many typical newspaper readers, including typical newspaper-reading bureaucrats and politicians. Eisenhower came to regret his resistance to U.S. foreign population aid. As if to make amends— but only after he left the White House—he became honorary cochairman of the Planned Parenthood Federation of America, along with former president Harry S. Truman.

Even the Catholic Church couldn't stop the momentum of U.S. concerns about population growth. John F. Kennedy, the former Massachusetts senator and first Catholic president, gave a green light to federal government action on world population. Like the national programs of India and Egypt, the U.S. program of international family planning assistance started out small and tentative. But within a decade the U.S. Agency for International Development (USAID) was supervising a $125 million program (worth over $585 million in 2007 dollars) to distribute U.S.-made contraceptives to countries around the world.

Despite Kennedy's initiative, population was no liberal Democratic issue. Democrats tended to line up with the labor movement's position that in numbers lie strength, not low wages. Republicans disagreed among themselves on whether population trends were worth worrying about. But most in Washington, D.C., who favored U.S. action on the issue were with the Grand Old Party. One of the strongest supporters in the House of Representatives from 1967 to 1970 was Republican George H. W. Bush, then representing the Seventh District of Texas and later president of the country. For his enthusiastic promotion of family planning at home and abroad, Bush earned the derisive nickname "Rubbers" from Wilbur Mills of Arkansas, the powerful Democratic chairman of the House Ways and Means Committee. (Mills's own career faded ignominiously after he was caught years later drunkenly carousing with a stripper named Fanne Fox.)[29]

Beyond U.S. shores, a United Nations conference on human rights, held in Tehran in 1968, established for the first time a basis in rights for the provision of family planning to all. "Parents have a basic human right to determine freely and responsibly the number and spacing of their children," the participating national delegations affirmed.[30] In the same year, Paul Ehrlich's book *The Population Bomb* was published, helping to mark an enduring divide between those who celebrated individual childbearing decisions as the basis of sustainable population and those who despaired about the demographic future no matter what options were available to childbearers. Writers who limned the perils of population growth took little interest in governmental efforts to enable couples to time and limit pregnancies. Some writers were frank in stating that much more urgent and direct action was needed to end world population growth.

In 1970, a U.S. Congress more sympathetic to the view of George H. W. Bush than to that of Wilbur Mills voted to offer family planning services to Americans with low incomes. Some supportive congressmen included the growth of U.S. population among the arguments for passage. The new law— Title X of the Public Health Service Act—brought within view and in her own country Margaret Sanger's dream of universal access to birth control. Federal largesse for family planning services, however, came nowhere near eliminating unintended pregnancy in the United States. Then, as now, nearly half of all pregnancies were wanted later or not at all by the women involved. But the new program undoubtedly contributed to the fall of U.S. total fertility rates from 2.5 children per woman in 1970 to fewer than 2 by 1980. Later Congresses were less enthusiastic about the program, however, which helps explain why U.S. fertility later rebounded, reaching 2.1 children per woman today.

The United Nations, USAID, and many of the world's governments operated on an assumption that contrasted with the view of so many population writers: that women able to decide at any given time whether to become pregnant would end up on average having two children. Even as early as the late 1960s, when Ehrlich and others were writing pessimistically about population growth, evidence was accumulating that this assumption was valid.

"Where in the world is there a country wherein people truly have the freedom and ability to control their fertility and where there is a continuing large excess use of their reproductive powers?" asked Reimert Ravenholt, director of USAID's Office of Population, in 1969. "In Japan and several countries of Eastern Europe the net reproduction rate has fallen below 1 [i.e., below replacement fertility], and social concern has shifted from the problem of too-great reproduction to concern for the possibly too-low reproductive rate."[31] Nearly forty years later, the close correlation between access to effective contraception and average family sizes of two children or less still holds true.

A Canny Strategy?

In 1969, one year after the Tehran declaration of family planning as a human right, the United Nations launched a Fund for Population Activities to consolidate monies from donor governments and distribute them to family planning programs in poor countries. For a decade or more, there wasn't much data to prove this was a canny strategy. Organizing, promoting, and providing family planning services is detail work, and the U.S. government paid for reams of technical reports to work out the minutiae.

The 1960s had seen the invention of the oral contraceptive pill and the IUD, revolutionary contraceptives that for the first time in human history assured reversible prevention of pregnancy without actually interfering with sex itself. But there were side effects to be considered, and training sufficient personnel to counsel users was a significant challenge. More and more women (and some men) showed up at clinics around the world, and many took home the contraceptives and started to use them. Still, throughout the late 1960s and early 1970s fertility and population growth rates in all but a few countries weren't changing enough to measure.

Ethical standards from the beginning stressed voluntarism in family planning programs, but in practice some promoters of family planning stretched the meaning of the word. Early on, a concept known as information, education, and communication, or IEC, evolved to help guide the promotion of contraceptive services. But the line in IEC campaigns that separated the benefits of contraception for clients from aggressive marketing and sometimes heavy-handed propaganda on the benefits of small families was never easy to draw. Pressured to show results, some programs and staff in parts of India and Bangladesh offered incentives to couples considering contraception. Most such incentives were fairly innocuous and arguably reasonable. Without a few rupees for bus fare, for example, many women found it impossible to visit a health clinic that might evaluate problems in pregnancy as well as help them prevent one.

Any money moving from family planning clinics to clients, however, risked the appearance of payments to prevent pregnancy. There's no convincing documentation that such incentives ever amounted to much more than small change. Some critics have nonetheless argued that potential clients in certain Asian programs outside of China, where examples of coercion are well documented even in recent years, felt browbeat or even bribed into using contraception.[32]

In India in 1976, family planning authorities, operating under a federal state of emergency, rounded up at least some men in low-income, high-fertility rural areas and forcibly vasectomized them. So enthusiastic were the some of the sterilizers that Shahu Laxman Ghalake, a peasant from the village in Kavhe in the state of Maharashtra, had his *vas deferens* clipped even though, as he insisted unsuccessfully to the doctor and the men who held him down, he had already been sterilized thirteen years earlier.[33] It has never been clear how many men were vasectomized. When the Indian government later offered compensation to men and women who could document having been forcibly sterilized during this period, few men and no women stepped forward, though fear of stigma may have discouraged potential claimants. But the incidents were enough to make the newspapers, alerting readers to the family planning movement's excesses. India's national family planning program has never quite recovered, and the stigma contributed to the defeat of Mrs. Gandhi and her party at the polls the next year.

In Bangladesh and Indonesia, women who sought to have IUDs removed from their uteruses, or Norplant rods from their upper arms, sometimes found to their dismay that physicians had received insufficient training or lacked experience in taking out the devices, despite their competence inserting them. In Peru, Mexico, and Brazil, physicians sometimes made their own decisions about what their patients needed—and surreptitiously tied the fallopian tubes of women just after childbirth.

In the context of large family planning programs in dozens of countries, such tactics were the exception. Much more common were clinics in which women's preferred contraceptive methods suddenly became unavailable, forcing them to choose a less desirable or inappropriate alternative or to give up on contraception altogether. Or poorly paid workers in poorly staffed clinics failed to give clients the personal attention they deserved and the contraceptives their circumstances warranted. These limitations are anything but history. When I traveled in Kenya in late 2006, I heard the stories of poorly supplied and staffed reproductive health clinics that were little different from those I had heard in other countries fifteen years earlier. If anything, in the wake of the shift in health spending toward HIV treatment and prevention in Kenya, family planning services in the country have deteriorated—a story matched, increasingly, elsewhere in Africa and other parts of the developing world.

Like India's, some family planning programs relied during the 1970s and 1980s mostly on sterilization. What young and newly sexually active women much more often needed was a way to delay their first pregnancy, not to end their childbearing altogether. A few programs were almost comically error-prone. In the early days of condom promotion in Thailand, sex workers were hired to measure the penises of their male clients so that condoms could be manufactured in the right sizes for the Thai market. The research results were only partially useful, however, because the women were unable to obtain measurements of a statistically significant sample of organs in their flaccid state.[34] In 1972, obstetrician-gynecologist Allan Rosenfield discovered that Thai women were less likely to keep using contraceptive pills when physicians prescribed them than when women could obtain the pills from midwives.[35] In Thailand, as elsewhere, "wise women" were the traditional keepers of knowledge about childbearing, including prevention. Rosenfield's revelation points to a pitfall of some early programs: too often, they failed to consider the traditions and preferences of the populations they served.

A Shy Revolution

Despite the half loaf of imperfect programs, however, the neo-Malthusian model of "population control" actually began to work. Population was not really controlled, of course. It never is. But gradually, and then at accelerating speeds in several countries, use of contraceptives went up, average family size went down, and population growth rates slowed. The mostly Roman Catholic island nation of Malta followed Japan's track to replacement fertility in the 1960s. Thailand, Taiwan, Singapore, Hong Kong, South Korea, Tunisia, Sri Lanka, and Colombia experienced comparable fertility falls in the 1970s and 1980s. From the late 1980s to 2005, Iran's fertility plummeted from nearly six children per woman to two, after the country's Shia Muslim government ordered contraceptive counseling and provision for all newlyweds. (The country's president, Mahmoud Ahmadinejad, called in 2006 for a higher rate of population growth, but his comments did not appear to undermine the country's family planning program.) And if Mexico once was characterized by large families, it is no longer: average fertility hovered in 2007 around 2.2 children per woman, leading some Mexican leaders to worry about population aging and even future decline. (This also suggests that the country will send fewer emigrants to the United States in future years.) Stories of family-size decline are similar in Morocco, Indonesia, and many other countries still considered part of the developing world.

Defying the expectations of economists, countries didn't even need to get wealthier to become less fertile. Cuba, its economy in tatters throughout the 1960s and 1970s, ended the latter decade with a fertility rate of two children per woman, half what the rate was at the time of the 1959 revolution. Per capita incomes barely budged in Bangladesh as fertility fell from five to three children per woman from the 1980s to today. The story was similar in Sri Lanka, Tunisia, and Kenya, where government commitment to family planning proved a far more important force for fertility decline than rising per capita income. Pioneers setting up new family planning clinics often were surprised to find crowds of women waiting in line, anxious to begin using contraception as soon as possible.

In the late 1990s, primatologist Jane Goodall and colleagues in Tanzania dispatched a team of health professionals to discuss family planning in villages surrounding the Gombe National Park, home of the chimpanzees Goodall has studied for several decades. The team members were unsure how the topic would fare among the devout Muslims, Catholics, and Seventh-day Adventists who lived (often side by side) in these communities. They needn't have worried. Goodall was on hand to hear from the team members after their first foray to the villages, and they were smiling: "Every single village said to us, 'Why didn't you come before? We need this information.'"[36]

By the 1980s it was obvious that women and many of their partners wanted later pregnancies and fewer of them. Where governments introduced family planning programs, contraceptive use rose almost immediately, followed not long after by falling fertility and population growth rates. The correlation among the three—government commitment to family planning programs, contraceptive prevalence, and completed family size—is more consistent than the commonly cited one between girls' average years of completed education and how many children they end up having.

The use of contraception expanded by 75 to 80 percent on average every decade beginning with the 1960s. Today more than three-fifths of reproductive-age women or their partners use contraception, a proportion made more impressive by the fact that another fifth of such women at any given time are either trying to get pregnant, are already pregnant, or are not engaging in heterosexual intercourse. One result of all this planning of families is that their size has shrunk in every part of the planet. The average women gave birth to five children in 1965. Today the average is just over half of that.

The difference that family planning programs have made to childbearing patterns—and the difference these have made to the world—are truly revolutionary. As revolutions go, however, this one has been pretty shy. No loyal constituency touts the fact that most acts of human sexual intercourse today are protected against the risk of conception. A handful of demographers and public health advocates point out that this means healthier mothers and children, fewer abortions, and more opportunities for women. Next to no one notices that the world's current total fertility rate (2.6 children per woman) is just one-quarter of a child—that impossible fraction again—above its replacement fertility rate (2.34, and much too high for comfort).

Policy makers and bureaucrats would have a hard time legislating as huge a change in childbearing patterns as has occurred voluntarily. China is a special case, with an ancient cultural preference for the collective over the individual good and a Communist government acutely aware of the pressure the country's 1.3 billion people exert on its natural resources. Even China's low fertility, however, arguably owes more to a growing preference for small families—true among Chinese populations in Taiwan and in other countries as well—than the government's unevenly enforced one-child policy.

It's not even clear that falling birthrates are the result, as is often claimed, of "changing ideas about the family." Sure, some ideas have changed, but did women and their partners around the world suddenly decide in the last three decades that large families weren't such a great idea after all? Not likely. The history of women's efforts to prevent pregnancy suggests that few have ever actually wanted frequent childbearing and large families, unless to conform to cultural norms. When researchers Bamikale Feyisetan and John Casterline studied the growing use of contraceptives in Latin America, Asia, and Africa from the 1970s through the 1990s, they found that downshifts in desired family size were much less influential than satisfaction of long pent-up demand for small families. The demand to time reproduction was already there—who knows for how long?—when contraception became at option.[37]

For the history of human population, the implications of this are significant but mostly unexplored. How much childbearing in excess of replacement fertility rates has arisen not out of women's intentions, but out of their inability to prevent unwanted pregnancy? What if the answer were "most"? What if that has been the answer for centuries? We can see the impact of contraception if we assume that most of the change in family size that has occurred since the 1970s stems from women's success at avoiding births they did not want. If fertility rates had not fallen as they did from the 1970s to the present, with all else equal, population would now total about 8.5 billion people, instead of 6.7 billion.[38] With a world population that size—growing economically at today's rates and with today's technologies—humanity would be a lot farther down the road toward a human-warmed planet, peak production of oil, freshwater scarcity, and the loss of nature and the wild. The baiji dolphin, recently judged extinct from its Chinese river habitat, might well be just one of several large animals never again to be with us on the planet.

One Hand Clapping

In the early years of the twenty-first century, organized family planning is in many ways a victim of its own success. Its adversaries remain the hierarchy of the Roman Catholic Church, joined by some evangelical Christian and Muslim leaders, and male political elites that see women's control of their own sexuality and childbearing as threats to dreams of national power.

"They plan . . . to block our growth," wrote the editor of El Salvador's *Diario de Hoy* of U.S. family planning advocates back in 1963, "slashing the wombs of Latin mothers, castrating Latin males, before we have grown sufficiently or taken possession of the vast empty lands of the continent."[39] Four and a half decades later, family planning services remain rare and underfunded in El Salvador, abortion is punitively criminalized, and the country's population has more than doubled since the editorial was written, from 3 million to 7 million people. Archaeological excavations suggest that people living fourteen centuries ago in what is now El Salvador ate more diverse diets and occupied sturdier and more comfortable housing than do most of those in the country today.[40] An additional 2 million or so Salvadorans now live in the United States, where they have taken possession not of vast empty lands, but of apartments that are often crowded and jobs that are often poorly paid.

The U.S. Supreme Court's 1973 decision legalizing abortion severed the population and family planning field from its early hopes of public acceptability. The Catholic hierarchy effectively directed its political influence against modern contraception and the contention that human population could ever grow too large—scientific views to the contrary. In 1994 the Pontifical Academy of Sciences shocked its patrons by concluding that advances in life-saving technologies "have made it unthinkable to sustain indefinitely a birth rate that notably exceeds the level of two children per couple." Replacement fertility rates, the advisory group insisted, were "the requirement to guarantee the future of humanity." Embarrassed and annoyed, Pope John Paul II immediately distanced himself from the findings and made sure the media registered his disapproval.[41]

After Ronald Reagan tapped George H. W. Bush to be his running mate in the 1980 presidential election, the former Congressman Rubbers told a friend there would be no more talk about population and family planning. Reagan built much of his political base among Americans embittered by legalized abortion, and Bush exploited the same base for his own ends when he succeeded Reagan as president—as did his son, the later President George W. Bush. Much of that base refuses to accept the logic that widespread use of birth control prevents abortions, preferring to believe that contraception just encourages sex, which ends up causing more abortions when contraception fails.

Hostility to family planning among U.S. leaders spreads like an infection among governments, sapping energy and funding from programs that could lead to both healthy reproduction and demographic stability. But poor leadership isn't the only problem. There's not much "followership" on the issue either. Few people are aware that easy access everywhere to good family planning services is most of what's needed to achieve a sustainable world population. As growth has slowed, news media worldwide—once influential in bringing the "population explosion" to public attention—have turned their attention to the seemingly fresher story of population aging and decline. Fully 45 percent of the world's population lives in countries in which total fertility rates are below their population-specific replacement fertility rates.[42] Unless fertility rebounds or immigration surges, these populations are poised to stop growing once today's childbearers grow old. Some countries—Russia, Germany, and Japan among them—are already losing population. If the story is population decline, for popular media that find nuance and internal contradiction challenging to convey, it can't also be population growth. How can the world be gaining 78 million people each year when "there's no more population 'explosion'"?[43] It can't be happening—or if it is, it's not news.

As in the media, so in the world. If they think about population growth at all, most policy makers tend to see it as a twentieth-century worry that never matched its crisis billing and is no longer an issue. The topic couldn't fade fast enough for many advocates of women's interests. Family planning suffers from its long association with "population control," a concept some see as an embarrassing relic of patriarchal attitudes long ago discarded. Rather than consider a strategic alliance with environmentalists and others who still express concern about human numbers, most advocates today prefer to leave population out of the picture altogether, discussing contraception as simply one aspect of women's reproductive health. Such views work their way into governments and related bodies and carry weight in international discussions and negotiations.

To some extent, the world's governments consciously chose to think of family planning removed from population growth. In 1994, the International Conference on Population and Development convened in Cairo to consider world population, and the meeting was noted in the media mostly for its rancorous battles over abortion. That issue came no closer to resolution than it ever has, but the conference did adopt the view that women, rather than population per se, should be the focus of "population policies." At the close of the conference, representatives of almost all the world's governments agreed to make family planning universally available by 2015 and to significantly expand assisted birth, improve maternal and child health, and prevent HIV and other sexually transmitted diseases. The agreement foresaw global spending of about $11.5 billion a year in 1994 dollars (nearly $16 billion in 2007 dollars) to make family planning fully available in developing countries. Spending has never approached even half that level, however, and it has been flat or declining since the conference took place.[44] Had governments enacted the agreement reached in Cairo, world population probably would now be poised to peak in the next few decades.

Despite high hopes, however, the common goals expressed by the Cairo conferees not only haven't been accomplished, they aren't even agreed on any more. Once most opinion leaders concluded by the mid- to late 1990s that population growth was no longer a pressing issue for the world, concern for women's health failed to motivate much more than paltry increases in funding for reproductive health—until the global HIV/AIDS pandemic was recognized and addressed. In 2000, when the United Nations governments crafted a set of Millennium Development Goals (MDGs) to take a big dent out of global poverty by 2015, most negotiators were weary and wary of the arguments on abortion that grafted themselves onto all discussions of population and reproductive health. The religious right argued that the very phrase *reproductive health* was code for abortion rights and amounted to a wink and a nod to promiscuity among teenagers. The entire concept was excluded from the MDGs, only to be squeezed into supporting language later by advocates who realized almost too late how badly they had been blindsided.

By abandoning the argument that slower population growth is one benefit of reproductive health services, these advocates let slip a line of reasoning that at least captures the attention of distracted public and policy audiences, most of them indifferent to the inherent values of healthy sexuality and reproduction. In 2006, President George W. Bush proposed cutting U.S. international family planning assistance from $436 million in the subsequent fiscal year to $357 million. An assistant administrator at USAID cited increases in spending to combat HIV and malaria, along with a program to reduce sexual violence in Africa, as evidence that the president had offered "a much better budget than we've had in the past for women's health."[45] On that turf, his argument was plausible, and no reproductive health advocates challenged him. But family planning is about not just women's health, but about all the options that women, their partners, and their children can enjoy in life. And it's about sex, and about a vision of human numbers steered by wanted rather than unwanted pregnancies. These broader connections have largely faded from the discussion, and the case for reproductive health is weaker as a result.

In some of the places where population growth chugs on most rapidly, demographic debates are more alive than ever. In the Philippines, facing 2 percent demographic growth and deepening poverty, legislators promoting bills to increase access to modern contraception face opposition from President Gloria Macapagal-Arroyo and the Catholic Church. In Pakistan, clerics are beginning to promote the benefits of family planning. The government recently considered offering free secondary-school education to families with only one child, a novel twist on China's population policy that at least relies on a positive incentive but that still bypasses the hard-slogging work of offering good family planning services throughout the country.[46]

In Yemen, a census completed in 2005 showed that the already water-scarce population of 19.7 million was growing at 3.2 percent annually, precisely the economic growth rate. Wealth was standing still, and water was receding. "We very badly need family planning," commented President Ali Abdullah Saleh. A survey a few months later, however, showed that use and awareness of reproductive health services was declining in the country, with only one in five married women using any kind of contraception.[47]

Despite gaining attention in a few countries, population dynamics and the expansion of family planning services are largely missing from discussions of public policy. In a recent survey of reproductive health insiders, researchers Amy Tsui and Ann Blanc provocatively asked whether the family planning movement is entering its "final stage"—demise—and suggested that any hope for its future lies in the rise of new leadership in the countries most in need of services.[48] No doubt that's true. But the efforts of countries like the Philippines, Pakistan, and Yemen, not to mention China, painfully demonstrate how much could be gained by more and better global cooperation on this preeminently global issue.

To the extent that policy makers in wealthy countries are thinking about population at all today, the talk is mostly of subsidizing childbearing domestically or attracting the best and brightest immigrants from developing countries. That's certainly one approach to population policy. But unless governments focus on creating the conditions by which births result from the conscious decisions of women and their partners to parent a child, there's no reason to be confident that global family size will

fall to a two-child average. Even if it does, the grand, one-time-only experiment—how many of us can the earth and we ourselves sustain?—will
continue, for a few decades at least, in the only available laboratory, the
only available home.

TEN

The Return of Nature

There has never in human history been a long term technological fix; there have merely been bridges to the next level of stress and crisis. We will only change this pro-gression when we understand our problems are those of human or cultural behavior, not inadequate machines.
   —George Brown Jr., chairman of the U.S. House Science Committee in the
   102nd and 103rd Congresses

Where women's status in every way approaches that of men, fertility rates most nearly approach the sustainable population "replacement" level.
   —Martha Farnsworth Riche, director of the U.S. Census
   Bureau from 1994 to 1998.

I n Greek legend, it was the blind seer Tiresias who revealed to King Oedipus of Thebes—an unwanted child abandoned at birth by his par-ents—that he had killed his father and married his mother. Sigmund Freud famously explained this myth as a metaphor for the male sexual unconscious. Rarely told, however, is how Oedipus's aged informant had lost his sight.

Years before he met up with Oedipus, Tiresias encountered two snakes copulating and tried to separate them with his staff. Undissuaded, the serpents simply writhed around the staff and each other, and the caduceus was born. Ultimately it became a winged scepter carried by Hermes (a god whose name derived from boundary stones adorned with erect phalluses). Through a twisting path, an ancient symbol rooted in animal sex—and a man's failed attempt to obstruct it—came to symbolize the healing arts early in the twentieth century after it was adopted by the U.S. Army Medical Corps. Someone in the corps, it seems, confused the caduceus with the ancient and less overtly sexual symbol of medicine, a single snake curling around a staff.

Tiresias's fate, however, had only begun to unfold. For his attempt to interfere with the sex of snakes, the gods turned him into a woman, and he walked the earth in female form for seven years until he (or she) once again saw two snakes in the act, and once again tried to separate them with a staff. This repeated gesture returned Tiresias to her (or his) male form. Having enjoyed sex throughout this uniquely transgendered experience, Tiresias qualified as the ideal judge when Zeus and Hera wanted to know whose orgasm, man's or woman's, was more satisfying. Tiresias declared the female orgasm the winner, explaining that men experienced just one-tenth of the pleasure available in sex, while women experienced the other nine-tenths. This response infuriated Hera, and she blinded the seer. Mythology scholar Walter Burkert finds Hera's anger inscrutable, but I can imagine her dismay.[1] Tiresias had given men yet another reason to resent, even while craving, the very act that regenerates humanity. Out of male resentment much female suffering arose.

The classical Greeks had an ambiguous relation to sex. Why, Greek men wondered, couldn't they just arrange with a priest to receive a son at the local temple and be done with the messy business of relating to women? This male discomfort with reproduction has helped shape population dynamics for a very long time; it's reflected in most of the world's great religions and in the modern culture of global commerce. That culture manages to shunt sexual and reproductive realities into the shadows, even while it uses adolescent sexual imagery to market products and equates population stability with the end of prosperity.

In this book I have suggested clues to the riddle of why men dominate women more often than the reverse, how that affects attitudes about sex and reproduction, and how all this has influenced the interaction of population and the environment. The ideas developed here don't assume differences between the genders aside from the obvious bodily ones: Women give birth. Men, on average, are bigger and stronger. On these two commandments, to paraphrase Jesus, hang all my hypotheses and speculations.

The skills human females developed to keep their offspring alive, from assisted birth to communicative group parenting, facilitated ancient bursts of population growth that eventually gave *Homo sapiens* earthly dominion. That growth helped give rise to art, technology, and new social organizations, but it also tended to push groups up against natural and social constraints. Women more than men understood the risks of childbearing during hard times—and the risks of frequent childbearing at all times. From as early as such thoughts could be formed, women would have sought ways to prevent pregnancy, childbirth, or (as a last resort) commitment to mothering a newborn child. Such endeavors, however, would have often run afoul of group interests in having more children and larger populations in order to supply leaders with workers, soldiers, subjects, and devotees. The development of agriculture led to the social arrangements that most effectively severed women from the realization of their reproductive intentions—until the breakthroughs of modern contraception and women's demands for equal rights over the last two centuries began to turn the tide.

Now the tide has indeed turned. Most women around the world use contraception, and women globally give birth to an average of just 2.6 children. Human population grows more slowly than it did forty years ago, but nonetheless is approaching 7 billion in a rapidly warming world. It's a good

time to ask: What next? Will fertility move lower still? Will human population eventually peak and then subside, but with fast-changing national and
ethnic balances because family size varies so much around the world? Or will
governments and the public continue to lose interest in population and family planning, leaving fertility to settle about where it is and population to keep
growing until rising death rates set in?

I don't know what *will* happen. I'm more interested in what *could*
unfold if societies choose to hasten the cresting of the demographic wave
by supporting women in timing their reproduction and in living as equals
with men. As British climate and energy specialist Michael Grubb has written, possible outcomes worth aiming for are "futures to guide us, not forecasts to fool us."[2]

Growth and Grandchildren

All historical eras are shaped by the material and environmental realities
of their time. Our own reflects the adjustments society and nature have made
to accommodate the unprecedented 6.7 billion human beings now alive. And
those changes are dramatic. The planet is warming dangerously as a result of
the heat-trapping byproducts of our daily lives. Half of the primeval forests
that existed at the end of the last ice age are gone. A mist of mercury and
other toxic metals from coal combustion falls continuously on land and
ocean, and to eat fish is to absorb these metals yourself. Half of us are now
urban, rarely if ever meeting up with creatures wilder than crows, cockroaches, and, in some cities, packs of feral dogs.

And this is just where we are *today*, while the beat of growth goes on.
Little if any of this would have transpired had human numbers peaked
long ago. Such a peak might have occurred by now, even with the gains in
life expectancy of the past century, if the status and reproductive intentions of women had found consistent support rather than silence and
censure.

Beginning little more than a century ago, social acceptance of contraception began to grow and to spread around the world. That led to dramatic declines in birthrates that gathered force as human population throttled past a few billion. Who knows how much closer we would be to a meltdown of Greenland's ice or the collapse of critical ocean fisheries had this collective wisdom—a public good derived from individuals acting in their private interest—not dampened the rise of population? Given the increasingly plausible threat of one or more interacting environmental catastrophes, the slowing of population growth is a triumph of human wisdom and good fortune. This realization is only slowly dawning, however, on the community of journalists and other opinion leaders.

The dominant concerns in many countries about population aging and decline are hardly baseless. These developments may well challenge societies. Populations may have more old people than young for a while, because yesterday's baby boomers are heading toward old age even as young women are having fewer children. Over time, however, extreme age disparities should subside as these large generations pass on, the more so when average fertility returns to close to two children per woman. Assuming it will.

Some demographers, eyeing the stubborn low fertility of women in most of Europe and parts of east Asia, are beginning to wonder if such a return to replacement fertility is possible. Some allude in cautionary tones to the possibility of a "low-fertility trap," a vast pool of demographic quicksand that prevents women from ever returning to replacement fertility once their childbearing average drops below about 1.5 births.[3] There's no real basis for such speculation, however. The world is too dynamic and our experience with intentionally low fertility far too new.

What might eventually unfold is something far more appealing: birth cohorts of consistently equal size across generations. The most demographically stable age structure for a population would be for each year's "class" of babies to be the same size as the one the year before, and ten, twenty-five, or fifty years before. No single age group, young or old, would naturally claim any more of society's attention than any other, at least based on their numbers. That's a population structure worth striving for.

For now, population aging is the inevitable outcome of two of the most positive developments of modern times: longer life spans and the realized intentions of women to have fewer children, later in their lives. Modern views on human rights and equality hardly would have allowed most women to continue giving birth to many more children than they wanted. And populations hardly could have continued growing in the twenty-first century at the same torrid pace as in the middle decades of the twentieth. Some populations had to be the first to experience the leveling off of growth and then decline, and in most cases this has occurred with no significant increases in death rates. That's rare, maybe even unprecedented, in human history.

Today, humanity still grows by 78 million people annually—the rough equivalent of a new Texas, California, and New York each year. Unless death rates rise catastrophically or birthrates plummet far more than anyone expects, the end of world population growth is still decades away. It's reasonable to expect that humanity will grow to 7 billion, 8 billion, or even higher before the number levels off for good reasons or bad.

What dominates our experience in the first decade of the third millennium are the technologies and institutions we have invented, disseminated, tinkered with, and improved over thousands of years to make human life on such scales possible. We've done well. Not only are more people alive than ever, but most of us live longer than our ancestors did. Quite a few of us spend our entire lives in comfort and with tools and toys that those ancestors never could have imagined.

I stress the adjustments we've made to adapt to our growing population because I grant Julian Simon, the late twentieth-century champion of perpetual population growth, this point: we human beings are, if not the "ultimate resource," at least awfully smart. When the going gets tough, the tough get patents. Had hunters and gatherers never run low on food and turned by necessity to cultivating it, we wouldn't have cities or symphonies or cell phones. I certainly wouldn't be typing on this laptop, anticipating a book that might appear in a bookstore window thousands of miles from my home. Innovation indeed is much of what makes human beings successful, but it also keeps the angels on the edge of their celestial seats, wondering, *Can they do it again?*

Each new pressure point creates the need for new innovation, and each new innovation produces effects of its own, many of them unintended and quite a few problematic. Why do things bite back, to borrow from the title of a recent book?[4] One reason (not actually mentioned in that book) is that it's getting crowded in here. In societies with low population densities relative to available natural resources, innovation's side effects often waft away, unimportant and unnoticed. In high-density societies, there's less tolerance for error, systems tend to be more sensitively balanced, and the scale of everything that people are doing is larger relative to the natural world. "When we try to pick out anything by itself," Scottish American conservationist John Muir wrote, "we find it is hitched to everything else in the Universe."[5] So what happens when 7 billion people pick out 7 billion things?

Losing Nature

We're finding out. Much of the human behavior we find unsustainable today is not so in its essence, but in its scale. Julian Simon used to say that more people leads paradoxically to more nature, but the history I've presented in this book makes clear that over the long sweep of time the trend is otherwise. The planet is in the early stages of a species extinction episode not seen since the dinosaurs disappeared. If you could somehow ask Mother Nature what she attributes this to, I think she'd likely say not just "people," but "this many people." Yes, some populous human societies plant trees to anchor vulnerable soils or set aside tracts of land for recreation or to preserve important ecosystems. How long the trees will grow remains a question, however. And the set-asides rarely protect all the land's wild inhabitants—not to mention the water or the steady climate that supports ecosystems over the long haul.

Protection is not necessarily forever. When the needs of growing populations press hard enough, in wealthy and poor countries alike, "set aside forever" often becomes a hollow promise. The biological reserve near where I swam years ago in southern Mexico is now pockmarked by the cleared land of impoverished squatters, whose needs can't ethically be denied or easily redirected to biologically less important land. Closer to my own home, the scarcity of affordable housing is undermining an agricultural reserve meant to save the last few farms of Montgomery County, Maryland. Wealthy societies tend to do a better job than poor ones of cleaning up environmental messes, but they rarely if ever improve upon what was there before the mess was made. Having more people might contribute in some cases to strengthening environmental protection, but not enough to matter over the long term.

In 1984 Simon and futurist Herman Kahn suggested that population growth can bring about more solitude, because more people own cars and elude the madding crowds on improved roads.[6] It would be interesting to poll drivers around the world about this assertion today. Earlier, Kahn had predicted dramatically new energy sources and undersea cities by the year 2000.[7] It's not just doomsayers on population and the environment whose forecasts sometimes don't pan out. So far, the twenty-first century is not proving at all kind to cornucopian predictions. While I was writing this book, the last backwaters of doubt that humans are propelling the planet toward uncontrolled warming dried up. Those who have claimed in the past that the environment just keeps getting better and better, thanks to wealth and technology, today seem strangely quiet.

"Ecosystems are at a tipping point," wrote the *Washington Post*, not usually known for tree-hugging advocacy, "verging on a collapse from which they won't recover." A front-page news story on "oil's new era" in the *Wall Street Journal* gave the last word on the subject to energy consultant Henry Groppe, who glumly suggested, "We have entered the era of scarcity and price rationing."[8]

I've been struck, too, by occasional expressions of almost hopeless inevitability about the impacts of population growth in the United States. "We're coming to the realization we can't meet the supply side" of drivers' demands for more roads, Ben Mannell, a Virginia Department of Transportation planning manager, told the *Washington Post*. "You can't put down enough pavement."[9]

A few years ago, Frank Wolf, a Republican congressman representing the northern Virginia suburbs of Washington, D.C., publicly switched sides on even discussing a new bridge across the Potomac River to supplement the routinely gridlocked one that carries the Beltway between Virginia and Maryland. Too many homeowners would be made anxious by the deliberation over alternate crossings, let alone the eventual bridge construction, Wolf wrote in a newspaper commentary. "What would be the effect on property values?" he asked. Homeowners ask the same question when utilities seek to string high-tension electric wires across metropolitan areas and energy companies plan new gasoline refineries.[10] New infrastructure that local population growth makes necessary, it seems, is now blocked by the rising property values that local population growth makes inevitable.

"You need to accept growth," Charles Walton, mayor of the Casa Grande, Arizona, told a *USA Today* reporter. "It's coming whether you want it or not." But he worried, too, that it would harm the quality of life for future generations. "I think I can tolerate it in my lifetime, but I feel very sorry for my grandchildren."[11] There's nothing inherently positive about continued population growth—quite the reverse—but by common perception it's inevitable, forever and ever, amen.

Perils of Adaptation

Despite the sense of dread and certainty, there don't seem to be any bright ideas for accommodating a lot more people, either in the United States or in the rest of the world. The gap between those with high and low incomes seems to grow wider by the year, driven at least in part by three megatrends closely related to population growth: rising housing costs, rising energy costs, and falling paychecks for unspecialized low-wage labor.

New housing starts are a good barometer of U.S. population growth. Divide each year's nearly 3 million additional U.S. inhabitants by two, about the average number of people moving into a new home, and you get 1.5 million housing starts. The number rises or falls depending on the state of the housing market, but it rarely strays far from that demo-graphically linked mark. If you own your shelter, your equity grows in tandem with its rising value. If you rent, it's your monthly payment that grows, and you have nothing to show for it other than a dwindling bank account. Home ownership is the greatest single wedge widening the U.S. wealth gap, and population growth is, over time, the heaviest hammer falling on it.

The same effect may operate abroad. A 2004 analysis by the International Monetary Fund found population growth to be second only to "bank cri-sis" among eight explanatory variables in the price of housing in industrial-ized countries. An increase in population growth rates by 1/4 percent will typically lead, the study predicted, to an increase in housing inflation by 1 percent.[12]

The adaptations we make to adjust to the growth of population tend to become problems themselves. As housing costs rise, owners and renters alike find themselves searching farther from downtowns for a place to live. Morning rush hour increasingly begins in the dark hours before dawn, but there are only so many of those hours available. People get by with less sleep, but they can't get by without any.[13] They pay for their longer commutes not only in lost time, but in greater use of gasoline—just as the cost per gallon is climbing. That, too, is driven up by population and economic growth not only in the United States but halfway around the world, where most of the 2.4 billion people living in China and India would like—and increasingly can afford—to drive automobiles. What happens when gasoline prices reach the point at which most workers can no longer afford to drive from exurban American homes to downtown offices and shops?

Even electricity is getting expensive in most of the United States, defying predictions that the utility deregulation of the 1990s would drive down rates. Demand rises consistently, largely because "consumers are buying more electronics, and there are more consumers," in the straightforward words of Douglas Faulkner, U.S. acting assistant secretary for energy efficiency in the Bush administration.[14] Not long ago, even environmentalists spoke hopefully of the Internet's capacity to knit the world together without killing trees for paper or sucking fossil fuels out of the earth's crust for transportation. But the sheer scale of computer use is shattering this promise. It's so easy to click on the little print icons on electronic documents that U.S. paper use is bigger than ever. Streaming videos, interactive games, Web pages, e-mails, and the computers that display all these have proliferated to such an extent that they suck up gigawatts of electricity, most of which is generated by burning fossil fuels. U.S.-based Internet companies that manage giant data centers now surf not the Web but the national electric grid for the cheapest juice they can find.[15]

In economics as in nature, scale matters. Growth in working-age populations tends to push down wages for work that requires few specialized skills, as evidenced by factories and call centers of Asia and lawns and offices of Los Angeles. Experts disagree about how strong this population-wage relationship is and how much of an economic problem results. But there's no doubt that the scale of recent immigration has led to wages below what they otherwise would be for many low-income Americans.[16] A point rarely made is that new arrivals also tend to reduce the wages of others who arrived just a bit earlier. "A hard worker used to be able to make $15 an hour here," a native of Tuxpan, Mexico, who owned a small gardening business on Long Island, told *Time*. "But there are too many workers here now. They're working for $10 an hour."[17] The same demographic forces make housing increasingly less affordable for immigrants as well as others. In the Washington, D.C., area, the Hispanic population fell 11 percent in Arlington, Virginia, from 2000 to 2005, a reflection of rising housing costs and redevelopment for affluent homebuyers there.[18]

I'm focusing on U.S. examples of the impacts of population growth in part because many of this book's readers may be able to look around and test what I'm saying against their own observations and experiences. It's a common view that population growth may be a problem in developing countries, but not in those industrialized ones where most of this book's readers probably live. That's oversimplified, of course. It's true that frustration over the local impacts of a large and growing U.S. population goes largely unexplored in the news media; but I suspect that it contributed to the outcry that crushed federal immigration reform while I was writing.

People feel the impacts of population growth all over the world. Even in Western Europe, whose population now grows by only 0.2 percent each year, centuries of much faster growth have left population density more than five times higher on average than in the United States. Truly wild land is all but nonexistent. If you can find a forest, the chances are good it's a rectangular field of trees machine-planted in orderly ranks, like transplanted hair plugs on a bald man's pate. Pavement and structures cover such a high proportion of the land that floodwaters tend to be swifter and more damaging to property than elsewhere in the world. A recent report on the "ecological footprint" of Europe calculated that the continent's people require the natural resources of more than two land masses its size.[19] Although per capita European energy and natural resource consumption is modest compared to that of the United States, this calculation suggests that Europeans nonetheless won't live sustainably until their population falls by half, assuming constant per capita consumption rates.

Faces of Want

In the industrialized world we feel the impacts of population growth and density in traffic congestion, in the inability to afford a home, or in paychecks we might have stretched further in a less crowded world. In many developing countries the toll is far higher and climbing faster. To explore this is to wade into the endless debate on the relative weight of the many causes of modern hunger, poverty, and violent conflict present in so many developing countries. Some points, however, are clear and well documented. Well over 800 million people—the number has been rising in recent years—are chronically undernourished, and during the 1990s the countries with the highest population growth rates made the least progress in reducing hunger.[20] Scarcities of water, closely tied to the tension between nature's fixed supply and the needs of growing human populations, are increasingly commonplace. Urban areas bid up water's price. Farmers lose access to water for irrigation precisely when rising food demand forces new production to rely on irrigation rather than rain. After generations of subdivision, farm plots are now so small in densely populated African countries that few young adults can hope to marry and launch families without moving to the city. "If I had known I would have so little land to pass down to my sons," a Zambian tribal chief once commented to his niece, my friend Wanga Grace Mumba, "I wouldn't have had so many sons."

Land shortage helps explain the genocidal conflict in Rwanda, which has one of the lowest ratios of cropland to people and the second lowest ratio of renewable freshwater to people in mainland Africa.[21] Such scarcities might also be behind the explosion of child abandonment seen most often among populations in which fertility is high and the use of contraceptives rare. Today some parents exile children they no longer want or no longer can support to urban streets. Or they sell them into early marriage, prostitution, or slavery.

Certainly the progressive degradation of cropland is among the reasons that the UN Population Division projects that in 2008, human beings will cross the threshold to being a mostly urban species. Cities have long stimulated the rich diversity of human culture, but in the world's most rapidly growing ones not many people are celebrating. Almost all urban expansions today are not planned neighborhoods, well supplied with infrastructure and services, but slums. Health indicators are often worse in cities than in the countryside that urban migrants left behind.[22] "I think we know cities in Kenya can hardly sustain the population they have," observed Doug Keating of Oxfam International on the prospects for rural exodus to cities as the organization helped pastoralist communities in northeast Kenya cope with a withering drought.[23]

The loss of forest cover, closely tied in developing countries to the ongoing need for more farmland, is among the biggest destroyers of species in a wave of extinctions comparable to those that occurred in the earth's remote and unpeopled past. It's an instructive irony that the places friendliest to the survival of biological diversity include the Demilitarized Zone between the two Koreas, various guerrilla-held areas of Colombia, and the "radioactive nature preserve" known as Chernobyl in the Ukraine.[24]

Without tree roots to anchor it, deforested soil easily changes form during heavy rains into flowing mud that seeks its own level—sometimes on top of a village. This is a sadly common story in densely populated and rapidly deforesting countries from the Philippines to Guatemala. The Ugandan farmers who hurt themselves falling off their steeply sloping fields, whose story opened this book, run the risks they do because nearby level land was deforested long ago and is already taken or has been farmed to exhaustion.

Human incursions into forests sometimes spur new pathogens to discover what a vast and inviting pool of protoplasm human bodies present. We're a bug's banquet. Our domesticated animal companions and livestock spread their own pathogens around in the wild, threatening species that have far smaller populations than theirs. We know from history that most infectious diseases tend to be closely related to population density and mobility, but the pace of pathogen exchange is occurring far more rapidly today than ever before. Malarial mosquitoes thrive in the pond waters of deforested land, and scientists are now confident that HIV/AIDS made its way from chimpanzees to humans a few decades ago, probably when a bushmeat hunter penetrated the forest, butchered his quarry, and absorbed some of its blood.[25]

In some places, even the traditional lifestyles of indigenous people who thrived in forests for centuries are no longer sustainable. Wildlife Conservation Society biologists Elizabeth Bennett and John Robinson calculated that tropical rainforests can support at most one subsistence hunter per square kilometer. "More than that and you're depleting the resource," Bennett told the *New York Times*. "There are few corners of the tropics at this moment that have so few people. You can probably still have it in remote sections of Amazonia. In Sarawak [in Malaysia], the indigenous people have the legal right to hunt. But there's been a population explosion, and there are three of them for every square kilometer of forest. That's three times the sustainable number. If they all employ their rights, they'll hunt out the forest."[26]

Bennett was not blaming indigenous people, who themselves suffer the effects of the growth of non-indegenous populations around them, for hunting out the forest. You might just as well blame an individual driver for a traffic jam. But the unsustainability is real, no matter how much we respect the dignity of indigenous individuals. It stems not from subsistence hunting itself, which is ancient, but from hunters' high population density, which is recent.

Bags of Ice

Thousands of years ago, subsistence hunters running out of prey, like those in Sarawak, became farmers whose descendents launched the world's great city-based civilizations. Such past adaptations made humans what we are today, but humanity stands in a quite different place now. Sum up the total mass of human beings, add all our pets and livestock (40 million farm animals are born each year in the United States alone[27]), and factor in our processing of energy and materials. We are a biological and geological force never previously witnessed. What once may have been win-win strategies of adaptation are now more often win-lose strategies—or desperation lose-lose plays. We are bulls in a china shop. Almost any turn we make sends the porcelain flying.

The use of fossil fuels and the Industrial Revolution itself began as science-based adaptations to energy scarcity and unsustainability. Coal, a dirty fuel long thought inferior to wood, was first used on a large scale around the sixteenth century as the forests of Europe were exhausted by large-scale land clearance for farming and the burning of wood for fuel and iron smelting. Today, the world burns nearly 5 billion metric tons of coal each year.[28] That's about three-quarters of a ton for each person on earth, with comparable combustion of oil and natural gas for each of us—all driving a human-induced warming of the planet whose endpoint we can't yet imagine. Even though the thought of tempering growth is not yet mainstream, the implausibility of growth without end is becoming more obvious in a closed-atmosphere, carbon-constrained world.

Humanity's energy dilemma becomes more obvious when we think clearly about alternative fuel sources. Adaptations, again, become problems. The sheer scale of human energy use is so vast that even today's small steps toward replacing fossil fuels with biofuels boost food prices and put ecologically valuable land at risk. The calories needed to keep a Hummer humming could feed a hundred humans. And anyone wealthy enough to own a Hummer can outcompete a hundred hungry people for the energy stored in plants. Enough solar energy to dent fossil-fuel use significantly would require panels and mirrors covering thousands of square miles of land, much of it valuable for other purposes. Enough windmills to do the same would draw howls of protest for visual pollution, their tendency to slice up heedless birds and bats, and the likelihood that large enough fields of turbines might even affect local weather.[29] Storing carbon in new forests will face the constraint that, as one analyst suggested glumly, "as the human population continues to grow . . . the earth's surface will be too disturbed."[30] Hydrogen as a fuel raises the question not only of what type of energy will be used to separate the element from water molecules, but of where that water will come from and what will be the impact of water vapor emitted by hundreds of millions of vehicles. Nuclear energy leaves us with the potential for proliferating weapons-grade plutonium and waste that takes hundreds of human lifetimes to become harmless. "No primary energy source, be it renewable or nonrenewable," write Jeffrey Chow, Raymond Kopp, and Paul Portney, analysts with the environmental think tank Resources for the Future, "is free of environmental or economic limitations."[31]

But suppose we fail to make this essential shift away from carbon-based fuels. Then, we can try to cool the earth's fevered surface literally with smoke and mirrors—massive injections of sulfur dioxide mist into the stratosphere, perhaps, or trillions of small reflective panels sent into orbit around the planet.[32] Feasible? Safe? Probably not, but such options are taken more seriously as the gap grows continually wider between actions taken and actions needed to avert future climate change.

One of my favorite Big Fixes is the oft-mentioned idea of towing polar icebergs to relieve freshwater scarcity. But how do you lasso an iceberg? How do you tow it, break it up, and distribute it? One group of scientists calculated recently that there's enough ice in the world's largest recorded iceberg—a frozen island the size of Jamaica that broke off the Ross Ice Shelf in Antarctica in March 2000—to provide everyone on earth a ten-pound bag of ice cubes every day for the next seventy-five years.[33] The scientists didn't account, of course, for population growth. But more to the point, what happens when the iceberg is used up? The world's people will be standing there, more numerous than ever and parched, waiting for bags of ice that will no longer arrive.

One way to reduce climate dangers, of course, is to disperse the risk of unintended consequences by diversifying the alternative sources of energy used. The more sources of energy, the less any one of them needs to be relied upon and scaled up to massive proportions. That makes dangerous side-effects and tipping points less likely. Another strategy for avoiding climate risk is simply to use less energy of all kinds through improving efficiency. There's plenty of room for that now. But just as dieting gets harder with each pound lost, the more efficient energy consumption gets, the harder it is to find the next improvement in energy efficiency. For long-term reductions in energy consumption, population decline counterbalances this problem nicely. The current momentum of population growth all but guarantees there won't be population declines for several decades. Those are precisely the decades during which humanity could make the easiest gains in energy efficiency. And just about when energy use is about as efficient as it can be in an imperfect world, human population could begin to shrink. That will remove much of the burden of squeezing additional water from the stone of a super-efficient global energy system. The need to reduce demand for fossil fuels will grow more urgent with each passing year as the global climate warms and the illusion of endless carbon-free energy gradually fades. And population decline reduces energy demand, all else equal, without any hardship for anyone.

This is a more sensible strategy than trying to turn icebergs into ice cubes, but that idea is at least innocuous. Other proposed Big Fixes—from genetic engineering to feed the hungry to nuclear energy to avoid toasting the planet—are dangerous.[34] As a species, we're running out of resilience to stand the cures for what ails us. Increasing numbers of people in all walks of life and all corners of the world are starting to know this in their guts, if not necessarily to think it through in their heads. About the most appealing vision on the horizon is the likelihood that rapid human population growth soon will be something for the history books. Just when we can see the wall we're hurtling toward, we're braking our demographic growth through the realized intentions of hundreds of millions of women and their partners to have just one or two children, when and only when it suits them to do so.

Dreams of People Everywhere

As a newspaper reporter in 1988, I interviewed atmospheric chemist David Lowe of New Zealand, whose paper on the human-related sources of methane had just been published in the journal *Nature*. Lowe regaled me with the many reasons that atmospheric concentrations of that powerful greenhouse gas were rising inexorably. Methane, I learned, flows into the air not only from the world's tens of thousands of landfills, but from its tens of millions of acres of irrigated rice fields and the guts of its billion or more cows and sheep. "It's simply a function of living, of people growing rice and raising cattle," Lowe commented. "What it says to me is that there are just too many people on the planet. You might be able to reduce your fossil fuel use, but with methane, you'd have to tell people to stop eating, and they're going to resist that. It's a colossal problem."[35]

A function of living. People have to eat. And find shelter. And while they're at it, they're probably going to want to cook their food, and heat their homes when they're cold, and cool them when they're warm. They may want to travel, using something other than their own legs; I certainly

do. "Our dreams are the dreams of people everywhere, aren't they?" a former copper mine manager named Kalala Budimbwa told author Howard
French in the Congo. "We want to be able to turn on the lights and read
to our children at night . . . We want roads so that we can truck our produce for sale in other markets, instead of seeing it spoil."[36] But what happens when the dreams of people everywhere become unsustainable—not
because of the nature of the dreams, but because of the numbers of the
dreamers?

There are good reasons why the importance of population growth to the
loss of nature is little studied and rarely remarked on. It's next to impossible to quantify or otherwise separate out the impact of demographic scale
from the many other reasons the environment appears to be crumbling
around us. But I suspect the larger problem is ignorance and the resulting
hopelessness about population growth ("you can't stop people from having
children") or, worse, the fear of blame. Who wants to be seen as implying that
parents who have three or more children and want decent lives for them are
somehow more at fault for our environmental problems than governments
or corporations or drivers of sport utility vehicles? It's not that there's any
compelling research absolving population growth as a long-term force in
environmental degradation. It's just that researchers don't like to risk their
reputations by appearing to hold prolific parents answerable for the sorry
state of nature. "No demographer," demographer Donald Bogue wrote
recently in challenging his colleagues to explore the social and environmental impacts of migration, "wants to be seen as a neo-nativist"—or even someone worried about population growth.[37]

This is not only understandable, in many ways it's commendable. The
history of science makes clear that we're in a far better place than we were
in the nineteenth century, when some biologists backed up racism with
dubious science. Most of us would rather err on the side of believing that
every human being is of equal worth and has an equal right to direct her

or his own life. The challenge is to maintain these convictions and yet objectively face the root causes of problems, striving to imagine ways to resolve them that are consistent with our values. Population is one realm where this is not only possible, but powerfully appealing—the success of a values-based strategy is already evident. Leave to women, more than to anyone else, the decision about when and how often to bear children. The history I've explored in this book suggests that doing so has moderated population growth in the past, and contemporary evidence makes clear that it does exactly that today.

Invisible Hand

There exists more potential than ever for women's reproductive intentions to support the sustainability of societies. Contraception is safer and more effective, and acceptance of its use in most societies is as high as it has ever been. In every country in which contraception and safe abortion (always needed, because contraceptive failure is always possible) are widely available, fertility has quickly fallen to replacement levels or close. Having high per capita income no doubt helps, but this seems much less important than nine or ten years of schooling for girls and a certain degree of women's decision-making autonomy.

Some who have probed modern population problems have argued that saving the lives of more infants and children is the most effective way to reduce fertility, but no significant research data support this optimistic conviction.[38] I say "optimistic" not only because saving lives is inherently good, but because this strategy would be much less controversial than making birth control and safe abortion available to all those who seek them. It was the greater survival of children, of course, that provided the biggest boost to population growth in the last century. The argument that raising child survival further would have the opposite effect today relies on the assumption that each life saved will prevent more than one future birth. Reducing infant and child mortality is a permanent objective of public health interventions everywhere. But only when parents are able to effectively plan their childbearing can they respond to improvements in child survival by having smaller families. The urgent need, as always, is for effective access to the means of managing childbearing and permission to use them.

When that access exists, women tend to take advantage of it no matter their economic or other social status relative to men. The long history of contraception and considerable recent evidence nonetheless suggest that women have greater success in timing their childbearing as their status moves closer to that of men. And since equality makes sense for so many other reasons—indeed, because it's simply right—it's worth embracing by anyone interested in sustainable population.

Family planning scarcely exists in a social vacuum. Women and men need protection from unintended pregnancy whether in stable monogamous marriages or any other sexual arrangement. Polygamous marriage is common in parts of Africa and western Asia. In some Shia Muslim communities "temporary marriage" is winked at by religious leaders. The International Center for Research on Women estimates that 51 million girls in developing countries were married as children, many to much older men.[39] Each year desperation pushes thousands of other girls and young women into the sex trade. Others make pacts with older men whose monetary gifts in exchange for sex help them through school or with child care. In Bangladesh, nearly half of all women reported they had been subjected to violence by their male partners. Such sexual violence results in millions of rapes each year and is a leading cause of death among young women in many countries. In South Africa, a rape takes place on average every six hours, and only 60 percent of those that go to trial end with a conviction.[40]

Over all of this hangs the spectral shadow of HIV/AIDS, now afflicting women in greater numbers and at younger ages worldwide than men and having reached its deadly peak in only a few countries. Many of the health systems that confront the pandemic are themselves in crisis. In Africa, where the needs are greatest, the World Health Organization reports that 1 million health workers whom the continent desperately needs are not there.[41] Many have moved to Europe, where the pay for nurses and other health professions is stratospheric compared to African salaries. Recent stalls in the decline of fertility in some countries probably stem in part from this erosion of health systems, in addition to the cooling since the mid-1990s of governments' ardor to fund family planning itself.

It's not easy to prioritize family planning when funds are scarce and needed to treat disease—not just AIDS, but malaria, dengue fever, tuberculosis, and more, plus disorders of affluence such as diabetes and heart disease. No government ministry even embraces the breadth of contraception's benefits, for the capacity to plan pregnancy relates to much more than health. Can a woman make ambitious plans? Can she wait to be a mother so she can go to school? Can she advance in her work when the opportunity is ripe? The fact that family planning straddles both health and the more abstract aspect of life we might call "opportunity" or "personal fulfillment" undermines government support for it. What government ministry has as its mission both health and personal fulfillment—not to mention demographic sustainability? On health grounds alone, family planning will never have the funding appeal of a crusade against a deadly disease. So, often, it's funded poorly or not at all.

In some cities in developing countries, sidewalk stalls peddling soft drinks and other sundries offer condoms for the equivalent of a few pennies. In rural areas, a particular villager may take on the task of distributing free or inexpensive contraceptives to her or his neighbors. Most women, however, must rely on health care clinics and providers for birth control. And those networks can be exceptionally difficult to access for those without means and education. Planning one's family is just easier when women enjoy status and social standing, legal protections, and the recognized capacity to make decisions for themselves.

As developing countries take ownership of their own health care systems, rather than simply fashioning them to please foreign donors, international cooperation to expand access to family planning is becoming more challenging, though no less needed. There is still plenty of work to do to make sure that effective family planning services are affordable and available to women and men in all countries of the world.

The Future of Population

In the meantime, there's far less to fear from the possibility of population decline than from ongoing growth. Here I will venture out on the limb of prediction, as it seems to me a stout branch. Very low fertility rates will bounce back to two-child-plus replacement values once populations actually decline significantly. That process is only just beginning, and only in a handful of countries. Thanks to immigration, the population momentum of past growth, and young age structures, the populations of most countries with subreplacement fertility are still growing. Others are just beginning to see their populations level off and a few have seen some demographic erosion.

When population really does decline, however, the laws of supply and demand will mean that land and housing will become more affordable, while employers will more highly value scarce young workers. Contrast Italy, where 90 percent of those aged twenty to twenty-four live with their parents (is it any wonder that Italian women have an average of 1.3 children?), to societies in which young people of modest means have their choice of inexpensive fixer-uppers for homes.[42] Unemployment will be lower, labor participation among adults of all ages and both sexes higher. Labor will be compensated more fairly. Savings rates will rise as older workers rely less on pay-as-you go social security systems, which will evolve toward needs-based supplemental income programs as their revenue base fails to keep pace with entitlement payments. Legacies divided into fewer parts than ever before (and think of the asset base that exists in the housing stock of a country like the United States) will convey even middle-class wealth down the generations.

Perhaps humanity will have succeeded in saving and healing much of nature and the environment. Perhaps women will feel they have not only economic security, but also the support of their partners and communities. If so, very many women will want—and have—two or maybe three children over their lifetimes. Other women will settle for one, or none at all. Some will find themselves in committed lesbian relationships. Some will adopt rather than give birth. Some will take advantage of the improving technology of fertility enhancement. And some will dream of Mary Wollstonecraft's houseful of babes, and their dream will come blissfully true. In a world of level and declining populations, intentional reproduction will mean never having to say you're sorry.

This looks like a world worth working toward, even if demography were unrelated to destiny. The vision won't address every population issue. Lower birth rates can't completely stop climate change or solve all the world's other environmental problems. We'll still have to learn how to moderate our consumption of materials and energy and to jumpstart new technologies that conserve them. The pressures to emigrate to find decent jobs won't go away any time soon, although they may be easing in some countries—Mexico is the best example—where the large proportion of young people is beginning to shrink at last. And we'll still have to coexist with widely varying views on abortion, which will always be an issue because there will always be a need for the procedure. Not everyone, of course, sees the logic of stressing both pregnancy prevention and safe options for terminating unwanted pregnancies as early as possible. But logical it is.

Reproductive health care for all will become a reality when it becomes a public and political priority. It will require significant but manageable global expenditures. Something like $45.8 billion dollars a year, spent wisely, could achieve universal access to comprehensive family planning and reproductive health services while also paying for prevention and treatment for HIV/AIDS in developing countries. That's less half what the U.S. government is spending for military activities in Iraq and Afghanistan each year as I write, and it compares with around $5 billion in annual population and reproductive health spending in developing countries today.[43]

To stabilize population, we'll need more than financial support. Men will also need to let go of ancient anxieties about where the combination of autonomous women and effective contraception might lead. Many already have-others are beginning the process. Walking with a village councilman on the Tanzanian shore of Lake Tanganyika in 2002, I asked him how things had gone since women had first run for and gained seats on the council a few years earlier.

"At first we thought it would waste our time, because women wouldn't know anything about how to run the village." he told me. "But we were surprised. The women on the council see things in different ways and come up with ideas none of the rest of us would have thought of. We wouldn't want to lose them now."

All of us will need to rise above our genes and their urge for self-replication. Is it critical that my "nation," however defined, survive for centuries or that my daughter carry on my own genetic lineage? Some elemental urge within me says yes. But that desire implies an *us* that at some point confronts a human *them*. Families, tribes, ethnic groups, and nations have accomplished great things, but frankly, not lately. Maybe we should simply appreciate their cultural and historical value, rather than putting all our resources into securing their long-term institutional future at the expense of humanity's as a whole.

Even in an ideal world, the gap between fertility intentions and outcomes can't be completely closed. In Europe, with its near-universal below-replacement fertility, surveys indicate that 10 percent or more of pregnancies are "accidents," the predictable outcomes of sudden sexual passion or contraceptive failure. But for the sake of women and their families, and with one eye toward humanity's survival on a finite planet, societies should work to make unintended pregnancy as rare as possible. Contraception doesn't need the "help" of coercion or incentives or propaganda. It just needs to be well advertised, inexpensive, safe, and *there*. That and the real recognition of women's equality are all we need to put human population on a sustainable path.

In 2006, evolutionary biologist Michel Raymond met a ninety-two-year-old women in a village in the Alps, where traditional agricultural practices had been common well into the 1980s. From her grandmother, the woman told him, she had learned about a plant whose berries could be used to make a potent contraceptive. The plant was a species of juniper, which pharmacological historian John Riddle has found to be pervasive in literature on herbal contraception since ancient times.[44] In the middle of Europe, with its modern reproductive health services and its subreplacement fertility, an elderly woman carried a reminder that her maternal ancestors had sought to manage the timing of childbearing for a very long time. We may see in this century what happens when that quest succeeds for all.

For most of the 6 million or so years than human-like creatures have stood on two feet, we walked in nature and fed ourselves from its bounty without overwhelming effort. By increments, learning all the way, we came to where we are today—with numbers and cleverness that give us the power to unwittingly submerge coastlines under rising seas and to untwist the thread of life itself. We'll never again know the paradise of plenty in which we once walked as prehistoric hunters and gatherers. The world of the future will be biologically poorer, warmer, and stormier than today's. But we can nonetheless begin the long process that will allow nature and its life-sustaining resources to reverse their retreat.

There is nothing about population, no looming crisis, that excuses us from our humanity and the moral responsibilities that accompany it. Life is far more about giving something of ourselves to the people around us than it is about assuring that fewer are born. Yet population, too, has always been a critical part of life. It always will be. Sex, reproduction, and the number of us on the planet are forever tangled up together, and peo-ple have always had to struggle with the untangling.

The clearest principle to guide us is that those who bear children should be the ones, more than anyone else, to decide when to do so. The rest will work itself out. We will not self-destruct through too much reproduction, nor will we fade sadly away through too little. With a bit of luck, an under-standing of our place in nature, and a grateful nod to the long line of suc-cessful mothers who preceded us, humanity's moment on this rich but finite planet instead may stretch out for longer than we can now imagine. Humanity really could be as countless as the stars—just not *all at once*, but over millennia to come. Wanting not more people, but more for all people, we might find ourselves at home again, with more nature than we thought possible, in an Eden we can keep.

Notes

Preface

1. Unless otherwise indicated, all population and vital statistics are from UN Department of Economic and Social Affairs (2007), *World Population Prospects*.

Introduction: Uncrowding Eden

Epigraphs: *Washington Post* (2007), Fee proposed to ease traffic in Manhattan, A11; Jaime Lerner, preface in M. Sheehan (2007), *State of the World 2007*, xx.

1. The Rwanda information is from Kinzer (2007), After so many deaths, too many births. The China data is from Barrionuevo (2007), China's appetites lead to changes in its trade diet, A1; and from Cody (2007), China's expansion puts workers in harm's way, A24.

2. Park (2007), 51 things we can do to save the environment; Cassady (2007), *The Carbon Boom*.

3. Biller (2000), *The Measure of Multitude*, 419.

4. U.S. Census Bureau (2003), Foreign-born a majority in six U.S. cities.

5. Longman (2005), Give more credit to prolific parents, B7.

6. Wattenberg, Ben J. (2004), *Fewer*.

7. Hansen quoted in Revkin (2007), A new middle stance emerges in debate over climate, A16.

8. Conniff, (2007), Death in Happy Valley.

9. Ekisa Anyara (2007), personal communication, February 5.

Chapter 1: Henrietta's Ideal

Epigraph: Pennington (2001), Hunter-gatherer demography, 170.

1. The Population Reference Bureau published figures on contraceptive prevalence for the world as a whole, the major world regions, and individual countries in its annual *World Population Data Sheet*, www.prb.org/Publications/Datasheets/2006/2006World PopulationDataSheet.aspx (accessed November 27, 2007).

2. Downs (2003), *Fertility of American Women: June 2002*, p. 3, table 2. The 18 percent figure is based on women aged 40–44, who are presumed to have completed their childbearing.

3. These replacement fertility rates and the related calculations that follow are from my work with Elizabeth Leahy at Population Action International in 2006 and are based on UN data. The material was presented in March 2006 as a poster session at the annual meeting of the American Public Health Association in Boston, and again in April 2006 at a session of the annual meeting of the Population Association of America in Los Angeles. See also Espenshade, Guzman, and Westoff (2003), The surprising global variation in replacement fertility.

4. Eaton and Mayer (1954), *Man's Capacity to Reproduce*; Lang and Gohlen (1985), Completed fertility of the Hutterites.

5. In her book *The Underside of History: A View of Women through Time* (1976), Elise Boulding coined the term *Mulier sapiens* to remind her readers that a member of our species is as likely to be a woman (*mulier*) as a man (*homo*). With a respectful nod to her reasoning, I use the conventional species name here.

6. UN Department of Economic and Social Affairs (2004), *World Population in 2300*; Lynch (2003), UN predicts much slower growth in population.

7. With 262,000 square miles of dry land, Texas has 167.6 million acres, or an eighth of an acre for every 5 people—a number not far from the average family size—of today's world population.

8. Meadows et al. (1972), *The Limits to Growth*.

9. Diamond (2005), *Collapse*, 311–28; Gasana (2002), Remember Rwanda?; Jeroen K. Van Ginneken and Margreet Wiegers (2005), Various causes of the 1994 genocide in Rwanda with emphasis on the role of population pressure, presentation during session

on the demography of political conflict and violence, annual meeting of the Population Association of America, Philadelphia. Canadian political scientist and author Thomas Homer-Dixon concluded in 1996, in a report with colleague Val Percival, that land scarcity induced by population growth was at most a marginal factor in the Rwandan genocide, but he has since changed his mind. See Percival and Homer-Dixon (1996), Environmental scarcity and violent conflict: The case of Rwanda; Homer-Dixon (2006), review of *States, Security, and Civil Strife in the Developing World*. On land subdivision in Malawi, see Cammack (2001), *Malawi at the Threshold*, 25.

10. No one, of course, really knows the exact world population at any particular time, but the educated guesses are probably close. The U.S. Census Bureau provides a world population clock at www.census.gov/ipc/www/popclockworld.html (accessed November 27, 2007).

11. Will (1993), In death, a return to randomness.

12. As an example, see Cammack (2001), *Malawi at the Threshold*, 25.

13. Zlotnick (2004), Population growth and international migration. Zlotnick actually reports a slight correlation between fertility rates in migrant-sending countries and the volume of emigration from these countries, but she judges it insignificant.

14. Demographic and Health Surveys and CARE International/Niger (1999), *Enquête Démographique et de Santé 1998*, 114.

15. The lower figure is from Jitendra Khanna, Paul F. A. Van Look, and P. David Griffin, eds., (1992), *Reproductive Health: A Key to a Brighter Future* (World Health Organization, Geneva), cited in World Health Organization (1992), *PROGRESS in Human Reproduction Research*, 4. The higher figure was calculated by Nada Chaya (2005), demographer at Population Action International, personal communication to Jennifer Dusenberry, research assistant for this book, May 24.

16. Alan Guttmacher Institute (1999), *Sharing Responsibility: Women, Society and Abortion Worldwide*.

17. World Health Organization (2004), *Unsafe Abortion*.

18. World Health Organization, Department of Reproductive Health and Research (2004), *Maternal Mortality Estimates in 2000*, 22.

19. Marston and Cleland (2003), Relationships between contraception and abortion; Bongaarts and Westoff (2000), The potential role of contraception in reducing abortion; Westoff (2005), Recent trends in contraception and abortion in 12 countries.

20. Potts (1997), Sex and the birth rate.

21. Becker (1960), An economic analysis of fertility; Pritchett (1994), Desired fertility and the impact of population policies.

22. Campbell et al. (n.d.), The impact of freedom on fertility transition. This unpublished paper was written after 2006.

23. Campbell, Sahin-Hodoglugil, and Potts (2006), Barriers to fertility regulation.

24. Nie and Wyman (2005), The one-child policy in Shanghai.

Chapter 2: The Population Growers

1. Tattersal (1998), *Becoming Human*, 49. Tattersal cites the English biographer James Boswell as his source for Benjamin Franklin's wordsmithing.

2. R. Weiss (2007), For first time, chimps seen making weapons for hunting.

3. The interpretation of human origins is ongoing, and key ideas were changing as I wrote this book. For a recent overview of current thought, see *Scientific American* (2006), Becoming human: Evolution and the rise of intelligence, special issue. Book-length overviews include Leakey and Lewin (1992), *Origins Reconsidered*; and Stringer and McKie (1997 [1996]), *African Exodus*. These accounts are based on the dominant scientific view that *Homo sapiens*, like most other hominid species, originated in Africa and spread from there to other continents. For the alternative view that *Homo sapiens* evolved concurrently in several parts of the Old World, see Wolpoff (2005), *Modern Human Origins*.

4. Gould (1980), introduction to *Dance of the Tiger: A Novel of the Ice Age*, xvii–xviii; Kipling (1994 [1902]), *Just So Stories*.

5. Jorde et al. (2001), Population genomics: A bridge from evolutionary history to genetic medicine; Harpending et al. (1998), Genetic traces of ancient demography. These sources mention 10,000 as the likely "effective," or breeding, human population around 70,000 years ago. Effective population size can be estimated to be half the total population size, according to J. Felsenstein (1971), Inbreeding and variance effective numbers in populations with overlapping generations, *Genetics* 68:581–97, cited in Harpending et al., ibid. Recent estimates suggest the number could have been as low as 5,000, according to Wade (2006), *Before the Dawn: Recovering the Lost History of Our Ancestors*.

6. The equation for such calculations is $P_2 = P_1 e^{rt}$, where P_1 is the first population, P_2 is the second, and e^{rt} is the exponential constant (which equals a bit less than 2.72) raised to the power of the rate of annual growth (r) multiplied by the number of years the growth occurs (t).

7. Coale (1974), The history of human population.

8. Lemonick and Dorfman (2006), What makes us different?

9. Brunet (2002), A new hominid from the Upper Miocene of Chad, Central Africa; Begun (2006), Planet of the apes.

10. Rosenberg and Trevathan (2001), The evolution of human birth, 72–77. The quotation is on p. 73.

11. Rosenberg and Trevathan (2001), 75.

12. Trevathan (1987), *Human Birth: An Evolutionary Perspective*, 94.

13. Rosenberg and Trevathan (2002), Birth, obstetrics and human evolution; Tattersal (1998), *Becoming Human*, 121–22.

14. See, for example, Musacchio (1999), *The Art and Ritual of Childbirth in Renaissance Italy*, 10–11, with a 1440s painting by Osservanza Master illustrating the birth of the Virgin Mary "in a fashionable fifteenth-century [Italian] interior. Indicative of the exclusively female nature of the event is the way in which Joachim [Mary's father] and his companion sit outside the bedchamber, eager to hear the news but unable to enter the room."

15. De Waal (2005), How animals do business.

16. Osrin et al. (2002), Cross sectional, community based study of care of newborn infants in Nepal.

17. Anne Pusey (2005), director of the Jane Goodall Institute's chimpanzee database at the University of Minnesota, interview with the author, July 8.

18. One list of sources on the *r* and *K* reproductive strategies is provided in Livi-Bacci (1992 [1989]), *A Concise History of World Population*, 2. Ansley J. Coale explains the importance of these strategies to demography in Coale and Cotts Watkins, eds., (1986), *The Decline of Fertility in Europe*, 7.

19. The 1999 edition of the *Guinness Book of World Records* (Bantam Books, New York), listed Leontina Albina of San Antonio, Chile, as the "most prolific mother." She claimed to have given birth to sixty-four children, of which fifty-five reportedly were documented. Most arrived in multiple births. A later edition of the book did not include her claim.

20. Erukhimovich et al. (1998), How many children can one man have? Einon was a coauthor of this paper and has advanced this argument elsewhere as well. By Einon's argument, the low sperm counts inherent in frequent male ejaculation combine with the low conception rates inherent in infrequent female sexual intercourse to make large harems a bad bet for high male fertility.

21. Zerjal et al. (2003), The genetic legacy of the Mongols; Sailer (2003), Genes of history's greatest lover found?

22. Dawkins (1989), *The Selfish Gene*; Robert L. Trivers, Parental investment and sexual selection, in Campbell, ed. (1972), *Sexual Selection and the Descent of Man 1871–1971*, 136–79.

23. Wells (2000), Natural selection and sex differences in morbidity and mortality in early life.

24. Thornhill and Palmer (2000), *A Natural History of Rape*.

25. Hrdy (1999), *Mother Nature*. The quotation is from p. 8.

26. I learned about the assisted births among tamarins and marmosets from College of William and Mary anthropologist and author Barbara J. King (2005), personal communication, March 2, and about the indri lemur fathers from park guide Julienne Racafindralandy (2003), in Mantadia National Park, Madagascar, October 11. Animal-behavior biologist Joyce Powzyk reports that indri males also are known to play with young and to offer alarm calls when predators are near. Powzyk (2005), personal communication, September 2. J. I. Pollock discusses paternal care of older offspring in this species in Field observations on *Indri indri*: A preliminary report, in Tattersal and Sussman, eds. (1975), *Lemur Biology*, 287–311.

27. Hrdy (1999), *Mother Nature*, 211, 226.

28. Hawkes et al. (1998), Grandmothering, menopause, and the evolution of human life histories; Packer (1998), Why menopause?

29. The Sicilian proverb is from Leonard Covello (1967), *The Social Background of the Italo-American School Child* (E. J. Brill, Leiden), 208–9, quoted in Joan Scott and Louise Tilly, Women's work and the family in nineteenth century Europe, in Rosenberg, ed. (1975), *The Family in History*, 159n44. The Swedish study referred to is U. Högberg and G. Brostrom (1985), The demography of maternal mortality: Seven Swedish parishes in the Nineteenth Century, *International Journal of Gynecology and Obstetrics* 23 (6): 489–97, cited in Mead Over, Randall P. Ellis, Joyce H. Huber, and Orville Solon, The consequences of ill health, in Feachem, Kjellstrom, Murray, Over, and Phillips, eds. (1992), *The Health of Adults in the Developing World*, 164. The Matlab results are from L .C. Chen, M. C. Gesche, S. Ahmed, A. I. Chowdhury, and W. H. Mosley (1974), Maternal mortality in rural Bangladesh, *Studies in Family Planning* 5, no. 11: 334–41, cited in Over, Ellis, Huber, and Solon, ibid., 164. The Eskimo customs are from Hart Hansen, Meldgaard, and Nordqvist (1985), The mummies of Qilakitsoq.

30. Richard J. Smith and William L. Jungers (1997), Body mass in comparative primatology, *Journal of Human Evolution* 32:523–59, cited in Wrangham et al. (1999), The raw and the stolen: Cooking and the ecology of human origins, *Current Anthropology* 40, no. 5: 567–94; Aiello and Wells (2002), Energetics and the evolution of the genus *Homo*, p. 325, table 1.

31. Lovejoy (1981), The origin of man; Frank Beach quoted in Leakey and Lewin (1992), *Origins Reconsidered*, 88; and in Sarah Blaffer Hrdy, The evolution of primate sexuality, in Bellig and Stevens (1988), *The Evolution of Sex*, 110.

32. Potts (1997), Sex and the birth rate. Hrdy (1999), *Mother Nature*, and several published papers, discuss possible reasons for the lack of estrus in humans, but there appears to be so single source that summarizes the range of views.

33. Sherwood L. Washburn and Chester S. Lancaster, The evolution of hunting, in Lee and DeVore, eds. (1968), *Man the Hunter*, 293–303.

34. Tanner and Zihlman (1976), Women in evolution.

35. Sarah Blaffer Hrdy, Comes the child before man: How cooperative breeding and prolonged postweaning dependence shaped human potentials, in Hewlett and Lamb, eds. (2005), *Hunter-Gatherer Childhoods*, 65–91.

36. Barbara Smuts (1992), Male aggression against women: An evolutionary perspective, *Human Nature* 3:1–44, cited in Wrangham et al. (1999), The raw and the stolen. See also Sarah L. Mesnick (1997), Sexual alliances: Evidence and evolutionary implications, in P. A. Gowaty, ed., *Feminism and Evolutionary Biology: Boundaries, Intersections and Frontiers* (Chapman and Hall, New York), 207–60, cited in Wrangham et al., ibid.

37. Boehm, trans. (2005), *A Woman in Berlin*, 115.

38. Wrangham et al. (1999), The raw and the stolen.

39. See, for example, Henry T. Bunn, essay in "Comments" section of Wrangham et al. (1999), The raw and the stolen, 579–80.

40. Brace from "Comments" section in Wrangham et al. (1999), The raw and the stolen, 577–79.

41. Aiello and Wells (2002), Energetics and the evolution of the genus *Homo*.

42. Saslow (2006), In prep cross-country, girls often face an uphill battle; T. Anderson (1996), Biomechanics and running economy.

43. Wall-Scheffler, Geiger, and Steudel-Numbers (2007), Infant carrying, 841.

44. Ambrose (2003), Did the super-eruption of Toba cause a human population bottleneck?

Chapter 3: Outbound

Epigraph: This verse opens one version of the old emigration lament:

My father he being a farmer, rare to industry,

He had four sons to manhood grown and lovely daughters three.

Our land's too small to serve us all, so some of us must roam.

Our friends may mourn, for we'll never return to Erin's lovely home.

1. Leonard (2002), Food for thought, 113. For a detailed treatment of more recent evidence on this great migration, see Wong (2006a), Stranger in a new land.

2. Wade (2003b), Why humans and their fur parted ways.

3. Morgan (1982), *The Aquatic Ape*.

4. Wall-Scheffler, Geiger, and Steudel-Numbers (2007), Infant carrying.

5. Adovasio, Soffer, and Page (2007), *The Invisible Sex*.

6. Leakey and Lewin (1978 [1977]), *Origins*, 137.

7. Christian, (1970), Social subordination, population density, and mammalian evolution, 84.

8. Gamble (1994), *Timewalkers*, 241, 245.

9. Wilford (2004), Experts place ancient toolmakers on a fast track to Northern China.

10. Wright (2005 [2004]), *A Short History of Progress*, 17.

11. Leonard (2002), Food for thought, 113.

12. Leakey and Lewin (1992), *Origins Reconsidered*, 172.

13. Revelations 6:1–8. The scriptural verses don't name what the horses represent, only the colors of their coats: white, red, black, and "pale." Red suggested to later interpreters bloodletting; black, pestilence; paleness, malnutrition or starvation; and white, the color of the shroud.

14. C. Richard Terman (1980), Behavior and regulation of growth in laboratory populations of prairie deermice, in Cohen, Malpass, and Klein, eds. (1980) *Biosocial Mechanisms of Population Regulation*, 23–36.

15. For an overview of selected literature on animal and human response to high population density, based on a 1978 interdisciplinary conference on the topic at the State University of New York in Plattsburgh, see Cohen, Malpass, and Klein, eds. (1980), *Biosocial Mechanisms of Population Regulation*.

16. Wade (2003c), We got rhythm; Wade (2003a), Early voices.

17. Knight (1991), *Blood Relations*.

18. Dunbar (1996), *Grooming, Gossip, and the Evolution of Language*; *The Economist* (2005–2006), Special "Christmas survey" on human evolution.

19. Lutz, Testa, and Penn (2006), Population density is a key factor in declining human fertility.

20. Primatologist Frans de Waal has spent much of his career documenting the behavior of chimpanzees, other apes, and monkeys, which like humans seem to have strong perceptions of fairness, even roots of what we might call a sense of morality, and which sometimes seem downright Machiavellian in calculating the impacts of their behavior on other members of their groups. See de Waal (1982), *Chimpanzee Politics*, and de Waal (1989), *Peacemaking among Primates*. Birds, too, in recent years have surprised researchers with their capacity for humanlike social behavior. See, for example, Heinrich (2000 [1999]), *Mind of the Raven*.

21. Robert H. Tamarin, Dispersal and population regulation in rodents, in Cohen, Malpass, and Klein, eds. (1980), *Biosocial Mechanisms of Population Regulation*,117–33; Jane M. Packard and L. David Mech, Population regulation in wolves, in Cohen, Malpass, and Klein, ibid., 135–50; Donald Stone Sade, Population biology of free-ranging rhesus monkeys on Cayo Santiago, Puerto Rico, in Cohen, Malpass, and Klein, ibid., 171–87; Christian (1970), Social subordination, population density, and mammalian evolution. Other significant population-control mechanisms in animals

include reductions in fertility or nursing of infants, maternal abandonment of infants, and reductions in immunity to infectious disease, all probably influenced by hormonal responses to the tactile and visual cues of crowding.

22. Tattersal (1998), *Becoming Human*; Tattersal (2000).

23. Christian (1970), Social subordination, population density, and mammalian evolution; John J. Christian, Endocrine factors in population regulation, in Cohen, Malpass, and Klein, eds. (1980), *Biosocial Mechanisms of Population Regulation*, 55–115.

24. Donald Stone Sade, Population biology of free-ranging rhesus monkeys on Cayo Santiago, Puerto Rico, in Cohen, Malpass, and Klein, eds. (1980), *Biosocial Mechanisms of Population Regulation*, 182.

25. Leakey and Lewin (1978 [1977]), *Origins*, 212.

26. Ardrey (1961), *African Genesis*; Lorenz (1966 [1963]), *On Aggression*; Montagu (1976), *The Nature of Human Aggression*.

27. Editors' note in Charles H. Southwick, Rhesus monkey populations in India and Nepal: Patterns of growth, decline and natural regulation, in Cohen, Malpass, and Klein, eds. (1980), *Biosocial Mechanisms of Population Regulation*, 161; Christian (1970), Social subordination, population density, and mammalian evolution.

28. Chernow (2004), *Alexander Hamilton*, 12–16. James L. Watson (1989), Self-defense corps, violence, and the bachelor subculture in South China: Two case studies, in *Proceedings of the Second International Conference on Sinology*, Academia Sinica, Taipei, Republic of China, June, 216, cited in Hudson and Den Boer (2002), A surplus of men, a deficit of peace, 18.

29. Wilford (2002a), Seeking Polynesia's beginnings in an archipelago of shards, D1.

30. Diamond (2005), *Collapse*, 88.

31. Vakua et al. (2002), A new skull of early *Homo*; Fischman (2000), Georgia on their mind; Wong (2006a), Stranger in a new land.

32. Harpending et al. (1998), Genetic traces of ancient demography.

33. Cavalli-Sforza, Menozzi, and Piazza (1993), Demic expansions and human evolution, 639.

34. Henshilwood et al. (2001), Blombos Cave, Southern Cape, South Africa.

35. Stringer and McKie (1997 [1996]), *African Exodus*, 12.

36. Henshilwood et al. (2004), Middle Stone Age shell beads from South Africa; Wilford (2006), Old shells suggest early human adornment.

37. Gore (2000), People like us.

38. Wong (2006b), The morning of the modern mind, 82. Wong cites Sally McBrearty of the University of Connecticut for the thought, 82. See also McBrearty, and Brooks (2000), The revolution that wasn't.

39. Shennan (2001), Demography and cultural innovation, 15.

40. J. L. Rosny-Aines wrote *La Guerre du Feu* in 1911, and the novel was the basis of the film *The Quest for Fire* in 1981; cited in Stringer and McKie (1997 [1996]), *African Exodus*, 12. Jean M. Auel's series of novels about interactions between Neanderthals and *Homo sapiens* began with *The Clan of the Cave Bear* (Crown Publishers, New York, 2001 [1980]).

41. Wolpoff quoted in Leakey and Lewin (1992), *Origins Reconsidered*, 233.

42. Brace quoted in Rudavsky (1991), The secret life of the Neanderthal, 56.

43. Kuhn and Stiner (2006), What's a mother to do?

44. Einwögerer (2006), Friesinger, Händel, Neugebauer-Maresch, Simon and Teschler-Nicola, Upper Palaeolithic infant burials.

45. McElvaine (2001), *Eve's Seed*.

46. Tudge (1999), *Neanderthals, Bandits and Farmers*.

47. Donlan (2007), Restoring America's big, wild animals, 70.

Chapter 4: The Grandmother of Invention

Epigraph: Tablet 1, lines 353–55 of the Atrahasis Epic, as quoted in Anne D. Kilmer (1972), The Mesopotamian concept of overpopulation and its solution as reflected in the mythology, *Orientalia* 41:160–76, cited in Cohen (1995), *How Many People Can the Earth Support?*, 5.

1. Ignatius (2006), Is it warm in here?

2. Jared Diamond describes several instances in which population growth combined with technological innovations to undermine cultures and civilizations in Diamond (2005), *Collapse*. Among others who have explored these connections in history and the present are Ponting (1993 [1991]), *A Green History of the World*; Perlin (1989), *A Forest Journey*; Tainter (1988), *The Collapse of Complex Societies*; and Homer-Dixon (1999), *Environment, Scarcity, and Violence*.

3. Hey (2005), On the number of New World founders.

4. Martin (1967), Prehistoric overkill; Martin and Wright, eds. (1967), *Pleistocene Extinctions*.

5. Alroy (2001), A multispecies overkill simulation of the end-Pleistocene megafaunal mass extinction. See also Wong (2001), Mammoth kill.

6. Stolzenburg (1994), New views of ancient times; *New York Times* (1988), Human hunters and pygmy hippos.

7. Rhys Jones cited in Tudge (1999), *Neanderthals, Bandits and Farmers*, 13–14. The rainfall reduction is discussed in Cowan (1998), If you don't spare the tree, you spoil more than the jungle.

8. Miller (2005), Ecosystem collapse in Pleistocene Australia and a human role in megafaunal extinction.

9. Barnosky (2004), Assessing the causes of late Pleistocene extinctions on the continents; Stuart et al. (2004), Pleistocene to Holocene extinction dynamics in giant deer and woolly mammoth.

10. Barnosky quoted in Gugliotta (2004), Suspects in the demise of giant mammals, A9.

11. Stiner (1999), Paleolithic population growth pulses evidenced by small animal exploitation; Stiner (2001), Thirty years on the "Broad Spectrum Revolution" and Paleolithic demography.

12. Terry Jones, ed., (1992), *Essays on the Prehistory of Maritime California* (Center for Archaeological Research, Davis, Calif.), cited in Diamond (2005), *Collapse*, 545; L. Mark Raab (1992), An optimal foraging analysis of prehistoric shellfish collecting on San Clemente Island, California, *Journal of Ethnobiology*, 12:63–80, cited in Diamond, ibid.; Gugliotta (2006), Indians depleted wildlife, too.

13. Boulding (1976), *The Underside of History*, 102.

14. McNeill (1991 [1963]), *The Rise of the West*, 86.

15. Eisler (1988 [1987]), *The Chalice and the Blade*. Swiss jurist Johann Bachofen first advanced the idea in the early nineteenth century that societies in which women were dominant preceded patriarchal culture in Europe. The primary elaborator of the modern conception was archaeologist Marija Gimbutas of the University of California–Los Angeles. See especially Gimbutas (1982 [1974]), *The Gods and Goddesses of Old Europe*. For an ambitious synthesis, outside the academic mainstream, of evidence that patriarchal societies violently overcame matriarchal or egalitarian ones in most of the world, see DeMeo (1998), *Saharasia: The 4000 BCE Origins of Child Abuse, Sex-Repression, Warfare and Social Violence in the Deserts of the Old World*.

16. Marshack (1978), *Ice Age Art*.

17. Karlen (2001 [1995]), *Plague's Progress*, 34–35.

18. Molleson quoted in Yale University Office of Public Information (1988), Bone deformities reveal grueling life of the world's early farmers.

19. Wilford (2002b), Don't blame Columbus for all the Indian's ills.

20. Ubelaker quoted in Rensberger (1998), In death, ancient peoples offer evidence that "progress" shortened life, H1.

21. Genesis 3:19 and 16. The wording "sweat of thy face" is from the King James Version. See McElvaine (2001), *Eve's Seed*, 97–102.

22. Genesis 2:10.

23. Hamblin (1987), Has the Garden of Eden been located at last?

24. Tudge (1999), *Neanderthals, Bandits and Farmers*, 36–37. For an overview of the idea that slow, cumulative population growth coupled with climate change to spur the invention of agriculture, see Pringle (1998), The slow birth of agriculture.

25. Tudge (1999), *Neanderthals, Bandits and Farmers*, 37.

26. Carneiro (2000), The transition from quantity of quality, 12929–30.

27. Carneiro (2000), The transition from quantity of quality; Diamond (1997), *Guns, Germs, and Steel*, 286; Dunbar (1996), *Grooming, Gossip, and the Evolution of Language*. The number of possible two-person relationships in a group equals half the product of the population of individuals in the group multiplied by that population minus one, or $(P*(P-1))/2$, where P stands for population.

28. Diamond (1997), *Guns, Germs, and Steel*, 281.

29. Wright (2005 [2004]), *A Short History of Progress*, 40.

30. Diamond (2005), *Collapse*, 509.

31. Part of this conversation is captured in a short film directed by Daniele Anastasion, (2004), *Finding Balance: Forests and Family Planning in Madagascar*, Population Action International, Washington, D.C.

32. Packer (2005), Ecological change, group territoriality, and population dynamics in Serengeti lions. The example of cockroach larvae is from Fountain (2006), Deciding on a roach motel by committee.

33. Goldman (2003), *Ancient Near Eastern Mythology*. The list is from Ebla, an ancient city-state in northern Syria, from the second half of the third millennium BC.

34. Feen (1996), Keeping the balance, 447–48.

35. Erle Leichty (1971), Demons and population control, in *Expedition* 13, no. 2 (Winter): 22–26, cited in Cohen (1995), *How Many People Can the Earth Support?*, 258; Anne D. Kilmer (1972), The Mesopotamian concept of overpopulation and its solution as reflected in the mythology, *Orientalia* 41:160–76, cited in Cohen, ibid.

Chapter 5: A Sense of Timing

Epigraphs: Multiple English translations of Ecclesiastes use this exact wording. Written before 180 BC, the verse fragment suggests that there are appropriate times for procreative sex and others for abstinence; see Buttrick (1984 [1952]), *The Interpreter's Bible*, vol. 5, p. 44, which cites earlier interpretations by Midrash Qoheleth Rabbah and Lukyn. The Mesopotamian proverb is from Kramer (1967), *Cradle of Civilization*, 127.

1. Kristen Patterson (2005), Peace Corps volunteer in Niger, personal communication, March 18.

2. Spencer et al. (2004), Social chemosignals from breastfeeding women increase sexual motivation.

3. Cleland, Bernstein, Ezeh, Foundes, Glasier, and Innis (2006), Family planning.

4. Van de Walle and Muhsam (1995), Fatal secrets and the French fertility transition, 271.

5. Pagels (1988), *Adam, Eve, and the Serpent*, 44.

6. Kauffmann Doig (1979), *Sexual Behaviour in Ancient Peru* Plate XVIII, 126–27.

7. Genesis 38:8–10.

8. Al-Jahiz, *Book of Animals*, cited in Musallam (1983), *Sex and Society in Islam*, 94.

9. Governor Bradford quoted in Himes (1970 [1936]), *Medical History of Contraception*, 225n.

10. Anonymous (1985 [1741]), *Histoire de dom Bougre, portier des Chartreux*, in *Oeuvres anonymes du XVIIIe siècle* (I), L'Enfer de la Bibliothèque Nationale 3 (Fayard, Paris), 29–236, cited in van de Walle and Muhsam (1995), Fatal secrets and the French fertility transition, 270.

11. Tattersal (1998), *Becoming Human*, 206.

12. Konner and Worthman (1980), Nursing frequency, gonadal function, and birth spacing among !Kung hunter-gatherers.

13. Riddle, Estes, and Russell (1994), Ever since Eve.

14. Riddle (1997), *Eve's Herbs*.

15. Foster and Duke (1990), *A Field Guide to Medicinal Plants*.

16. Riddle (1992), *Contraception and Abortion from the Ancient World to the Renaissance*, 66–69; Himes (1970 [1936]), *Medical History of Contraception*; Noonan (1986 [1965]), *Contraception*.

17. Christine Mauck (2007), physician and researcher specializing in HIV and reproductive health, personal communication, March 28.

18. Himes (1970 [1936]), *Medical History of Contraception*, 187–88.

19. Ibid., 18–19.

20. See, for example, Caldwell (2004), Fertility control in the classical world.

21. Cleland, Bernstein, Ezeh, Foundes, Glasier, and Innis (2006), Family planning, 1813.

22. Riddle (1992), *Contraception and Abortion from the Ancient World to the Renaissance*, 145.

23. Boonstra et al. (2006), *Abortion in Women's Lives*. In the spring of 2006, the U.S. Centers for Disease Control and Prevention and several private health organizations advised all sexually active, fecund women to consider themselves pregnant or about to become so, relative to their own behavior and any health treatment. The reason: almost half of all pregnancies in the United States take women by surprise. See Payne (2006), Forever pregnant.

24. Martin Daly and Margo Wilson, A sociobiological analysis of human infanticide, in Hausfater and Hrdy, eds. (1984), *Infanticide*, 487–582.

25. Gies and Gies (1990), *Life in a Medieval Village*, 169; Claudia Opitz, Life in the late Middle Ages, in Klapisch-Zuber, ed. (1994 [1992]), *A History of Women in the West*, 291.

26. UN Wire (2000), Bolivia: Infanticide rate reaches 16% in some areas.

27. Harris and Ross (1987), *Death, Sex, and Fertility*.

28. Denham (1974), Population structure, infant transport, and infanticide among Pleistocene and modern hunter-gatherers.

29. Hammond (2004), *From Yao to Mao*.

30. Molleson discussed in Hodder (2005), Women and Men at Çatalhöyük, 37; Xenophon cited in Boulding (1976), *The Underside of History*, 20.

31. For an overview of dozens of anthropological surveys of indigenous hunter-gatherer societies and female status, see Sanday (1996 [1981]), *Female Power and Male Dominance*. Sanday defines male dominance as "the exclusion of women from political and economic decision making [and/or] male aggression against women" (164).

32. McNeill (1991 [1963]), *The Rise of the West*, 13, 19.

33. Adams (2000), *Neolithic Europe*.

34. McNeill (1991 [1963]), *The Rise of the West*, 26.

35. See, for example, Anderson and Zinsser (1988), *A History of Their Own*, 13.

36. McNeill (1991 [1963]), *The Rise of the West*, 26.

37. Amanda Giles (1999), Gender dynamics in the past: Insights from a Darwinian study of human ornamentation, master's dissertation, Institute of Archaeology, University College London, p. 40, cited in Shennan (2002), *Genes, Memes and Human History*, 202–4.

38. Sanday (1996 [1981]), *Female Power and Male Dominance*, 81–82.

39. I'm grateful to Scott Denman, of the Wallace Global Fund, for pointing out the etymological connection.

40. Wilford (2003), Lost no more.

Chapter 6: Axial Age

1. S. D. Eisenstadt, Introduction: The Axial Age breakthroughs, in Eisenstadt, ed. (1986), *The Origins and Diversity of Axial Age Civilizations*, 1. The ideas in this paragraph and several that follow are drawn generally from this essay and others in this book.

2. Noble (2002), *The Foundations of Western Civilization*.

3. Hermann Kulke, The historical background of India's Axial Age, in Eisenstadt (1986), *The Origins and Diversity of Axial Age Civilizations*, 378.

4. Armstrong (2001), *Buddha*, 10, 23; Harris (1991 [1977]), *Cannibals and Kings*, 179, 214, and 216.

5. Armstrong (2001), *Buddha*, xxviii.

6. Hammond (2004), *From Yao to Mao*.

7. Eliade (1959 [1957]), *The Sacred and the Profane*, 126.

8. Armstrong (2001), *Buddha*, 151–56.

9. The censuses, probably the earliest ever recorded, are described in Numbers chapters 1 and 26. God's promise to Abraham is in Genesis 15:5.

10. Karlen (2001 [1995]), *Plague's Progress*, 59–60; Bowra et al. (1965), *Classical Greece*, 118; Cantor (2001), *In the Wake of the Plague*, 188.

11. Caldwell (2004), Fertility control in the classical world.

12. Hamilton (1942), *Mythology*, 50; Riddle (1992), *Contraception and Abortion from the Ancient World to the Renaissance*, 26, 33.

13. Jacob A. Adetunji (2006), Rising popularity of injectable contraceptives in sub-Saharan Africa, paper presented at annual meeting of the Population Association of America, March, Los Angeles.

14. Riddle, Estes, and Russell (1994), Ever since Eve; Riddle (1992), *Contraception and Abortion from the Ancient World to the Renaissance*; Riddle and Estes (1992), Oral contraceptives in ancient and medieval medicines.

15. In Clucas, *Versions of Catullus*, the poem title is translated as "How Many Kisses Satisfy?"

16. Herodotus, *The History*, book 1, chapter 136, quoted in Hutchinson (1967), *The Population Debate*, 8.

17. Genesis 19:23–26.

18. Genesis 13:6–11; Malthus (1927 [1914]), *An Essay on Population*, 59.

19. Plato, Republic V 460:a, in Hamilton and Cairns, eds. (1971 [1961]), *The Collected Dialogues of Plato*, 699; Kingsley Davis (1974), The migrations of human population; Thomas Cahill (2003), *Sailing the Wine-Dark Sea*, 83; Plato, Critias 110:e–112:e, in Hamilton and Cairns, ibid., 1216.

20. Aristotle, Politics 7.16, 1335b, cited in Noonan (1986), *Contraception*, 18; Aristotle, *History of the Animals* 7.3, 583a, cited in Noonan, ibid., 15.

21. Kautilya and Han Fei Tzu described in Nathan Keyfitz, in Peterson, ed. (1972), *Readings in Population*, 41–69;

22. Some Muslims acknowledge this tendency of female subordination in Islam. See Hirsi Ali (2007), *Infidel*. "It spreads a culture that is . . . fixated on controlling women," Ali writes of the Qur'an, the holy book of Islam, the religion in which she was raised (272).

23. Chandler (1987), *Four Thousand Years of Urban Growth*.

Chapter 7: Punishing Eve

Epigraph: Joni Mitchell (1994), The Magdalene Laundries, *Turbulent Indigo*, Reprise Records, Crazy Crow Music, used by permission.

1. Cahill (1996 [1995]), *How the Irish Saved Civilization*, 178.

2. Finnegan (2004 [2001]), *Do Penance or Perish*.

3. Aristotle (1809), *The History of the Animals of Aristotle, and His Treatise on Physiognomy*, 268; Lloyd (1983), *Science, Folklore and Ideology*, 170–71; Anderson and Zinsser (1988), *A History of Their Own*, 28.

4. Luke 8:1–3; John 8:11.

5. Pope Clement quoted in Pagels (1988), *Adam, Eve, and the Serpent*, 29.

6. Potts (1997), Sex and the birth rate.

7. Pagels (1988), *Adam, Eve, and the Serpent*, 110–11, 21.

8. Georges Duby, J. Dunnett, trans. (1994), *Love and Marriage in the Middle Ages* (Cambridge University Press, Cambridge), quoted in Biller (2000), *The Measure of Multitude*, 185. The Biller quotations are on the same page, emphasis in original.

9. Biller (2000), *The Measure of Multitude*, 138, 173–76. The quotation is on p. 176.

10. Gies and Gies (1990), *Life in a Medieval Village*, 106.

11. Ecclesiastical court record quoted in Riddle (1997), *Contraception and Abortion from the Ancient World to the Renaissance*, 22–24. Biller (2000), *The Measure of Multitude*, 139–40, also provides an account of the story of Béatrice. Riddle reports that use of *Ferula asafedia* survived in the modern era, with women simply wearing it as an amulet around their necks, possibly a case of mimicking the irrelevant secondary behavior rather than the effective primary one—insertion into the "abdomen" as a pessary. Riddle (2006), personal communication, October 6.

12. Plato, Theaetetus 149c–d, in Hamilton and Cairns (1971), *The Collected Dialogues of Plato*, 854.

13. Achterberg (1990), *Woman as Healer*, 121. The cited document is called Sloane 2463 and is rendered here in modern English.

14. The comment on land boundaries is from Gies and Gies (1990), *Life in a Medieval Village*, 18. "Beating the bounds" is from BBC (2003), Boys "bounced" in bizarre tradition. The quotation is from Cantor (2001), *In the Wake of the Plague*, 8.

15. Wills (1997), *Yellow Fever, Black Goddess*; Cantor (2001), *In the Wake of the Plague*.

16. Information on dowers and inheritance is from Cantor (2001), *In the Wake of the Plague*, 127, 203. The Bristol study is from Maryanne Kowaleski (1984), Exeter, Bristol and Dartmouth, paper delivered at the Berkshire Conference on the History of Women, Smith College, Northampton, Mass., June, cited in Anderson and Zinsser (1988), *A History of Their Own*, 360.

17. Fry (1967), *Rulers of Britain*, 64–65; Cantor (2001), *In the Wake of the Plague*.

18. Jean Bodin (1606 [1576]), *The Six Books of a Commonwealth*, trans. Richard Knolles (London), quoted in Hutchinson (1967), *The Population Debate*. I have modernized the seventeenth-century English translation Hutchinson provides.

19. Chaucer (1983), *The Canterbury Tales.* I have modernized Chaucer's Middle English, 1032–33.

20. Pearsall (1992), *The Life of Geoffrey Chaucer*; Cantor (2001), *In the Wake of the Plague*, 219; Ruiz (1996), *Medieval Europe.*

21. Cologne's midwives from Heinsohn and Steiger (2004), *Witchcraft, Population Catastrophe and Economic Crisis in Renaissance Europe*, 18; and from Riddle (1997), *Eve's Herbs*, 113. New England accused witches from Karlsen (1989 [1987]), *The Devil in the Shape of a Woman*, 47 and 142. Grace Sherwood from Shapira (2006), After toil and trouble, "witch" is cleared.

22. Ehrenreich and English (1973), *Witches, Midwives, and Nurses.* For an opposing view, see Harley (1990), Historians as demonologists.

23. Heinsohn and Steiger (2004), *Witchcraft, Population Catastrophe and Economic Crisis in Renaissance Europe*; Heinsohn and Steiger (1982), The elimination of Medieval birth control and the witch trials of modern times; Riddle (1997), *Eve's Herbs.*

24. Summers, trans. (1928), *Malleus Maleficarum*, xliii.

25. Ibid., 66.

26. Oster (2004), Witchcraft, weather and economic growth in Renaissance Europe.

27. Heinsohn and Steiger (2004), *Witchcraft, Population Catastrophe and Economic Crisis in Renaissance Europe.*

28. Domning (1997), Pope's cultural critique lacks perspective.

29. Defoe quoted in Shorto (2006), Contra-contraception, 48; and in Riddle (1997), *Eve's Herbs*, 155.

Chapter 8: Age of Enlightenment

Epigraph: Timothy Sellers (song composer and lyricist) (2005), Thomas Robert Malthus, *26 Scientists Volume One: Anning–Malthus*, Greeen Records, used by permission. Actually, Malthus was the second son of seven children. Until corrected by surgery, his cleft palate affected his speech, though whether he stuttered is less certain.

1. Himes (1970 [1936]), *Medical History of Contraception*, 9.

2. Niccolò Machiavelli (1512–17), *Discourses on the First Ten Books of Livy*, book 2, chapter 5, quoted in Hutchinson (1967), *The Population Debate*, 17; Sir Walter Raleigh (1650), *Discourse of War in General*, quoted in Hutchinson, ibid., 34.

3. Sir Matthew Hale (1673), A Discourse Touching Provision for the Poor, London, quoted in Hutchinson (1967), *The Population Debate*, 56.

4. Graunt quoted in Hutchinson (1967), *The Population Debate*, 45–46; Smith (1992), *Formal Demography*, 2; Behar (1987), Malthus and the development of demographic analysis.

5. Fénelon quoted in Hutchinson (1967), *The Population Debate*, 30; Franklin quoted in Hutchinson, ibid., 116.

6. Lütken quoted in Saether (1993), Otto Diederich Lütken, 511.

7. James (1979), *Population Malthus*, 46.

8. Malthus (1926 [1798]), *First Essay on Population*, 139.

9. Schabas (2005), *The Natural Origins of Economics*, 106.

10. Bryson (2003), *A Short History of Nearly Everything*, 65–66, 60–62. A metric ton amounts to 2,205 pounds.

11. Wrigley and Schofield (1981), *The Population History of England, 1541–1871*; Gay (1966), *Age of Enlightenment*, 107; Uglow (2002), *The Lunar Men*, 165.

12. There are several modern editions of Malthus's Essay on the Principle of Population in print. It's important to see which of the seven original editions is reproduced in each case. The actual "principal of population" is most clearly stated about four pages into the opening chapter of the first edition (often called the "first essay"), and the principal was recapitulated in somewhat different terms in later editions. The second through the seventh original editions are all considered versions of the "second essay," because they represent an altogether new work with only slight variations among them. I have used a publication of the first edition from 1926 and a publication of the seventh edition from 1927. A contemporary republication of the first essay, with selections from the second and related writings on population by other authors (including this one), is Appleman (2004), *An Essay on the Principle of Population*. The complete text of the first edition can also be found at http://socserv2.socsci.mcmaster.ca/~econ/ugcm/3||3/malthus.popu.txt (accessed November 27, 2007).

13. For details of Malthus's life I have drawn from James (1979), *Population Malthus,* and from a variety of shorter biographical works, especially W. T. Layton, introduction, in Malthus (1927 [1914]), *An Essay on Population*, vii–xv; James Bonar, Notes on Malthus's first essay, in Malthus (1926 [1798]), *An Essay on Population*, i–xxv; and Parsons (1998), *The Reverend Thomas Robert Malthus.*

14. Karl Marx (1861–63), *Theories of Surplus Value*, vol. 2, quoted in Meek, ed. (1971), *Marx and Engels on the Population Bomb*, 129.

15. For his reaction to inequality of property, see Malthus (1926 [1798]), *First Essay on Population*, 287n–288n. For a view on death as a punishment, see Malthus, ibid., 256. On a national education system, see Malthus (1927 [1872]), *An Essay on Population*, 212–15. On women's intellectual faculties, see Malthus (1926 [1798]), *First Essay on Population*, 238. On workers collectively reducing their working hours to gain higher wages, see Malthus (1927 [1914]), *An Essay on Population*, 298.

16. Wood (1998), A theory of preindustrial population dynamics, 131.

17. Writing about the Black Death in fourteenth-century Europe, for example, authors John Kelly and Norman F. Cantor both use *Malthusian* to describe the conditions experienced by populations that were outgrowing their agricultural resource base. Kelly (2005), *The Great Mortality*; Cantor (2001), *In the Wake of the Plague*. Wood (1998), A theory of preindustrial population dynamics, synthesizes the work of Malthus and some of his critics to come up with a "theory of preindustrial population dynamics . . . in Malthusian systems," 99. Gregory Clark's argument about the "Malthusian trap" in Clark (2007), *A Farewell to Alms*.

18. Engels (1844), The myth of overpopulation, from *Outlines of a Critique of Political Economy*, in Meek, ed. (1971), *Marx and Engels on the Population Bomb*, 59, 57.

19. Simon (1996), *The Ultimate Resource 2*, 73; David Coleman (2006), personal communication, September 25.

20. Barta (2007), Crop prices soar, pushing up the cost of food globally.

21. Malthus (1926 [1798]), *First Essay on Population*, 249.

22. Story of Merian from Schiebinger (1993), *Nature's Body*, 210. The Linnaean name of the plant is *Caesalpihia pulcherrima*.

23. Bryson (2003), *A Short History of Nearly Everything*, 374–75, 356–57.

24. Schiebinger (1993), *Nature's Body*, 40–74.

25. Ibid., 11–39.

26. Himes (1970 [1936]), *Medical History of Contraception*, 194–95; van de Walle and Muhsam (1995), Fatal secrets and the French fertility transition.

27. Malthus (1927 [1914]), *An Essay on Population*, 52.

28. Parsons (1998), *The Reverend Thomas Robert Malthus*, 34–35.

29. James (1979), *Population Malthus*, 364–65.

30. McEvedy and Jones (1978), *Atlas of World Population History*, 179–81; Harris and Ross (1987), *Death, Sex, and Fertility*, 98–99. Harris and Ross cite Susan B. Hanley and Kozo Yamamura (1977), *Economic and Demographic Change in Preindustrial Japan 1600–1868* (Princeton University Press, Princeton, N.J.), 182, for the detail about congratulatory customs after a birth.

31. I'm grateful to Fabian Drixler of Harvard University for sharing an image of this scroll and its story, part of his doctoral dissertation research.

32. Bengtsson and Dribe (2006), Deliberate control in a natural fertility population, all quotations 728.

33. Wollstonecraft (2004 [1792]), *A Vindication of the Rights of Women*, 238.

34. Schiebinger (1993), *Nature's Body*, 35; Godwin quotation, 56.

35. Biller (2000), *The Measure of Multitude*, 155.

Chapter 9: Zen and the Art of Population Management

Epigraphs: Mead (2001 [1949]), *Male and Female*, 208; Levenson was an American comic and frequent television performer who died in 1980. This line is widely attributed to him, but I have not been able to find a reliable citation.

1. Apologies for the chapter name go to author Robert Pirsig, Pirsig (1984 [1974]), *Zen and the Art of Motorcycle Maintenance*.
2. For Francis Place and the historical developments discussed in this and the next few paragraphs, see Himes (1970 [1936]), *Medical History of Contraception*, 209–59; and Noonan (1986 [1965]), *Contraception*, 392–407.
3. Speert (2004), *Obstetrics and Gynecology: A History and Iconography*, 443.
4. Garrett Hardin, Second thoughts on "The Tragedy of the Commons," in Daly, ed. (1980), *Economics, Ecology, Ethics*, 118.
5. Potts (1997), Sex and the birth rate.
6. Besant (1878), *The Law of Population*, 26–36 and dedication page.
7. Himes (1970 [1936]), *Medical History of Contraception*, 228–29.
8. Gifford quoted in Gordon (1993), *The Alarming History of Medicine*, 146.
9. Noonan (1986 [1965]), *Contraception*, 407–8.
10. Ibid., 412–13.
11. Riddle (1997), *Eve's Herbs*, 246.
12. A rich literature covers the life, career, and impact of Margaret Sanger—along with some vitriolic Web pages that vilify her as a racist eugenicist. I recommend studying her times and reading her words. I have relied primarily on Sanger (2003 [1922]), *The Pivot of Civilization*; Katz et al., eds. (2003), *The Selected Papers of Margaret Sanger*; Reed (2003), *Margaret Sanger*; Chesler (1992), *Woman of Valor*; McCann (1994), *Birth Control Politics in the United States, 1916–1945*; and Gordon (1980 [1974]), *Woman's Body, Woman's Right*.
13. "Tell Jake to sleep on the roof" from Sanger (1938), *Margaret Sanger*, 91.
14. Katz et al. (2003), *The Selected Papers of Margaret Sanger*, 457–59; Piotrow (1973), *World Population Crisis*, 8.
15. Chesler (1992), *Woman of Valor*, 258–59.
16. Eugenics in Brazil from Gibson (2006), Race in Brazil.
17. Chesler (1992), *Woman of Valor*, 182.
18. Sanger (2003 [1922]), *The Pivot of Civilization*, 185.
19. Ibid., 122.
20. For accounts of the impact of the eugenics movement in the United States, see Kevles (1985), *In the Name of Eugenics*; and Larson (1995), *Sex, Race, and Science*. For an account of forced eugenic sterilizations in the United States (the focus is North Carolina), see Schoen (2005), *Choice and Coercion*.

21. McCann (1994), *Birth Control Politics in the United States, 1916–1945*, 152. The account and the text of King's speech are available at Planned Parenthood, www.plannedparenthood.org/about-us/who-we-are/the-reverend-martin-luther-king-jr.htm (accessed November 27, 2007).

22. Zeisel, ed. (1984), *Censorship*, 311.

23. Grossman (1995), *Reforming Sex*, 153.

24. Sanger (1920), *Woman and the New Race*, 151; United States Holocaust Memorial museum (2004), Deadly Medicine: Creating the Master Race, exhibition at the Museum, Washington, D.C., April 22, 2004, to October 16, 2005.

25. Several books document the history of the international population and family planning movement. In addition to Piotrow (1973), *World Population Crisis*, I have relied on Kantner and Kantner (2006), *The Struggle for International Consensus on Population and Development*; Harkavy (1995), *Curbing Population Growth*; and Donaldson (1990), *Nature Against Us*.

26. Bloom, Canning, and Sevilla (2003), *The Demographic Dividend*; Birdsall, Kelley, and Sinding, eds. (2001), *Population Matters*.

27. President's Committee to Study the United States Military Assistance Program (1959), *Composite Report*, 96. Draper had served under Eisenhower during the war and under George Marshall after it. He spent much of the rest of his career promoting assistance from industrialized countries for family planning services in developing ones. In 1965 he helped found the Population Crisis Committee, which became Population Action International.

28. Eisenhower quotation from Piotrow (1973), *World Population Crisis*, 36–45.

29. Micklethwait and Wooldridge (2004), *The Right Nation*, 33.

30. UN Population Fund (2004), *The Cairo Consensus at 10*, 5.

31. Ravenholt (1969), AID's family planning strategy.

32. For an account of rather mild excesses in the 1970s family planning program in Bangladesh, illustrating both the desperation of rural women to postpone pregnancies and the ham-fisted tactics and indifferent attitudes of some family planning providers, see Hartmann and Boyce (1983), *A Quiet Violence*.

33. Bird (1976), Indira Gandhi uses force.

34. D'Agnes (2001), *From Cabbages to Condoms*, 213–14.

35. Ibid., 166n.

36. Goodall (2003), Bridging the chasm, 3.

37. Feyisetan and Casterline (2000), Fertility preferences and contraceptive change in developing countries.

38. Heuveline (1999), The global and regional impact of mortality and fertility transitions, 1950–2000. I have taken the liberty of adjusting Heuveline's population total conservatively to account for the higher world population at the time of writing.

39. Editorial quoted in J. Mayone Stycos, Ideology, faith, and population growth in Latin America, in Peterson (1972), *Readings in Population*, 349.

40. Roach (1997), New world Pompeii.

41. Pontifical Academy of Sciences quoted in Cowell (1994), Scientists linked with Vatican call for population curbs.

42. Calculation by Elizabeth Leahy and Robert Engelman (2006), Population Action International.

43. Samuelson (2006), Behind the birth dearth.

44. Speidel (2006), Population donor landscape analysis for review of Packard Foundation international grantmaking in population, sexual and reproductive health and rights.

45. Dugger (2006), U.S. cuts funds for family planning overseas, stirring opposition.

46. Indo-Asian News Service (2006), Mosques in Pakistan to preach family planning; Global News Wire/Africa Asia Intelligence Wire (2006), Pakistan offers free education to one-child families.

47. UN IRIN (2005), Yemen: Population grows to 19.7 million.

48. Blanc and Tsui (2005), The dilemma of past success.

Chapter 10: The Return of Nature

Epigraphs: Brown (1992), The objectivity crisis, 780; Brown was a long-time Democratic congressman from California. Riche (2001), A woman's status in European life, 16.

1. Burkert (1979), *Structure and History in Greek Mythology and Ritual*, 30–31; Grimal (1996 [1951]), *The Dictionary of Classical Mythology*, 193; Hamilton (1942), *Mythology*, 256–59. The image of two snakes entwined around a staff is even older than Greek civilization, having appeared in Mesopotamian art in the third millennium BC.

2. Grubb (2004), Power to the people, 469.

3. Balter (2006), The baby deficit.

4. Tenner (1996), *Why Things Bite Back*.

5. Muir (1988), *My First Summer in the Sierra*, 110.

6. Simon and Kahn (1984), *The Resourceful Earth*, 7.

7. Kahn and Wiener (1967), *The Year 2000*.

8. *Washington Post* (2006), Oceans in peril, A14; Groppe quoted in Bahree, and Cummins (2006), In oil's new era, power shifts to countries with reserves, A1.

9. Mannell quoted in Carr (2004), On the road, B1.

10. Wolf (2001), Why I changed my mind on a new river crossing, B8; Barbaro (2003), Selling the public on more lines.

11. Walton quoted in El Nasser (2006), A nation of 300 million.

12. Terrones (2004), What explains the recent run-up in house prices?, 74–76.

13. E. Weiss (2002), The coffee is hot, and so is pre-dawn business; O'Connor (2004), Wakefulness finds a powerful ally.

14. Faulkner quoted in Wald (2005), I vant to drink your vatts.

15. Delaney and Smith (2006), Surge in Internet use, energy costs has big tech firms seeking power.

16. Irwin and Kang (2006), Well-paid benefit most as economy flourishes.

17. Native of Tuxpan, Mexico, quoted in Thornburgh (2006), Inside the life of the migrants next door, 39.

18. Gowen (2007), A second migration.

19. Wackernagel et al. (2005), *Europe 2005*, p. 3, figure 2.

20. UN Food and Agriculture Organization (2004), Population aspects in the reduction of hunger.

21. Des Forges (2005), Ordinary men, 3; Engelman et al. (2006 [2000]), *People in the Balance*.

22. Martine (2007), *State of World Population 2007*.

23. Keating quoted in Wax (2006), Dowries running dry in drought-stricken East Africa, A1.

24. Chivers (2005), A tour of Chernobyl.

25. Wills (1998), *Yellow Fever, Black Goddess*; Vittor et al. (2006), The effect of deforestation on the human-biting rate of *Anopheles darlingi*, the primary vector of falciparum malaria in the Peruvian Amazon; Keele et al. (2006), Chimpanzee reservoirs of pandemic and nonpandemic HIV-1.

26. Bennett quoted in Dreifus (2006), A global advocate for the meal that cannot speak for itself.

27. Stecklow (2006), U.S. falls behind in tracking cattle to control disease. Geographer Vaclav Smil estimates that livestock outweigh the planet's wild animals by a factor of 20. Reported in Radford (2004), Touching the void. Environmental scientist Susan Suback and colleagues estimated in 1994 that there were 60 million bison in the continental United States in preindustrial times, compared to 1.4 billion ruminant livestock worldwide today. Cited in Keppler (2007), Ruminant rumination, 16.

28. Perlin (1989), *A Forest Journey*; Ponting (1993 [1991]), *A Green History of the World*; Weber (n.d.), *Population and Energy*, 15; U.S. Energy Information Agency (2006), *International Energy Outlook 2006*, 51, short tons converted to metric tons.

29. Fountain (2004), Catch the wind, change the weather.

30. Schlesinger (1990), Vegetation an unlikely answer.

31. Chow, Kopp, and Portney (2003), Energy resources and global development, 1528.

32. Broad (2006), How to cool a planet (maybe).

33. Stone (2005), Drip, drip, drip.

34. Feder (2006), Technology's future.

35. Engelman (1988), Scientists think they've identified unexpected source of methane.

36. Budimbwa quoted in Rosenblum (2004), Dark years on the dark continent.

37. Bogue (2006), review of *The American People: Census 2000*, 172.

38. Larry Brilliant, a physician and executive director of Google.org, called child survival "by far the most important" way to slow the growth of population. "In a community in which childhood death rates hover near one-third, most parents will opt to overshoot their internal targets on their own most desired family size. They will have replacement births, insurance births, lottery births—and the population will soar." He conceded that "the data from Africa appears to contradict the child survival hypothesis"—but stuck by his point. Brilliant (2007), Climate, poverty and health.

39. International Center for Research on Women (2005), State Department forum stresses need for NGOs and governments to address child marriage and improve options for girls, 1.

40. Reuters (2000), Bangladesh has worst violence against women; Reuters (2005), South Africa spouse killings epidemic.

41. Reuters (2006), Creaking health systems hampering AIDS battle.

42. Information on Italy from Martinelli (2003), Why do they do it in the road?

43. Speidel (2006), Population donor landscape analysis for review of Packard Foundation international grantmaking in population, sexual and reproductive health and rights.

44. Raymond (2006), The birth of contraception.

Bibliography

Achterberg, Jeanne. 1990. *Woman as Healer*. Shambhala, Boston.

Adams, Jeremy. 2000. *Neolithic Europe*. The Teaching Company, Chantilly, Va.

Adovasio, J. M., Olga Soffer, and Jake Page. 2007. *The Invisible Sex: Uncovering the True Roles of Women in Prehistory*. Smithsonian Books, New York.

Aiello, Leslie C., and Jonathan C. K. Wells. 2002. Energetics and the evolution of the genus *Homo*. *Annual Review of Anthropology* 31:323–38.

Alan Guttmacher Institute. 1999. *Sharing Responsibility: Women, Society and Abortion Worldwide*. Alan Guttmacher Institute, New York.

Alroy, John. 2001. A multispecies overkill simulation of the end-Pleistocene megafaunal mass extinction. *Science* 292, no. 5523 (June 8):1893–96.

Ambrose, Stanley. 2003. Did the super-eruption of Toba cause a human population bottleneck? Reply to Gathorne-Hardy and Harcourt-Smith. *Journal of Human Evolution* 45: 231–37.

Anderson, Bonnie S., and Judith P. Zinsser. 1988. *A History of Their Own: Women in Europe from Prehistory to the Present*. Vol. 1. Harper & Row, New York.

Anderson, Tim. 1996. Biomechanics and running economy. *Sports Medicine* 22 (2): 76–89.

Appleman, Philip, ed. 2004 [1976]. *An Essay on the Principle of Population*. Norton, New York.

Ardrey, Robert. 1961. *African Genesis: A Personal Investigation into the Animal Origins and Nature of Man*. Macmillan, London.

Aristotle. 1809. *The History of Animals of Aristotle, and His Treatise on Physiognomy*. Trans. Thomas Taylor. Robert Wilks, London.

Armstrong, Karen. 2001. *Buddha*. Viking, New York.

Bahree, Bushan, and Chip Cummins. 2006. In oil's new era, power shifts to countries with reserves. *Wall Street Journal*, June 14, A1.

Bakalar, Nicholas. 2005. Unrelated adults at home increases risk for children. *New York Times*, November 8, D8.

Balter, Michael. 2006. The baby deficit. *Science* 312, no. 5782 (June 30): 1894–97.

Barbaro, Michael. 2003. Selling the public on more lines. *Washington Post*, August 20, E1.

Barnosky, Anthony D., Paul L. Koch, Robert S. Feranec, Scott L. Wing, and Alan B. Shabel. 2004. Assessing the causes of late Pleistocene extinctions on the continents. *Science* 306, no. 5693 (October 1): 70–75.

Barrionuevo, Alexei. 2007. China's appetites lead to changes in its trade diet. *New York Times*, April 6, A1.

Barta, Patrick. 2007. Crop prices soar, pushing up cost of food globally. *Wall Street Journal*, April 9, A1.

BBC. 2003. Boys "bounced" in bizarre tradition, June 7, http://news.bbc.co.uk/1/hi/wales/south_east/2969750.stm (accessed November 27, 2007).

Becker, Gary S. 1960. An economic analysis of fertility. In National Bureau of Economic Research. *Demography and Economic Change in Developed Countries*. 209–40. Princeton University Press, Princeton, N.J.

Begun, David R. 2006. Planet of the apes. *Scientific American* 16, no. 2 (special edition): 4–13.

Behar, Cem L. 1987. Malthus and the development of demographic analysis. *Population Studies* 41:269–81.

Bellig, Robert, and George Stevens. 1988. *The Evolution of Sex: Nobel Conference XXIII*. Harper & Row, San Francisco.

Bengtsson, Tommy, and Martin Dribe. 2006. Deliberate control in a natural fertility population: Southern Sweden, 1766–1864. *Demography* 43 (4): 727–46.

Besant, Annie, 1878. *The Law of Population: Its Consequences and Its Bearing upon Human Conduct and Morals*. Asa K. Butts, New York.

Biller, Peter. 2000. *The Measure of Multitude: Population in Medieval Thought*. Oxford University Press, Oxford.

Bird, Kai. 1976. Indira Gandhi uses force. *The Nation*, June 19, 747–49.

Birdsall, Nancy, Allen C. Kelley, and Steven W. Sinding, eds. 2001. *Population Matters: Demographic Change, Economic Growth, and Poverty in the Developing World*. Oxford University Press, Oxford.

Blanc, Ann K., and Amy O. Tsui. 2005. The dilemma of past success: Insiders' views on the future of the international family planning movement. *Studies in Family Planning* 36, no. 4 (December): 263–76.

Bloom, David E., David Canning, and Jaypee Sevilla. 2003. *The Demographic Dividend: A New Perspective on the Economic Consequences of Population Change*. Rand, Santa Monica, Calif.

Boehm, Philip, trans. 2005. *A Woman in Berlin: Eight Weeks in the Conquered City*. Metropolitan Books, New York.

Bogue, Donald J. 2006. Review of *The American People: Census 2000*. *Population and Development Review* 32, no. 1 (March 1):169–73.

Bongaarts, John, and Charles F. Westoff. 2000. The potential role of contraception in reducing abortion. *Studies in Family Planning* 31, no. 3 (September): 193–202.

Boonstra, Heather D., Rachel Benson Gold, Cory L. Richards, and Lawrence B. Finer. 2006. *Abortion in Women's Lives*. Guttmacher Institute, New York.

Bowra, C. M. 1965. *Classical Greece*. Time-Life Books, New York.

Boulding, Elise. 1976. *The Underside of History: A View of Women through Time* Westview Press, Boulder, Colo.

Brilliant, Larry. 2007. Climate, poverty and health: Time for preventive medicine. John H. Chafee Memorial Lecture on Science and the Environment, presented at the Seventh National Conference on Science, Policy, and the Environment, National Council for Science and the Environment, Washington, D.C., February 1.

Broad, William J. 2006. How to cool a planet (maybe). *New York Times*, June 27, F1.

Brown, George E., Jr. 1992. The objectivity crisis. *American Journal of Physics* 60, no. 9 (September):779–81, 780.

Brunet, Michel, et al. 2002. A new hominid from the Upper Miocene of Chad, Central Africa. *Nature* 418:145–51.

Bryson, Bill. 2003. *A Short History of Nearly Everything*. Broadway Books, New York.

Burkert, Walter. 1979. *Structure and History in Greek Mythology and Ritual*. University of California Press, Berkeley.

Buttrick, George Arthur. 1984 [1952]. *The Interpreter's Bible: A Commentary in Twelve Volumes*. Abingdon Press, Nashville.

Cahill, Thomas. 1996 [1995]. *How the Irish Saved Civilization: The Untold Story of Ireland's Heroic Role from the Fall of Rome to the Rise of Medieval Europe*. Anchor Books, New York.

——. 2003. *Sailing the Wine-Dark Sea: Why the Greeks Matter.* Nan Talese Press/Doubleday, New York.

Caldwell, John C. 2004. Fertility control in the classical world: Was there an ancient fertility transition? *Journal of Population Research* 21 (1): 1–17.

Cammack, Diana. 2001. *Malawi at the Threshold: Resources, Conflict and Ingenuity in a Newly Democratic State.* Committee on International Security Studies, American Academy of Arts and Sciences, Cambridge, Mass.

Campbell, Bernard, ed. 1972. *Sexual Selection and the Descent of Man 1871–1971.* Heinemann, London.

Campbell, Martha, Nuriye Nalan Sahin-Hodoglugil, and Malcolm Potts. 2006. Barriers to fertility regulation: A review of the literature. *Studies in Family Planning* 37, no. 2 (June): 87–98.

Campbell, Martha, Ndola Prata, Anke Hemmerling, and Malcolm Potts. N.d. The impact of freedom on fertility transition: Revisiting the theoretical framework. Unpublished paper, University of California, Berkeley.

Cantor, Norman F. 2001. *In the Wake of the Plague: The Black Death and The World It Made.* Free Press, New York.

Carneiro, Robert L. 2000. The transition from quantity to quality: A neglected causal mechanism in accounting for social evolution. *Proceedings of the National Academy of Sciences* 97 (23): 12926–31.

Carr, Martha Randolph. 2004. On the road. *Washington Post*, September 5, B1.

Cassady, Alison. 2007. *The Carbon Boom: State and National Trends in Carbon Dioxide Emissions Since 1990.* U.S. PIRG Education Fund, Washington, D.C.

Cavalli-Sforza, Luigi L., Paolo Menozzi, and Alberto Piazza. 1993. Demic expansions and human evolution. *Science* 259, no. 5095 (January 29):639–46.

Chandler, Tertius. 1987. *Four Thousand Years of Urban Growth: An Historical Census.* St. David's University Press, Lewiston, N.Y.

Chaucer, Geoffrey. 1983. *The Canterbury Tales.* Vol. 2. The Franklin Library, Franklin Center, Pa.

Chernow, Ron. 2004. *Alexander Hamilton.* Penguin Press, New York.

Chesler, Ellen. 1992. *Woman of Valor: Margaret Sanger and the Birth Control Movement in America.* Simon & Schuster, New York.

Chivers, C. J. 2005. A tour of Chernobyl, radioactivity included. *New York Times*, *Süddeutsche Zeitung* supplemental ed., June 27, 3.

Chow, Jeffrey, Raymond J. Kopp, and Paul R. Portney. 2003. Energy resources and global development. *Science* 302, no. 5650 (November 28): 1528–31.

Christian, John J. 1970. Social subordination, population density, and mammalian evolution. *Science* 168, no. 3927 (April 3): 84–90.

Cincotta, Richard P., and Robert Engelman. 2000. *Nature's Place: Human Population and the Future of Biological Diversity*. Population Action International, Washington, D.C.

Clark, Gregory. 2007. *A Farewell to Alms: A Brief Economic History of the World*. Princeton University Press, Princeton, N.J.

Cleland, John, Stan Bernstein, Alex Ezeh, Anibal Foundes, Anna Glasier, and Jolene Innis. 2006. Family planning: The unfinished agenda. *The Lancet* 368, no. 9549 (November 18): 1810–27.

Clucas, Humphrey. 1985. *Versions of Catullus: Translation*. Hippopotamus Press, Frome, UK.

Coale, Ansley J. 1974. The history of human population. In *The Human Population*. Freeman and Co. for *Scientific American*, San Francisco.

Coale, Ansley J., and Susan Cotts Watkins, eds. 1986. *The Decline of Fertility in Europe*. Princeton University Press, Princeton, N.J.

Cody, Edward. 2007. China's expansion puts workers in harm's way. *Washington Post*, April 26, A24.

Cohen, Joel E. 1995. *How Many People Can the Earth Support?*. Norton, New York.

Cohen, Mark Nathan, Roy S. Malpass, and Harold G. Klein, eds. 1980. *Biosocial Mechanisms of Population Regulation*. Yale University Press, New Haven, Conn.

Conniff, Richard. 2007. Death in Happy Valley. *Smithsonian* (February), 40–51.

Cowell, Alan. 1994. Scientists linked with Vatican call for population curbs. *New York Times*, June 16, A6.

Cowan, Robert C. 1998. If you don't spare the tree, you spoil more than the jungle. *Christian Science Monitor*, January 13, 14.

D'Agnes, Thomas. 2001. *From Cabbages to Condoms: An Authorized Biography of Mechai Viravaidya*. Post Books, Bangkok.

Daly, Herman E., ed. 1980. *Economics, Ecology, Ethics: Essays Toward a Steady-State Economy*. W. H. Freeman, New York.

Davis, Kingsley. 1974. The migrations of human population. In *The Human Population*. Freeman and Co. for *Scientific American*, San Francisco.

Dawkins, Richard. 1989 [1976]. *The Selfish Gene*. Oxford University Press, New York.

de Waal, Frans. 1982. *Chimpanzee Politics: Power and Sex Among Apes*. Harper & Row, New York.

———. 1989. *Peacemaking Among Primates*. Harvard University Press, Cambridge, Mass.

———. 2005. How animals do business. *Scientific American* 292, no. 4 (April): 73–77.

Delaney, Kevin J., and Rebecca Smith. 2006. Surge in Internet use, energy costs has big tech firms seeking power. *Wall Street Journal*, June 13, A1.

DeMeo, James. 1998. *Saharasia: The 4000 BCE Origins of Child Abuse, Sex-Repression, Warfare and Social Violence in the Deserts of the Old World*. Orgone Biophysical Research Lab, Ashland, Ore.

Demographic and Health Surveys and CARE International/Niger. 1999.*Enquête Démographique et de Santé 1998*. Macro International, Calverton, Md.

Denham, Woodrow W. 1974. Population structure, infant transport, and infanticide among Pleistocene and modern hunter-gatherers. *Journal of Anthropological Research* 30 (3): 191–98.

Des Forges, Alison. 2005. Ordinary men. Review of *Machete Season: The Killers in Rwanda Speak*, by Jean Hatzfeld. *Washington Post*, August 21, Book World p. 3.

Diamond, Jared. 1997. *Guns, Germs, and Steel: The Fate of Human Societies*. W. W. Norton, New York.

———. 2005. *Collapse: How Societies Choose to Fail or Succeed*. Viking, New York.

Domning, Daryl P. 1997. Pope's cultural critique lacks perspective. *National Catholic Reporter*, September 19.

Donaldson, Peter J. 1990. *Nature Against Us: The United States and the World Population Crisis, 1965–1980*. University of North Carolina Press, Chapel Hill.

Donlan, C. Josh. 2007. Restoring America's big, wild animals. *Scientific American* 296, no. 6 (June): 70–77.

Downs, Barbara. 2003. *Fertility of American Women: June 2002*. Current Population Reports, P20-548. U.S. Census Bureau, Washington, D.C.

Dreifus, Claudia. 2006. A global advocate for the meal that cannot speak for itself. *New York Times*, June 6, F2.

Dugger, Celia W. 2006. U.S. cuts funds for family planning overseas, stirring opposition. *New York Times*, February 15, A7.

Dunbar, Robin. 1996. *Grooming, Gossip, and the Evolution of Language*. Harvard University Press, Cambridge, Mass.

Eaton, Joseph W., and Albert J. Mayer. 1954. *Man's Capacity to Reproduce: The Demography of a Unique Population*. Free Press, Glencoe, Ill.

The Economist. 2005–2006. Special "Christmas survey" on human evolution. December 24 to January 6, pp. 3–12.

Ehrenreich, Barbara, and Dierdre English. 1973. *Witches, Midwives, and Nurses: A History of Women Healers*. Feminist Press, Old Westbury, N.Y.

Einwögerer, Thomas, Herwig Friesinger, Marc Händel, Christine Neugebauer-Maresch, Ulrich Simon and Maria Teschler-Nicola. 2006. Upper Palaeolithic infant burials. *Nature* 444, no. 7117 (November 16): 285.

Eisenstadt, S. N., ed. 1986. *The Origins and Diversity of Axial Age Civilizations*. State University of New York Press, Albany.

Eisler, Riane. 1988 [1987]. *The Chalice and the Blade: Our History, Our Future*. Harper & Row, San Francisco.

El Nasser, Haya. 2006. A nation of 300 million. *USA Today*, July 5, 1A.

Eliade, Mircea. 1959 [1957]. *The Sacred and the Profane: The Nature of Religion*. Harcourt, New York.

Engelman, Robert. 1988. Scientists think they've identified unexpected source of methane. Scripps Howard News Service, April 7.

Engelman, Robert, Daniele Anastiasion, Eric Steiner, Sara Haddock, and Elizabeth Leahy. 2006 [2000]. *People in the Balance: Population and Natural Resources in the New Millennium*. Updated Web ed. Population Action International, Washington, D.C. http://216.146.209.72/Publications/Reports/People_in_the_ Balance/Interactive/peopleinthebalance/pages/index.php (accessed DNovember 27, 2007).

Erukhimovich, I. Y., A.R. Khokhlov, T.A. Vilgis, A. Ramzi, F. Boue, D. Einon. 1998. How many children can one man have? *Evolution and Human Behavior* 19:413–26.

Espenshade, Thomas J., Juan Carlos Guzman, and Charles F. Westoff. 2003. The surprising global variation in replacement fertility. *Population Research and Policy Review* 22:575–83.

Feachem, Richard G.A., Tord Kjellstrom, Christopher J.L. Murray, Mead Over, and Margaret A. Phillips, eds. 1992. *The Health of Adults in the Developing World*. Oxford University Press, Oxford.

Feder, Barnaby J. 2006. Technology's future: A look at the dark side. *New York Times*, May 17, G4.

Feen, Richard Harrow. 1996. Keeping the balance: Ancient Greek philosophical concerns with population and environment. *Population and Environment* 17 (6): 447–58.

Feyisetan, Bamikale, and John B. Casterline. 2000. Fertility preferences and contraceptive change in developing countries. *International Family Planning Perspectives* 26 (3): 100–9.

Fischman, Josh. 2000. Georgia on their mind. *U.S. News & World Report* 128, no. 29 (May 22): 65.

Finnegan, Frances. 2004 [2001]. *Do Penance or Perish: Magdalen Asylums in Ireland*. Oxford University Press, New York.

Foster, Steven, and James A. Duke. 1990. *A Field Guide to Medicinal Plants: Eastern and Central North America*. Houghton Mifflin, Boston.

Fountain, Henry. 2004. Catch the wind, change the weather. *New York Times*, November 2, F3.

———. 2006. Deciding on a roach motel by committee. *New York Times*, April 4, D3.

Fry, Plantagenet Somerset. 1967. *Rulers of Britain*. Paul Hamlyn, London.

Gamble, Clive. 1994. *Timewalkers: The Prehistory of Global Colonization*. Harvard University Press, Cambridge, Mass.

Gasana, James. 2002. Remember Rwanda? *World Watch* 15, no. 5 (Sepember/October): 24–33.

Gay, Peter. 1966. *Age of Enlightenment*. Time-Life Books, New York.

Gibson, Lydialyle. 2006. Race in Brazil. *University of Chicago Magazine* 98, no. 5 (June): 21–24.

Gies, Frances, and Joseph Gies. 1990. *Life in a Medieval Village*. Harper & Row, New York.

Gimbutas, Marija. 1982 [1974]. *The Gods and Goddesses of Old Europe: 6500–3500 B.C., Myths and Cult Images*. Updated ed. University of California Press, Berkeley.

Global News Wire/Africa Asia Intelligence Wire. 2006. Pakistan offers free education to one-child families. July 5.

Goldman, Shalom L. 2003. *Ancient Near Eastern Mythology*. The Teaching Company, Chantilly, Va.

Goodall, Jane. 2003. Bridging the chasm: Helping people and the environment across Africa. *Environmental Change and Security Program Report* 9: 1–5.

Gordon, Linda. 1980 [1974]. *Woman's Body, Woman's Right: A Social History of Birth Control in America*. Penguin, Harmondsworth, UK.

Gordon, Richard. 1993. *The Alarming History of Medicine*. St. Martin's Press, New York.

Gore, Rick. 2000. People like us: The dawn of humans. *National Geographic* 198, no. 1 (July): 95–117.

Gould, Stephen Jay. 1980. Introduction to *Dance of the Tiger: A Novel of the Ice Age*, by Björn Kurtén. Random House, New York.

Gowen, Annie. 2007. A second migration. *Washington Post*, March 8, B1.

Grimal, Pierre. 1996 [1951]. *The Dictionary of Classical Mythology*. Trans. A. R. Maxwell-Hyslop. Blackwell, Malden, Mass.

Grossman, Atina. 1995. *Reforming Sex: The German Movement for Birth Control and Abortion Reform, 1920–1950*. Oxford University Press, New York.

Grubb, Michael. 2004. Power to the people. *Nature* 428, no. 1 (April 1): 469–70.

Gugliotta, Guy. 2004. Suspects in the demise of giant mammals. *Washington Post*, October 11, A9.

———. 2006. Indians depleted wildlife, too. *Washington Post*, February 20, A9.

Hamblin, Dora Jane. 1987. Has the Garden of Eden been located at last? *Smithsonian* 18, no. 2 (May): 127–35.

Hamilton, Edith. 1942. *Mythology*. New American Library, New York.

Hamilton, Edith, and Huntington Cairns, eds., 1971 [1961]. *The Collected Dialogues of Plato*. Princeton University Press, Princeton, N.J.

Hammond, Kenneth J. 2004. *From Yao to Mao: 5000 Years of Chinese History*. The Teaching Company, Chantilly, Va.

Harkavy, Oscar. 1995. *Curbing Population Growth: An Insider's Perspective on the Population Movement*. Plenum Press, New York.

Harley, David. 1990. Historians as demonologists: The myth of the midwife-witch. *Social History of Medicine* 3 (1): 1–26.

Harpending, Henry C., Mark A. Batzer, Michael Gurven, Lynn B. Jorde, Alan R. Rogers, and Stephen T. Sherry. 1998. Genetic traces of ancient demography. *Proceedings of the National Academy of Sciences* 95 (4): 1961–67.

Harris, Marvin. 1991 [1977]. *Cannibals and Kings: The Origin of Cultures.* Vintage, New York.

Harris, Marvin, and Eric B. Ross. 1987. *Death, Sex, and Fertility: Population Regulation in Preindustrial and Developing Societies.* Columbia University Press, New York.

Hart Hansen, Jens P., Jørgen Meldgaard, and Jørgen Nordqvist. 1985. The mummies of Qilakitsoq. *National Geographic* 167, no. 2 (February): 191–207.

Hartmann, Betsy, and James T. Boyce. 1983. *A Quiet Violence: View from a Bangladesh Village.* Zed Press, London.

Hausfater, Glenn, and Sarah Blaffer Hrdy, eds. 1984. *Infanticide: Comparative and Evolutionary Perspectives.* Aldine, New York.

Hawkes, K., J.F. O'Connell, N.G. Blurton Jones, H. Alvarez, and E.L. Charnov. 1998. Grandmothering, menopause, and the evolution of human life histories. *Proceedings of the National Academy of Sciences* 95 (3): 1336–39.

Heinrich, Bernd. 2000 [1999]. *Mind of the Raven: Investigations and Adventures with Wolf-Birds.* HarperCollins, New York.

Heinsohn, Gunnar, and Otto Steiger. 1982. The elimination of medieval birth control and the witch trials of modern times. *International Journal of Women's Studies* 5, no. 3 (May 3):193–214.

———. 2004. *Witchcraft, Population Catastrophe and Economic Crisis in Renaissance Europe: An Alternative Macroeconomic Explanation.* With an appendix by John M. Riddle. Institut für Konjunktur und Strukturforschung Discussion Paper No. 31. University of Bremen.

Henshilwood, Christopher. S., J.C. Sealy, R.J. Yates, K. Cruz-Uribe, P. Goldberg, F.E. Grine, R.G. Klein, C. Poggenpoel, K.L. van Niekerk, and I. Watts. 2001. Blombos Cave, Southern Cape, South Africa: Preliminary report on the 1992–1999 excavations of the middle stone age levels. *Journal of Archaeological Science* 28:421–48.

Henshilwood, Christopher, Francesco d'Errico, Marian Vanhaeren, Karen van Niekerk, and Zenobia Jacobs. 2004. Middle Stone Age shell beads from South Africa. *Science* 304, no. 5669 (April 16): 404.

Heuveline, Patrick. 1999. The global and regional impact of mortality and fertility transitions, 1950–2000. *Population and Development Review* 25, no. 4 (December): 681–702.

Hewlett, Barry, and Michael Lamb, eds. 2005. *Hunter-Gatherer Childhoods: Evolutionary, Developmental, and Cultural Perspectives*. Aldine Transaction, New Brunswick, N.J.

Hey, Jody. 2005. On the number of New World founders: A population genetic portrait of the peopling of the Americas. *PLoS Biology* 3. no. 6 (June): e193.

Himes, Norman E. 1970 [1936]. *Medical History of Contraception*. Schocken Books, New York.

Hirsi Ali, Ayaan. 2007. *Infidel*. Free Press, New York.

Hodder, Ian. 2005. Women and Men at Çatalhöyük. *Scientific American* 15, no. 1 (January): 34–41.

Homer-Dixon, Thomas F. 1999. *Environment, Scarcity, and Violence*. Princeton University Press, Princeton, N.J.

———. 2006. Review of *States, Security, and Civil Strife in the Developing World*, by Colin H. Kahl. *Population and Development Review* 32, no. 3 (September): 585–87.

Hrdy, Sarah Blaffer. 1999. *Mother Nature: A History of Mothers, Infants, and Natural Selection*. Pantheon, New York.

Hudson, Valerie M., and Andrea Den Boer. 2002. A surplus of men, a deficit of peace: Security and sex ratios in Asia's largest states. *International Security* 26 (4): 5–38.

Hutchinson, E. P. 1967. *The Population Debate: The Development of Conflicting Theories Up to 1900*. Houghton Mifflin, Boston.

Ignatius, David. 2006. Is it warm in here? *Washington Post*, January 18, A17.

Indo-Asian News Service. 2006. Mosques in Pakistan to preach family planning. December 18.

International Center for Research on Women. 2005. State Department forum stresses need for NGOs and governments to address child marriage and improve options for girls. *ICRW Newsletter* (Washington, D.C.), October.

Irwin, Neil, and Cecilia Kang. 2006. Well-paid benefit most as economy flourishes. *Washington Post*, July 10, A1.

James, Patricia. 1979. *Population Malthus: His Life and Times*, Routledge & Kegan Paul, London.

Jorde, L. B., W.S. Watkins, and M.J. Bamshad. 2001. Population genomics: A bridge from evolutionary history to genetic medicine. *Human Molecular Genetics* 10 (20): 2199–2207.

Kahn, Herman, and Anthony J. Wiener, 1967. *The Year 2000: A Framework for Speculation on the Next 33 Years*. Macmillan, New York.

Kantner, John F., and Andrew Kantner. 2006. *The Struggle for International Consensus on Population and Development*. Palgrave Macmillan, New York.

Karlen, Arno. 2001 [1995]. *Plague's Progress: A Social History of Man and Disease*. Phoenix, London.

Karlsen, Carol F. 1989 [1987]. *The Devil in the Shape of a Woman: Witchcraft in Colonial New England*. Vintage, New York.

Katz, Esther, Cathy Moran Hajo, and Peter C. Engelman., eds. 2003. *The Selected Papers of Margaret Sanger*. University of Illinois Press, Urbana.

Kauffmann Doig, Federico. 1979. *Sexual Behaviour in Ancient Peru*. Kompactos, Lima.

Keele, Brandon F., et al. 2006. Chimpanzee reservoirs of pandemic and nonpandemic HIV-1. *Science* 313, no. 5789 (July 28): 523–26.

Kelly, John. 2005. *The Great Mortality: An Intimate History of the Black Death, the Most Devastating Plague of All Time*. HarperCollins, New York.

Keppler, Frank. 2007. Ruminant rumination. Reply to letter. *Scientific American* 296. no. 6 (June):16.

Kevles, Daniel J. 1985. *In the Name of Eugenics: Genetics and the Uses of Human Heredity*. Knopf, New York.

Kinzer, Stephen. 2007. After so many deaths, too many births. *New York Times*, February 11, The Week in Review, 14.

Kipling, Rudyard. *Just So Stories*. 1994 [1902]. Puffin, London.

Klapisch-Zuber, Christiane, ed. 1994 [1992]. *A History of Women in the West, II. Silences of the Middle Ages*. Belknap Press of Harvard University Press, Cambridge, Mass.

Knight, Chris. 1991. *Blood Relations: Menstruation and the Origins of Culture*. Yale University Press, New Haven, Conn.

Konner, Melvin, and Carol Worthman. 1980. Nursing frequency, gonadal function, and birth spacing among !Kung hunter-gatherers. *Science* 207, no. 4432 (February 15): 788–91.

Kramer, Samuel Noah. 1967. *Cradle of Civilization*. Time-Life Books, New York.

Kuhn, Steven L., and Mary C. Stiner. 2006. What's a mother to do? The division of labor among Neandertals and modern humans in Eurasia. *Current Anthropology* 47, no. 6 (December): 953–81.

Lang, Hartmut, and Ruth Gohlen. 1985. Completed fertility of the Hutterites: A revision. *Current Anthropology* 26, no. 3 (June): 395.

Larson, Edward J. 1995. *Sex, Race, and Science: Eugenics in the Deep South*. Johns Hopkins University Press, Baltimore.

Leakey, Richard E., and Roger Lewin. 1978 [1977]. *Origins: What New Discoveries Reveal About the Emergence of Our Species and Its Possible Future*. E. P. Dutton, New York.

———. 1992. *Origins Reconsidered: In Search of What Makes Us Human*. Doubleday, New York.

Lee, Richard B., and Irven DeVore, eds., 1968. *Man the Hunter*. Aldine, Chicago.

Lemonick, Michael D., and Andrea Dorfman. 2006. What makes us different? *Time*, October 9, 44–53.

Leonard, William R. 2002. Food for thought: Dietary change was a driving force in human evolution. *Scientific American* 287, no. 6 (December): 106–15.

Livi-Bacci, Massimo, 1992 [1989]. *A Concise History of World Population*. Blackwell, Cambridge, Mass.

Lloyd, G. E. R. 1983. *Science, Folklore and Ideology: Studies in the Life Sciences in Ancient Greece*. Cambridge University Press, Cambridge, U.K.

Longman, Phillip. 2005. Give more credit to prolific parents. *Washington Post*, January 9, B7.

Lovejoy, Owen. 1981. The origin of man. *Science* 211, no. 4480: 341–50.

Lorenz, Konrad. 1966 [1963]. *On Aggression*. Trans. Konrad Lorenz, Harcourt, New York.

Lutz, Wolfgang, Maria Rita Testa, and Dustin Penn. 2006. Population density is a key factor in declining human fertility. *Population and Environment* 28, no. 2 (November): 69–81.

Lynch, Colum. 2003. U.N. predicts much slower growth in population. *Washington Post*, December 9, A20.

Malthus, Thomas Robert. 1926 [1798]. *First Essay on Population*. Revised ed. Macmillan, London.

———. 1927 [1872]. *An Essay on Population*. J. M. Dent & Sons, London.

Marshack, Alexander. 1978. *Ice Age Art: 35,000–10,000 B.C.* Exhibit catalog. American Museum of Natural History, New York.

Marston, Cicely, and John Cleland. 2003. Relationships between contraception and abortion: A review of the evidence. *International Family Planning Perspectives* 29, no. 1 (March): 6–13.

Martin, Paul S. 1967. Pleistocene overkill. *Natural History* 76 (December): 32–38.

Martin, Paul S., and H. E. Wright, eds. 1967. *Pleistocene Extinctions: The Search for a Cause*. Vol. 6 of *Proceedings of the Seventh Congress of the International Association for Quaternary Research*. Yale University Press, New Haven, Conn.

Martine, George. 2007. *State of World Population 2007: Unleashing the Potential of Urban Growth*. UN Population Fund, New York.

Martinelli, Nicole. 2003. Why do they do it in the road? *Newsweek*, March 31, 12.

McBrearty, Sally, and Alison S. Brooks. 2000. The revolution that wasn't: A new interpretation of the origin of modern human behavior. *Journal of Human Evolution* 39, no. 5 (November): 453–563.

McCann, Carole R. 1994. *Birth Control Politics in the United States, 1916–1945*. Cornell University Press, Ithaca, N.Y.

McElvaine, Robert. 2001. *Eve's Seed: Biology, the Sexes, and the Course of History*. McGraw-Hill, New York.

McEvedy, Colin, and Richard Jones. 1978. *Atlas of World Population History*. Facts on File, New York.

McNeill, William H. 1991 [1963]. *The Rise of the West: A History of the Human Community*. University of Chicago Press, Chicago.

Mead, Margaret. 2001 [1949]. *Male and Female*. HarperCollins, New York.

Meadows, Donella H., Dennis L. Meadows, Jørgen Randers, and William W. Behrens III. 1972. *The Limits to Growth: A Report for the Club of Rome's Project on the Predicament of Mankind*. Universe Books, New York.

Meek, Ronald L., ed. 1971. *Marx and Engels on the Population Bomb: Selections from the Writings of Marx and Engels Dealing with the Theories of Thomas Robert Malthus*. Ramparts Press, Berkeley.

Micklethwait, John, and Adrian Wooldridge. 2004. *The Right Nation: Conservative Power in America*. Penguin Press, New York.

Miller, Gifford H., Marilyn L. Fogel, John W. Magee, Michael K. Gagan, Simon J. Clarke, and Beverly J. Johnson. 2005. Ecosystem collapse in Pleistocene Australia and a human role in megafaunal extinction. *Science* 309, no. 5732 (July 8): 287–90.

Montagu, Ashley. 1976. *The Nature of Human Aggression*. Oxford University Press, Oxford.

Morgan, Elaine. 1982. *The Aquatic Ape*. Stein & Day, New York.

Muir, John. 1988 [1911]. *My First Summer in the Sierra*. Sierra Club Books, San Francisco.

Musallam, B. F. 1983. *Sex and Society in Islam: Birth Control before the Nineteenth Century*. Cambridge University Press, Cambridge.

Musacchio, Jacqueline Marie. 1999. *The Art and Ritual of Childbirth in Renaissance Italy*. Yale University Press, New Haven, Conn.

New York Times. 1988. Human hunters and pygmy hippos. December 20, C7.

Nie, Yilin, and Robert J. Wyman. 2005. The one-child policy in Shanghai: Acceptance and internalization. *Population and Development Review* 31, no. 2 (June): 313–36.

Noble, Thomas F. X. 2002. *The Foundations of Western Civilization*. The Teaching Company, Chantilly, Va.

Noonan, John T.1986 [1965]. *Contraception: A History of Its Treatment by the Catholic Theologians and Canonists*. Enlarged ed. Harvard University Press, Cambridge, Mass.

O'Connor, Anahad. 2004. Wakefulness finds a powerful ally. *New York Times*, June 29, D1.

Osrin, David, Kirti M Tumbahangphe, Dej Shrestha, Natasha Mesko, Bhim P. Shrestha, Madan K. Manandhar, Hilary Standing, Dharma S. Manandhar, and Anthony M. de L. Costello. 2002. Cross sectional, community based study of care of newborn infants in Nepal. *British Medical Journal* 325, no. 7372 (November 9): 1063.

Oster, Emily. 2004. Witchcraft, weather and economic growth in Renaissance Europe. *Journal of Economic Perspectives* 18, no. 1 (Winter): 215–28.

Packer, Craig. 1998. Why menopause? *Natural History* 107 (6): 24–26.

Packer, Craig, Ray Hilborn, Anna Mosser, Bernard Kissui, Markus Borner, Grant Hopcraft, John Wilmshurst, Simon Mduma, and Anthony R.E. Sinclair. 2005. Ecological change, group territoriality, and population dynamics in Serengeti lions. *Science* 307, no. 5708 (January 21): 390–93.

Pagels, Elaine. 1988. *Adam, Eve, and the Serpent.* Random House, New York.

Park, Alice, et al. 2007. 51 things we can do to save the environment. *Time*, April 9, 69–100.

Parsons, Jack. 2000. *The Reverend Thomas Robert Malthus, AM, FRS: Demi-deDvil, Saint, or Merely Great Benefactor?* edited version of a lecture delivered at Cardiff University, March 10, 1998. Population Policy Press, Llantrisant, Wales.

Payne, January W. 2006. Forever pregnant. *Washington Post*, May 16, F1.

Pearsall, Derek. 1992. *The Life of Geoffrey Chaucer: A Critical Biography.* Blackwell, Oxford.

Pennington, Renee. 2001. Hunter-gatherer demography. In Catherine Panter-Brick, Robert H. Layton and Peter Rowley-Conwy, eds., *Hunter-gatherers: An Interdisciplinary Perspective.* 170–204. Cambridge University Press, Cambridge, UK.

Percival, Val, and Thomas Homer-Dixon. 1996. Environmental scarcity and violent conflict: The case of Rwanda. *The Journal of Environment & Development* 5 (3): 270–91.

Perlin, John. 1989. *A Forest Journey: The Role of Wood in the Development of Civilization.* W. W. Norton, New York.

Peterson, William, ed. 1972. *Readings in Population.* Macmillan, New York.

Piotrow, Phyllis Tilson. 1973. *World Population Crisis: The United States Response.* Praeger, New York.

Pirsig, Robert M. 1984 [1974]. *Zen and the Art of Motorcycle Maintenance: An Inquiry into Values.* Bantam, New York.

Ponting, Clive. 1993 [1991]. *A Green History of the World: The Environment and the Collapse of Great Civilizations.* Penguin Books, New York.

Potts, Malcolm. 1997. Sex and the birth rate: Human biology, demographic change, and access to fertility-regulation methods. *Population and Development Review* 23, no. 1 (March): 1–39.

President's Committee to Study the United States Military Assistance Program. 1959. *Composite Report of the President's Committee to Study the United States Military Assistance Program.* Vol. 1. The White House, Washington, D.C.

Pringle, Heather. 1998. The slow birth of agriculture. *Science* 282, no. 5393 (November 20): 1446–450.

Pritchett, Lant H. 1994. Desired fertility and the impact of population policies. *Population and Development Review* 20 (1): 1–55.

Radford, Tim. 2004. Touching the void. *The Guardian*, July 22, Life, 4.

Ravenholt, Reimert, T. 1969. AID's family planning strategy. *Science* 163, no. 3683 (January 10):124–27.

Raymond, Michel. 2006. The birth of contraception. *Nature* 444 (December 7): 685.

Reed, Miriam. 2003. *Margaret Sanger: Her Life in Her Words.* Barricade Books, Fort Lee, N.J.

Rensberger, Boyce. 1998. In death, ancient peoples offer evidence that "progress" shortened life. *Washington Post*, May 13, H1.

Reuters. 2000. Bangladesh has worst violence against women: Report. September 20.

——. 2005. South Africa spouse killings epidemic. May 23.

——. 2006. Creaking health systems hampering AIDS battle: WHO. July 21.

Revkin, Andrew C. 2007. A new middle stance emerges in debate over climate. *New York Times*, January 1, A16.

Riche, Martha Farnsworth. 2001. A woman's status in European life. Letter to the editor. *New York Times*, January 14, p. 16.

Riddle, John M. 1992. *Contraception and Abortion from the Ancient World to the Renaissance.* Harvard University Press, Cambridge, Mass.

——. 1997. *Eve's Herbs: A History of Contraception and Abortion in the West.* Harvard University Press, Cambridge, Mass.

Riddle, John M., and J. Worth Estes. 1992. Oral contraceptives in ancient and medieval medicines. *American Scientist* May/June, 226–33.

Riddle, John M., J. Worth Estes, and Josiah C. Russell. 1994. Ever since Eve: Birth control in the ancient world. *Archaeology* 47, no. 2 (March/April): 29–35.

Roach, Mary. 1997. New world Pompeii. *Discover*, February, 74–80.

Rosenberg, Charles E., ed. 1975. *The Family in History.* University of Pennsylvania Press, Philadelphia.

Rosenberg, Karen R., and Wenda R. Trevathan. 2001. The evolution of human birth. *Scientific American* 285, no. 5 (November): 72–77.

Rosenberg, Karen, and Wenda Trevathan. 2002. Birth, obstetrics and human evolution. *BJOG: An International Journal of Obstetrics and Gynaecology* 109 (November): 1199–1206.

Rosenblum, Mort. 2004. Dark years on the dark continent. Review of *A Continent for the Taking: The Tragedy and Hope of Africa*, by Howard W. French. *Washington Post*, July 7, C8.

Rudavsky, Shari. 1991. The secret life of the Neanderthal. *Omni*, October, 42–56.

Ruiz, Teofilo F. 1996. *Medieval Europe: Crisis and Renewal.* The Teaching Company, Chantilly, Va.

Saether, Arild. 1993. Otto Diederich Lütken—40 years before Malthus? *Population Studies* 47 (3): 511–17.

Samuelson, Robert J. 2006. Behind the birth dearth. *Washington Post*, May 24, A23.

Sailer, Steve. 2003. Genes of history's greatest lover found? United Press International, February 6.

Sanday, Peggy Reeves. 1996 [1981]. *Female Power and Male Dominance: On the Origins of Sexual Inequality*. Cambridge University Press, Cambridge.

Sanger, Margaret.1920. *Woman and the New Race*. Brentano's, New York.

———. 1938. *Margaret Sanger: An Autobiography*. W. W. Norton, New York.

———. 1969 [1931]. *My Fight for Birth Control*. Maxwell Reprint Co., Elmsford, N.Y.

———. 2003 [1922]. *The Pivot of Civilization*. Humanity Books, Amherst, N.Y.

Saslow, Eli. 2006. In prep cross-country, girls often face an uphill battle. *Washington Post*, September 16, A1.

Schabas, Margaret. 2005. *The Natural Origins of Economics*. University of Chicago Press, Chicago.

Schiebinger, Londa. 1993. *Nature's Body: Gender in the Making of Modern Science*. Beacon Press, Boston.

Schlesinger, William H. 1990. Vegetation an unlikely answer. *Nature* 348. no 6303 (December): 679.

Schoen, Johanna. 2005. *Choice and Coercion: Birth Control, Sterilization, and Abortion in Public Health and Welfare*. University of North Carolina Press, Chapel Hill.

Scientific American. 2006. Becoming human: Evolution and the rise of intelligence. Special issue, vol. 16, no. 2 (September).

Shapira, Ian. 2006. After toil and trouble, "witch" is cleared. *Washington Post*, July 12, B1.

Sheehan, Molly O'Meara, ed. 2007. *State of the World 2007: Our Urban Future*. W. W. Norton, New York.

Shennan, Stephen. 2001. Demography and cultural innovation: A model and its implications for the emergence of modern human culture. *Cambridge Archaeological Journal* 11 (1): 5–16.

Shennan, Stephen. 2002. *Genes, Memes and Human History: Darwinian Archaeology and Cultural Evolution*. Thames & Hudson, London.

Shorto, Russell. 2006. Contra-contraception. *New York Times Sunday Magazine*, May 7, 48–55, 68, 83.

Simon, Julian. 1996. *The Ultimate Resource 2*. Princeton University Press, Princeton, N.J.

Simon Julian L., and Herman Kahn. 1984. *The Resourceful Earth*. Basil Blackwell, Oxford.

Smith, David P. 1992. *Formal Demography*. Plenum Press, New York.

Speert, Harold. 2004. *Obstetrics and Gynecology: A History and Iconography*. Parthenon Publishing, New York.

Speidel, J. Joseph. 2006. Population donor landscape analysis for review of Packard Foundation international grantmaking in population, sexual and reproductive health and rights. Written for presentation to a task force of The David and Lucile Packard Foundation, September 6. www.packard.org/assets/files/population/program%20review/pop_rev_speidel_030606.pdf (accessed November 27, 2007).

Spencer, Natasha A., Martha K. McClintock, Sarah A. Sellergren, Susan Bullivant, Suma Jacob, and Julie A. Mennella. 2004. Social chemosignals from breastfeeding women increase sexual motivation. *Hormones and Behavior* 46:362–70.

Stecklow, Steve. 2006. U.S. falls behind in tracking cattle to control disease. *Wall Street Journal*, June 6, A1.

Stiner, Mary C. 2001. Thirty years on the "Broad Spectrum Revolution" and Paleolithic demography. *Proceedings of the National Academy of Sciences* 98 (13): 6993–96.

Stiner, Mary C., Natalie D. Munro, Todd A. Surovell, Eitan Tchernov, and Ofer Bar-Yosef. 1999. Paleolithic population growth pulses evidenced by small animal exploitation. *Science* 283, no. 5399 (January 8): 190–94.

Stolzenburg, William. 1994. New views of ancient times. *Nature Conservancy*, September/October, 10–15.

Stone, Emily. 2005. Drip, drip, drip. *Chicago Tribune Magazine*, November 17, 12–28.

Stringer, Christopher, and Robin McKie, 1997 [1996]. *African Exodus: The Origins of Modern Humanity*. Henry Holt/John Macrae, New York.

Stuart, Anthony J., P. A. Kosintsev, T. F. G. Higham, and A. M. Lister. 2004. Pleistocene to Holocene extinction dynamics in giant deer and woolly mammoth. *Nature* 431, no. 7009 (October 7): 684–89.

Summers, Montague, trans. 1928. *Malleus Maleficarum*. R. Clay & Sons, Bungay, England.

Tainter, Joseph A. 1988. *The Collapse of Complex Societies*. Cambridge University Press, Cambridge.

Tanner, Nancy and Adrienne Zihlman. 1976. Women in evolution, part I: Innovation and selection in human origins. *Signs: Journal of Women in Culture and Society* 13 (1): 558–608.

Tattersal, Ian. 1998. *Becoming Human: Evolution and Human Uniqueness*. Harcourt, New York.

——. 2000. Once we were not alone. *Scientific American* 282, no. 1 (January): 56-62.

Tattersal, Ian, and R. W. Sussman, eds., 1975. *Lemur Biology*. Plenum Press, New York.

Tenner, Edward. 1996. *Why Things Bite Back: Technology and the Revenge of Unintended Consequences*. Knopf, New York.

Terrones, Marco. 2004. What explains the recent run-up in house prices? *World Economic Outlook September 2004: The Global Demographic Transition*, International Monetary Fund, Washington, D.C.

Thornburgh, Nathan. 2006. Inside the life of the migrants next door. *Time*, February 6, 34–45.

Thornhill, Randy, and Craig Palmer. 2000. *A Natural History of Rape: Biological Bases of Sexual Coercion*. MIT Press, Cambridge, Mass.

Trevathan, Wenda R. 1987. *Human Birth: An Evolutionary Perspective*. Aldine de Gruyter, Hawthorne, N.Y.

Tudge, Colin. 1999. *Neanderthals, Bandits and Farmers: How Agriculture Really Began*. Yale University Press, New Haven, Conn.

Uglow, Jenny. 2002. *The Lunar Men: Five Friends Whose Curiosity Changed the World*. Farrar, Straus and Giroux, New York.

UN Department of Economic and Social Affairs. 2004. *World Population in 2300: Proceedings of the United Nations Expert Meeting on World Population in 2300*. ESA/P/WP.187/Rev. 1. United Nations, New York. www.un.org/esa/population/publications/longrange2/2004worldpop2300reportfinalc.pdf (accessed November 27, 2007).

——. 2007. *World Population Prospects: The 2006 Revision*. United Nations, http://esa.un.org/unpp (accessed November 27, 2007).

UN Food and Agriculture Organization. 2004. Population aspects in the reduction of hunger. Paper prepared for the Seminar on the Relevance of Population Aspects for the Achievement of the Millennium Development Goals, United Nations, November 17–19, UN/POP/PD/2004/4.

UN IRIN (UN Integrated Regional Information Networks). 2005. Yemen: Population grows to 19.7 million. March 21.

UN Population Fund. 2004. *The Cairo Consensus at Ten: Population, Reproductive Health and the Global Effort to End Poverty (State of World Population 2004)*. United Nations, New York.

UN Wire. 2000. Bolivia: Infanticide rate reaches 16% in some areas—study, summarizing story in La Paz, Bolivia, newspaper *Los Tiempos*. May 24.

U.S. Census Bureau. 2003. Foreign-born a majority in six U.S. cities. Press release CB03-194, December 17, Washington, D.C.

U.S. Energy Information Agency. 2006. *International Energy Outlook 2006*. Washington, D.C. www.eia.doe.gov/oiaf/archive/ieo06/index.html (accessed on November 27, 2007).

van de Walle, Etienne, and Helmut V. Muhsam. 1995. Fatal secrets and the French fertility transition. *Population and Development Review* 21 (2): 261–79.

Vekua, Abesalom, et al. 2002. A new skull of early *Homo* from Dmanisi, Georgia. *Science* 297, no. 5578 (July 5): 85–89.

Vittor, Amy Yomiko, Robert H. Gilman, James Tielsch, Gregory Glass, Tim Shields, Wagner Sánchez Lozano, Viviana Pinedo-Cancino, and Jonathan A. Patz. 2006. The effect of deforestation on the human-biting rate of *Anopheles darlingi*, the primary vector of falciparum malaria in the Peruvian Amazon. *American Journal of Tropical Medicine and Hygiene* 74, no. 1 (January): 3–11.

Wackernagel, Mathis, Daniel Moran, Steven Goldfinger, Chad Monfreda, Aaron Welch, Michael Murray, Susan Burns, Carl Königel, Jules Peck, Paul King, and Marta Ballesteros. 2005. *Europe 2005: The Ecological Footprint*. World Wide Fund for Nature European Policy Office, Brussels.

Wade, Nicholas. 2003a. Early voices: The leap to language. *New York Times*, July 15, D1.

——. 2003b. Why humans and their fur parted ways. *New York Times*, August 19, D1.

——. 2003c. We got rhythm; the mystery is how and why. *New York Times*, September 16, D1.

——. 2006. *Before the Dawn: Recovering the Lost History of Our Ancestors*. Penguin Press HC, New York.

Wald, Matthew L. 2005. I vant to drink your vatts. *New York Times*, November 17, D1.

Wall-Scheffler, C. M., K. Geiger, and K. Steudel-Numbers. 2007. Infant carrying: The role of increased locomotory costs in early tool development. *American Journal of Physical Anthropology* 133 (2): 841–46.

Washington Post. 2006. Oceans in peril. Editorial. January 23, A14.

——. 2007. Fee proposed to ease traffic in Manhattan. April 23, A11.

Wattenberg, Ben J. 2004. *Fewer: How the New Demography of Depopulation Will Shape Our Future*. Ivan R. Dee, Chicago.

Wax, Emily. 2006. Dowries running dry in drought-stricken East Africa. *Washington Post*, March 20, A1.

Weber, Michael. N.d. *Population and Energy*. National Audubon Society, Washington, D.C.

Weiss, Eric M. 2002. The coffee is hot, and so is pre-dawn business. *Washington Post*, June 10, A1.

Weiss, Rick. 2007. For first time, chimps seen making weapons for hunting. *Washington Post*, February 23, A1.

Wells, Jonathan C. K. 2000. Natural selection and sex differences in morbidity and mortality in early life. *Journal of Theoretical Biology* 202:65–76.

Westoff, Charles F. 2005. Recent trends in contraception and abortion in 12 countries. *DHS Analytical Studies*, No. 8, ORC Macro, Calverton, Md.

Wilford, John Noble. 2002a. Seeking Polynesia's beginnings in an archipelago of shards. *New York Times*, January 8, D1.

——. 2002b. Don't blame Columbus for all the Indians' ills. *New York Times*, October 29, F1.

——. 2003. Lost no more: an Etruscan rebirth. *New York Times*, April 15, D1.

——. 2004. Experts place ancient toolmakers on a fast track to Northern China. *New York Times*, October 5, F3.

——. 2006. Old shells suggest early human adornment. *New York Times*, June 23, A6.

Will, George. 1993. In death, a return to randomness. *Washington Post*, December 12, C7.

Wills, Christopher. 1997. *Yellow Fever, Black Goddess: The Coevolution of People and Plagues*. Addison Wesley, New York.

Wolf, Frank. 2001. Why I changed my mind on a new river crossing. Letter to the editor. *Washington Post*, June 3, B8.

Wolpoff, Millard H. 2005. *Modern Human Origins: The Other View*. Aldine de Gruyter, Hawthorne, N.Y.

Wollstonecraft, Mary. 2004 [1792]. *A Vindication of the Rights of Women*. Revised ed. Penguin Books, London.

Wong, Kate. 2001. Mammoth kill. *Scientific American* 284, no. 2 (February): 22.

——. 2006a. Stranger in a new land. *Scientific American* 16, no. 2 (September 19): 38–47.

——. 2006b. The morning of the modern mind. *Scientific American* 16, no. 2 (special edition): 74–83.

Wood, James W. 1998. A theory of preindustrial population dynamics: Demography, economy, and well-being in Malthusian systems. *Current Anthropology* 39 (1): 99–135.

World Health Organization. 1992. *PROGRESS in Human Reproduction Research*. No. 21. World Health Organization, Geneva.

World Health Organization. 2004. *Unsafe Abortion: Global and Regional Estimates of the Incidence of Unsafe Abortion and Associated Mortality in 2000*. 4th ed.World Health Organization, Geneva.

World Health Organization, Department of Reproductive Health and Research. 2004. *Maternal Mortality in 2000: Estimates Developed by WHO, UNICEF, UNFPA*. World Health Organization, Geneva.

Wrangham, Richard W., James Holland Jones, Greg Laden, David Pilbeam, and NancyLou Conklin-Brittain. 1999. The raw and the stolen: Cooking and the ecology of human origins. *Current Anthropology* 40 (5): 567–94.

Wright, Ronald. 2005 [2004]. *A Short History of Progress*. Carroll & Graf, New York.

Wrigley, E. A., and R. S. Schofield. 1981. *The Population History of England, 1541–1871*. Harvard University Press, Cambridge, Mass.

Yale University Office of Public Information. 1988. Bone deformities reveal grueling life of the world's early farmers. News release, May 12 .

Zeisel, William, ed. 1984. *Censorship: 500 Years of Conflict*. New York Public Library, New York.

Zerjal, Tatiania, et al. 2003. The genetic legacy of the Mongols. *American Journal of Human Genetics* 72:717–21.

Zlotnick, Hania. 2004. Population growth and international migration. In Douglas S. Massey and J. Edward Taylor, eds., *International Migration: Prospects and Policies in a Global Market*, 13–34. Oxford University Press, Oxford.

Index

About Island Press

Island Press is the only nonprofit organization in the United States whose principal purpose is the publication of books on environmental issues and natural resource management. We provide solutions-oriented information to professionals, public officials, business and community leaders, and concerned citizens who are shaping responses to environmental problems.

Since 1984, Island Press has been the leading provider of timely and practical books that take a multidisciplinary approach to critical environmental concerns. Our growing list of titles reflects our commitment to bringing the best of an expanding body of literature to the environmental community throughout North America and the world.

Support for Island Press is provided by the Agua Fund, The Geraldine R. Dodge Foundation, Doris Duke Charitable Foundation, The Ford Foundation, The William and Flora Hewlett Foundation, The Joyce Foundation, Kendeda Sustainability Fund of the Tides Foundation, The Forrest & Frances Lattner Foundation, The Henry Luce Foundation, The John D. and Catherine T. MacArthur Foundation, The Marisla Foundation, The Andrew W. Mellon Foundation, Gordon and Betty Moore Foundation, The Curtis and Edith Munson Foundation, Oak Foundation, The Overbrook Foundation, The David and Lucile Packard Foundation, Wallace Global Fund, The Winslow Foundation, and other generous donors.

The opinions expressed in this book are those of the author and do not necessarily reflect the views of these foundations.